A New Theory
of Information
& the Internet

Steve Jones
General Editor

Vol. 66

The Digital Formations series is part of the Peter Lang Media list.
Every volume is peer reviewed and meets
the highest quality standards for content and production.

PETER LANG
New York • Washington, D.C./Baltimore • Bern
Frankfurt • Berlin • Brussels • Vienna • Oxford

Mark Balnaves & Michele Willson

A New Theory
of Information
& the Internet

Public Sphere meets Protocol

PETER LANG
New York • Washington, D.C./Baltimore • Bern
Frankfurt • Berlin • Brussels • Vienna • Oxford

Library of Congress Cataloging-in-Publication Data

Balnaves, Mark.
A new theory of information and the Internet: public sphere meets protocol /
Mark Balnaves, Michele Willson.
p. cm. — (Digital formations; vol. 66)
Includes bibliographical references and index.
1. User interfaces (Computer systems). 2. Internet searching.
3. Computer network resources—Public opinion.
I. Willson, Michele A. II. Title.
QA76.9.U83B34   025.04–dc22   2011008412
ISBN 978-1-4331-1063-4 (hardcover)
ISBN 978-1-4331-1062-7 (paperback)

Bibliographic information published by **Die Deutsche Nationalbibliothek**.
Die Deutsche Nationalbibliothek lists this publication in the "Deutsche
Nationalbibliografie"; detailed bibliographic data is available
on the Internet at http://dnb.d-nb.de/.

The Last Judgement in Cyberspace. By Chinese New Media artist,
Miao Xiaochun. Reproduced with permission.

The paper in this book meets the guidelines for permanence and durability
of the Committee on Production Guidelines for Book Longevity
of the Council of Library Resources.

Contents

Acknowledgements

The idea for this book emerged during a discussion at an AoIR conference in Milwaukee, late 2009. One of the authors had just presented a paper on Habermas, protocol, and the materiality of the Internet. The other author was interested in Habermas's understanding of information and the notion of the informed citizen. Since then, and about the time of the finalising of this book manuscript, the WikiLeaks saga has started unfolding on the public stage (with the trial and possible extradition of Julian Assange still being discussed). The international furore and public debates around WikiLeaks highlights the centrality of many of the core concerns of this book: questions about understandings of information, the notion of a public sphere and informed citizenry, and the importance of understanding and taking into account the material possibilities and constraints of the Internet.

As is often the case, this book would not have been possible without the contributions, goodwill and assistance of other people. The authors are grateful to Professor Matthew Allen, Internet Studies, Curtin University and Dr Debbie Rodan, School of Communications and Arts, Edith Cowan University, for their permission to use the following joint works. These include work adapted from Allen, M. & Balnaves, M. (2009). "Is e-governance a function of government or media? Some directions for future research and development of electronically mediated citizen participation." *Internet Research 10.0–Internet: Critical.* (AoIR), 7–10 October, Milwaukee; Balnaves, M. & Allen, M. (2009). "E-governance as digital ecosystem: A New Way to Think About Citizen Engagement and the Internet?" *ICEG: 5th International Conference on e-Government,* 19–20 October, Boston; and Rodan, D. & Balnaves, M. (2009). Democracy to come: Active forums as indicator suites for e-participation and e-governance. In A. Macintosh and E. Tambouris (eds.) *ePart 2009, LCNCS 5694,* (pp. 175–185), Springer-Verlag, Heidelberg. Mark Balnaves acknowledges the Communication Policy Research Forum and Network Insight for the opportunity to adapt for the book parts of the paper "The Internet aggregators" presented at the *Communication Policy Research Forum,* Sydney, 15–16 November 2010.

The authors would like to thank Dr Tama Leaver, Internet Studies, Curtin University for his permission to use some of their joint work, Balnaves, M., T.

Leaver, & M. Willson. "Habermas and the Net," *International Communications Association Conference*, Singapore, 22–26 June, 2010. They would also like to acknowledge the support of the Australian Research Council (ARC) LP100200803 "Transitions to a Sustainable City—Geraldton WA: An applied study into co-creating sustainability though civic deliberation and social media."

Many of the URL examples related to e-democracy were originally researched by Adam Swift at Queensland University of Technology (QUT), as part of preparation for an Australian Research Council (ARC) grant with Professor Terry Flew and Associate Professor Axel Bruns (QUT) and Professor Matthew Allen (Curtin University). The authors acknowledge Adam for his work and the QUT team for providing an environment of stimulating thought and collaboration.

The authors would also like to extend their thanks to new media artist Miao Xiaochun for generously allowing the use of an image of his work, *The Last Judgement in Cyberspace, the below view*, for the cover image. Thanks also must go to the production team at Peter Lang, and in particular, to Mary Savigar and Steve Jones. Thanks too, to Monika Strzalkowska for the refining, formatting and cross-checking of many of the references, and to Frank Smith for speedy and comprehensive indexing.

Last, and very importantly, the authors would like to thank their families: Kim, Dash, Xavier and Charlie; and Tony, Asha and Ben.

CHAPTER ONE

Introduction

Today I discovered the danger of changing my Facebook profile. My fiancee and I decided that showing our engagement in Facebook gave out a little too much personal information. But I did not realize that unchecking "Thomas Crampton is engaged to Thuy-Tien Tran" would send a message to every Facebook friend that "Thomas Crampton and Thuy-Tien Tran are no longer engaged". A little broken heart accompanied the message in our newsfeed, for added emotion. Within minutes an email arrived from a friend in San Francisco asking if I was doing ok and offering emotional support at this trying time.

—Crampton (2007)

The Internet is not simply one big neutral space that people can enter. It is made up of thousands upon thousands of menus to choose from and, as Thomas Crampton found out, many of those menus and choices might have unforeseen consequences. Alexander Galloway (2004) argued that protocol is important to our understanding of the Internet because things happen to our communication or to the social distribution of knowledge independently of the content of the Internet. The very material structures of the Internet have their own effects, from routers to drop-down menus. For Crampton, his engagement to Thuy-Tien Tran is of primary relevance to his life and the no-longer-engaged message produced by Facebook was an imposed relevance. Life on the Internet is a balance of intrinsic and imposed relevances and interests.

This book *is* about the material consequences of the Internet but it is also more than that. The authors look at the disciplines that debate the existence of information and the nature of human communication, from computing to librarianship, electronic engineering to cognitive psychology. They argue that it is important to have an historical understanding of the various notions of information and communication that in turn underpin the design, functions and uses of the Internet.

It is the concept of information, especially, that has captured the imagination of theorists. Beniger (1986), Campbell (1982), Stonier (1983; 1986), and

Wiener (1950; 1951), for example, have advanced general theories of information. They hold information to be a real entity, an object with temporal extension, capable of transforming physical, economic and social relations. The Soviet information theorist and philosopher Ursul, for instance, said that information is, and has always been, the ideal physical factor in the development of societies because it intensifies human activity and leads gradually to "a single (or unitary) system of intensification of human activity" (1983: 5). Thus information is not only a direct production force, but also the effective cause of intensive development and change in a community (1983: 6).

It was Claude Shannon's algorithms in electronic engineering that started the idea that information is a quantity. That idea was then taken up by cyberneticians. Information became a thing within a thing, a real entity occupying the place of other entities yet not identical with them. These historical origins of information as a phenomenon are important to understand because they highlight the complexity of the sciences behind the Internet and the consequences of their conceptions of information for understanding the human mind. These disciplinary ideas are important because they have a direct effect on how people think about the Internet: that information is a quantity is now taken for granted as is the understanding that the more information you have access to, the better. It is assumed that the Internet has lots of 'information' in 'networks'.

The major information and communication disciplines also contribute to the design and operation of the Internet. Computing and artificial intelligence work in particular have their own conceptions of knowledge representation and these affect what counts as intelligence and how that intelligence works. As the Internet becomes more intelligent the modern citizen is offered ever more user friendly options. By user friendly, the authors mean that the citizen does not understand or does not need to know the deeper infrastructure or mechanics that provide a service: it is 'black boxed'. A web browser is an example of such black boxing: the browser is a 'location' that assists the user in navigating the intricacies of the Internet's IP addresses and domain names. The user does not have to know the specific IP address of a particular website nor does s/he need to understand or navigate directly with the underlying programming languages and instructions. Instead the interface of a web browser provides the user with a translation that they are able to understand and use. This 'black box' aspect to the Internet has played a vitally important role in increasing the uptake of Internet users and in affording access to people from all walks of life. This black-boxing continues to expand across the

Internet at many levels and within other mobile technologies that increasingly engage with the Internet.

Historically early Internet users were largely homogenous in terms of their demographics: young, white, male, Western, largely from middle class socio-demographics. They shared competencies in terms of their ability to navigate online and to create the navigation systems and the computing behind them. They were both creators and users. The introduction of web browsers and graphical interfaces enabled an opening up of that communicative space to a broader range of people, but in that process it took away the need for some of the competencies.

This type of engagement with citizens has continued to the point where the generalisation of competencies for the Internet is limited to only a relative few. Most people learn the procedures for the software or hardware they are using: in this book, we refer to this type of knowledge or understanding as recipe knowledge. Most people are unable to judge the competencies of those creating the software and hardware or the appropriateness of the systems created. They can simply assert that it is useful for their purposes or not. This general level of competency has ramifications for any idea of participation in the public sphere, Jürgen Habermas's (1989) concept of genuine participative spaces, or becoming an informed citizen where common intrinsic interests can be expressed. Alfred Schutz's (1946) concept of common intrinsic interests, like Habermas's idea of the public sphere, rely heavily on the proposition that what is relevant to people works within processes of knowledge representation, or schema, and within communicative spaces that limit distortion by power, force, coercion or violence.

The Internet involves different kinds of mediation and action in communicative spaces, than in traditional broadcasting or the codex book. When you pick up a codex book, the book does not record your identity and continually capture your movements, for instance. Let us look at a composite profile of one kind of Internet user, taken from actual case studies:

> Mary has a computer at work and at home. She belongs to *Insurgent Desire*, a green anarchist, anti-technology group. Her work computer bans her access to this group under the 'criminal activity' rules for the system. Her local ISP, however, does not have a problem with it. Mary accesses the site frequently from home to engage in discussion and to read the latest news. Mary guesses that her ISP may be recording her surfing habits but she is not aware that major aggregators like Acxiom are also collecting and on-selling her personal details. Mary uses Windows Live, email and chat, for discussions with her group. Recently, however, one of the members of the group has been posting lewd material and insulting members of the group. Mary decides that she wants to close her whole account. She spends 3 hours reading the instructions on

how to close the account, only to find that when she follows procedure the account does not close. She decides instead to re-customise the site to limit anyone seeing her profile.

Since joining the international online group, Mary has had problems with endless spam and unsolicited materials from other political groups. She emailed the senior members of the collective but has only got automated replies. Mary wants to talk to the senior members of the collective to ask them about whether they are collecting information about her but also to get to know them and to become more involved in the international activities. While she does not get a reply from the main office, she still get emails asking her to pursue particular issues and to take actions locally.

Mary is an Internet junkie—she belongs to rsvp.com.au, an Internet dating site, and belongs to a large range of Internet groups. She is willing to trade her personal information for access to sites that she really wants to use. Her personal profile is available on Facebook and MySpace and her professional profile is with LinkedIn. She uses Wikipedia as her major source of information on anarcho-primitivism because she cannot afford access to the online journals available through the publishers. Her local university does not provide public access to the online journals and the local library has limited Internet access. She joins every online competition that she can and has amassed a large mobile bill from her SMSs to competition hotlines. Google already has specific ads targeted to Mary. She has noticed recently that Amazon has also been posting recommendations to her for books on activism.

Mary has adopted typifications from the Internet. Typification is Schutz's term for particular types of knowledge schema derived from social interaction. Equally, spammers and direct mail have already classified Mary as a particular type of user. What are not so obvious are the political implications of some of these understandings. The parameters are not necessarily clear because many of the typifications associated with either information or the Internet have become commonsensical, such as user friendly, knowledge is power, consumer choice, in order to make a decision all you need is (the right) information. But the conditions under which that information is developed, archived, accessed or engaged with are not always transparent and those conditions have ramifications for the future of the Internet and for the possibilities of an informed citizenry.

Information, Communication and the Internet

Information emerged as a universal principle at work in the world, giving shape to the shapeless, specifying the peculiar character of living forms and even helping to determine, by means of special codes, the patterns of human thought. In this way, information spans the disparate fields of space-age computers and classical physics, molecular biology and human communication, the evolution of language and the evolution of man [sic]. (Campbell, 1982: 16)

If we could construct a community in which it was universally believed that there was one overriding human purpose, then all that would matter would be to find the right ways of attaining that universally accepted end. In the Information Age, for Campbell it appears that there will be no gap between society's culminating purpose and the means toward it, because information is conceived as both the means and the end. According to Campbell, for example, we live in a "second-theorem" society, one where the mathematical formula for entropy (the measure of uncertainty, randomness) in information theory helps to provide the basis for a social theory of variety and choice (1982: 254–265). "Such a theory would be a way of escaping the stale alternatives of traditional capitalism and traditional socialism, because it would pose an altogether different question: how much variety do we want in a society, and how much control?" (1982: 264). For Campbell, society can be analysed by reference to *information*, a single organising, and generalised explanatory, principle.

Campbell is not alone in supposing that analysis of information may be fundamental to our understanding of social, or individual, action. Writers on the information society like Bell (1973), Porat (1978), Smith (1980), Stonier (1983), and others, have also challenged traditional approaches to economics, social analysis and, more particularly, Marxist labour theory. Marx argued that, if we bear in mind that the value of commodities has a purely social reality, and that they acquire this reality only insofar as they are expressions or embodiments of one social characteristic, that is, *human labour*, then it follows as a matter of course, that value can only manifest itself in the social relation of commodity to commodity (1906: 55). However, post-industrial theorists argue that contemporary society is characterised not by a labour theory but by an information theory of value. Stonier wrote, for example, that tools and machinery may be stored-up labour, but they are also

and more significantly, stored-up information! This is true for capital, the productivity of land and any other aspect of economics which invokes stored labour. There exist no productive labour inputs which do not, at the same time, involve inputs of information. Furthermore, information, like capital, can be accumulated and stored for future use. In a post-industrial society, a country's store of information is its principal asset, its greatest potential source of wealth. (1983: 11–12)

Bell, similarly, described the shift to a post-industrial society as a changeover from a "goods-producing society to an information or knowledge society" (1973: 487). But what kind of 'good' is information? According to Smith

> A piece of information acquired from an ancient manuscript may pass into a learned paper, then into a biography, then into the treatment of a television programme, then a cinema film and end up a videodisc or video-cassette.... At each point information is the linkage between states; it is a kind of raw material itself which is contained within the product whose manufacture has depended upon it. Manufactured goods are in many senses frozen information. (1980: 112)

In this example, information is presumed to be an object with temporal extension; a physical object that occupies the place of other physical objects, but cannot be said to be identical with them. Porat suggested that the most serious characteristic of this 'good' is that it lends itself poorly to the classical economic and legal concepts of *property rights*, because it is exclusion which separates private from public goods. "One cannot easily own information, because the act of theft is difficult to detect and even more difficult to prove. As simultaneous ownership is possible, there is no clear way of claiming or proving sole ownership" (1978: 35).

There is no shortage of analyses of, or statements about the information society, the post-industrial society (see for example, Bearman, 1987; Cronin, 1986; Lyon, 1988; Masuda, 1981; Toffler, 1980) or the networked information society (Benkler, 2006) The concept of 'information' has also been investigated or discussed elsewhere, for example by Lamberton (1984) and Melody (1987) and by Machlup in his seminal works on knowledge production (1980; 1982; 1984) (see also Machlup and Mansfield 1983 in an interdisciplinary context). However, the various claims made about information require detailed attention and investigation. This is especially the case when information is taken to be an actor in, and an explanatory principle in analysis of, social relations. According to Braman, for instance, argument over how to define information is critical because that definition is central to an emerging information policy regime (1989: 234). Thus she created a hierarchy of four categories of definitions of information, the standard-setting category being that which defined information as a constitutive force in society. Information "is not just affected by its environment, but is itself an actor affecting other elements in the environment. Information is that which is not just embedded within a social structure, but creates that structure itself" (Braman, 1989: 239). The concept of 'communication' is also relevant to an analysis of the concept of 'information' because communication is often associated with information: "The functioning of society depends upon information and its effective communication among society's members" (Melody, 1987: 1313).

Historically, introductory texts to communication theory, such as those produced by Fiske (1982), Littlejohn (1983), Rogers (1962), and McQuail (1994), treat the ideas of communication and information in different ways.

For example, for Fiske (1982), on the one hand, the study of semiotics is the study of communication. For Littlejohn (1983), on the other hand, the study of communication embraces general systems theory, cybernetics, persuasion, theories of perception, and so on.

James Carey has called these two approaches to the study of communication the 'ritual' and the 'transmission' views.

> American studies are grounded in a transmission or transportation view of communication. They see communication, therefore, as a process of transmitting messages at a distance for the purpose of control....By contrast, the preponderant view of communication in European studies is a ritual one: communication is viewed as a process through which a shared culture is created. (1977: 412)

Littlejohn has suggested that communication theory remains fragmented and that "the fragmented nature of communication theory detracts from a well co-ordinated effort to understand the basic or central processes common to all communication. Fragmentation also creates terminology confusion" (1983: 303). The concept information is seen as one of the reasons for this fragmentation and confusion. "Is information a product of perception or cognition, or is it an inherent part of the stimulus field? Actually, this issue is a subset of the larger issue of what defines information. Theorists thus disagree over the locus of information" (1983: 306).

This book shares the concern of introductory communication texts with the need to clarify the locus of information. Indeed, with the rise of the Internet as a major intermediary in the social distribution of knowledge, this task has become even more important. In this book, the authors will analyse the disciplinary and institutional contexts within which the concepts of communication and of information are acquired, used and especially *reduced*.

If the concept information can be substituted with other concepts, without any significant loss of meaning, then it is the reduction that constitutes the true meaning of the concept. For example, black cannot be reduced to white. Information in some contexts can be reduced to knowledge and in others it cannot. The authors side with Strawson's assertion that ordinary language has no exact logic (1950: 344).

This book differs from previous analyses because it adopts a phenomenological approach to the study of information as a phenomenon, of the typifications of information. Bell, for example, emphasised in his work that he used post-industrial society as an ideal type, "a construct, put together by the social analyst, of diverse changes in the society which, when assembled, becomes more or less coherent when contrasted with other conceptual constructs" (1973: 487). This book, however, does not seek to formulate an ideal type of post-industrial society or more recently, a network society (see for example, Castells, 2001 or Benkler, 2006) but rather to explore the meanings, interests, preferences and purposes that may attach themselves to these concepts of information and communication.

Bates (1988: 91) wrote that an equitable distribution of information can only be achieved if we can agree on the nature of information and determine its "true value." Information, according to Bates, has a unique nature, physical and non-physical, and unique properties which make it both a private and a public good (1988: 76). It is not the purpose of this book to derive comprehensive and exhaustive answers to these questions. The book will provide a framework within which such questions can be usefully discussed by investigating how authors and practitioners characterise information, its role, value and existential characteristics and how these characterizations affect our views of the Internet as key to the social distribution of knowledge. The authors' key argument is that *information does not exist, only informed people exist*. This might appear to be a radical position to take, but information as you will see should *not* be taken to be a social actor in its own right. Any theorization of the Internet as a social phenomenon, similarly, should ignore any claims that information has agency in its own right.

In the following chapters, the authors present the historical emergence of the scientific, mathematical, computing and human communication disciplinary discussions on information, together with the rise of the idea of information as a resource and as a commodity. The authors argue that the contemporary situation has not changed in terms of resolving exactly what information might be as a real thing. For example, Bates in 2005 argues that "Information is not tangible, and objects are. Intangible things seem less real to us, therefore less valuable." (2005: 5). This type of conception, of course, is a *legerdemain*, a sleight of hand. It avoids discussing what "intangible" but "real" might mean in practice. Raber, on the science side, recounts the mathematical theory, in his *The Problem of Information* (Raber, 2003). The disciplinary split on conceptions of information, therefore, remains. What has changed, the authors would argue, is that the idea that information is a resource and a commodity has basically become so common that it is now a cultural trope, a standard way of looking at information. But this view distorts how knowledge has been treated in law.

The idea that the community owns published knowledge is enshrined in law. Intellectual property law tries to protect the individual and the community interest in knowledge. There is no freedom of access to what a person knows, for example, unless that person publishes what he or she knows. Under common law you own your own ideas completely until they are published. "Ideas are free; but while the author confines them to his study they are like birds in a cage, which none but he can have a right to let fly; for, till he thinks properly to emancipate them, they are under his own dominion" (Briggs, 1906: 19). People who decide to "let fly" their ideas gain a reward because of their contribution to the public domain. "Copyright, which defines the right of an author with regard to his production, is undoubtedly given him to recompense for his creative work" (Briggs, 1906: 22). While the right to tangible expression of knowledge is called a property right, it is more precisely a right to reward those who surrender their exclusive control of their own thoughts. Freedom of access to the public domain, to the totality of published works, refers to access to the tangible expressions of knowledge, such as documents, signals and data structures.

Barry Hindess (1988), in his critique of rational choice theory, advanced a minimal concept of the actor as a site of decision and action, where the action is in some sense a consequence of the actor's decision. "Actors do things as a result of their decisions. We call those things actions, and the actor's decisions play a part in their explanation. Actors may also do things that do not result from their decisions, and their explanation has a different form" (Hindess, 1988: 44–45). Hindess argued that a capacity to make decisions is an integral part of anything that might be called an actor. State agencies, political parties, football clubs, churches and tenants' associations are all examples of actors in the minimal sense, in that, "They all have means of reaching decisions and of acting on at least some of them" (Hindess, 1988: 46). The actions of a tenants' association, a corporate actor, is of course, always dependent upon the actions of others such as managers, elected officers, employees and other organisations. The authors agree with Hindess and propose a nominalist approach to information as a social actor.

Technological Code

The Internet is used differently by different people and means different things to them as a result. Some use it for finding answers to a question or to keep themselves informed about particular states of affairs. Others use the Internet primarily for financial transactions: buying and selling on eBay; purchasing books from Amazon; undertaking online banking transactions. Still others use the Internet for social debate and discussion; to communicate with others locally or far away. And others use the Internet for entertainment: downloading movies or music; uploading videos to YouTube or immersing themselves in a massively multiplayer online role-playing game (MMORPG) such as World of Warcraft. Most users would not turn to the Internet for just one type of engagement—most would undertake a number of different engagements though the degree to which they do this may differ across applications. All of these uses involve communication or the transfer of information between persons mediated through a computer or mobile technologies or the communication of information between a person and a technology (e.g., database, online game, search engine).

These engagements with technologies or people mediated through technological means bring certain issues to the forefront; issues that may exist in less technologically mediated engagements but less obviously or less frequently. These are issues surrounding authenticity, veracity, intent, and usefulness. Key processes that are used to address these issues in less mediated environs have been developed over time. These include things like peer review, legal oversight, institutional reputation and the power of association, physical identification systems (ID cards, signatures, etc), physical 'locatedness', and so on. Some of these issues are slowly being addressed with technological developments online—increasing acceptance of online journals, the use of digital signatures, a growing familiarity with and acceptance of online engagements and an accumulated recognition of online brands (such as Amazon) and trust in their representation (and corresponding trust or reputation systems such as those used on eBay).

One of the main differences about technologically mediated interaction, apart from the removal of face-to-face presence, is that there are various layers of technological interface and of action. By this, the authors are referring to the fact that not only is the engagement mediated through hardware—cables, satellite signals, PC, routers and so forth—but there are other layers that manage, convert, and transport this engagement through the Internet to another person or persons or to other technological locations.

These layers in the form of software or technical code written to perform acts and limit others, and algorithmic functions programmed into these systems, are vital for the functioning of the Internet as we know it. However, as noted above, these layers are often either invisible or incomprehensible to many users. Some may be more obvious such as in the transparent recording of wiki transactions. However, most people would not be able to tell you how Google's search engine produces the search items on their computer screen or how it decides what is on the first page or the third. Others of course make it their business to know this, and there is a flourishing industry around ensuring visibility and page rank on search engines such as Google. However, in the main, these layers only become obvious when they do not work as well as they should or are expected to, when they do not produce expected responses, or when the users is disturbed in the flow of their surfing behaviour and required to log in, to tick acknowledgement boxes, or restricted in their access by a filter. For example, when Facebook users suddenly found that their daily activity on their pages was fed via a newsfeed to everyone who was listed as their friend, people became indignant and reactive, demanding that Facebook reverse the action and respect their privacy. They wanted to be able to choose what they did or didn't see of their friends and likewise did not wish everything they did to be broadcast. Or to be clear about what they want to broadcast, as Thomas found in the opening quotation at the beginning of this book. In these instances, their 'page' moves from being their familiar and individually activated site to one whereby other agencies become obvious.

There are numerous typologies employed to describe these layers: Galloway notes at least four layers, recounted here to give the reader an idea as to the scope and method, but there are undoubtedly many others that could be employed. Taken from an RFC on "Requirements for Internet hosts," he lists these basic layers: "(1) the application layer, (e.g., telnet, the Web), (2) the transport layer (e.g., TCP), (3) the Internet layer (e.g., IP), and (4) the link (or media-access) layer (e.g., Ethernet)" (Galloway, 2004: 39). We could add another layer to refer to the performance or public space where data is inputted and text is written and exchanged: possibly a 'content' layer. The language of layers enables discussion of the various processes that take place in online engagements across these various layers. While the user may be able to freely converse in an online space though possibly constrained by social norms and etiquettes at one level, this action is controlled at other levels according to the possibilities of the software, the performance of the connection, the protocols that enable the communication to pass between computers, routers and so forth. To understand the Internet as a site and medium for democratic civic processes, the various layers and the material effects of these layers also need to be addressed. This book, in the process of examining the understanding of information and communication, investigates the notion of an informed citizenry within the context of the increasingly ubiquitous place of the Internet in social, informational life.

Chapter Outline

The next chapter, Chapter Two: Information and Its Realities, explores key historical accounts and discourses in the disciplines of electronic engineering and language to show that the major debates about the nature of information in the key information and communication disciplines always take the same form—those who think of information as an object that has temporal extension (and can be measured and quantified as a result) and those who do not.

Chapter Three: Networks and Relevance takes these explorations of the ideas of information and communication further, discussing the ways in which these ideas have developed in the fields of computing, artificial intelligence and information retrieval. Each of these disciplines adopted particular approaches to information as a phenomenon and these approaches have a direct bearing on what Internet networks, now and in the future, will look like.

Chapter Four: The Informed Citizen, explores Habermas's theory of information and the theoretical context from which it is derived. In this chapter, the authors look at knowledge schema and their role in understanding the Internet as a mediator in the social distribution of knowledge. Jürgen Habermas is famous for his idea of the public sphere and both the phrase and the idea are now used to describe many different things. But it is Habermas's and Alfred Schutz's theorizing about being informed that provides tantalizing insights into how structured subjective spaces that benefit open communication in fact work

Chapter Five: Protocol and Machinic Infrastructure looks more closely at the materiality of the Internet and the extent to which it meets the claims of the utopians and the extent to which it can be called a public sphere. In this chapter, the authors discuss how Galloway and Habermas talk about space, time and place and the empirical examples they use, including the Internet. They suggest that any discussion of the Internet, the possibilities for an informed citizenry and the potentialities of collaborative spaces need to engage not only with the social, cultural and political actions by human agents that take place directly in online environs, but also take into account the material processes and possibilities engendered by the technology.

Chapter Six: Trading Spaces examines this issue of collaboration and open spaces in more detail. The architecture of the Internet, as the authors will have shown in previous chapters, is driven at present not by policies or regulations that want to expand a public sphere but mostly by techniques or logics of ease and opportunity. These logics are not necessarily evil and nor are they part of a capitalist conspiracy to restrict access or to control people. They do have an effect, though, on how collaborative rules might be possible. This chapter explores some of these spaces and describes some of the practices, the possibilities, and the problems in relation to open communicative spaces in action.

Chapter Seven: Collaborative Rules explores some of those communicative spaces on the Internet that *have* established collaborative rules that best approximate the structural conditions required for a public sphere. As you will see, the vernacular surrounding those communicative spaces differs radically from the language surrounding other spaces.

The Conclusion reasserts the importance of considering both the material environment of the Internet—the software, the hardware and the infrastructure—as well as the intents of actors that engage within and through this environment. It suggests that there are different futures that are possible and that forms of these differing futures are all evident now in various ways. But it also suggests that while in some ways these futures have already been determined—by the adoption of particular understandings of information and communication and also by the lack of generalized competencies amongst citizens more broadly, in other ways there are opportunities to expand these engagements, to generate common intrinsic interests, and to strengthen the possibilities for the enactment of public spheres and an informed citizenry.

The Internet is a complex, differentiated environment that affords many practices and constrains others. It is not as simple as saying that it is bad or it is good; that it is public or private, commercial or communal: all of these characteristics or tendencies exist together—often within the same space or engagement. The challenge is to develop languages and tools to critically engage with these environments and to find a way to navigate the topology of being a citizen in a technologically mediated environment. The following pages begin to undertake such a task.

Information and Its Reality (Definitions, Disciplines and Dichotomies)

The Internet has quickly become one of the most prevalent and important media technologies in contemporary life.

—Geiger (2009)

There can be little doubt that the Internet is important to the social distribution of knowledge and, indeed, important to society as a means of communication. Information and communication as phenomena are intimately linked together and the reality of the one affects the reality of the other.

The study of information is generally taken to be an exact science, with research leading to insights not only about the physical nature of information and its properties but also about the transformative effects of information in human, social, action and relations (see for example, Kochen, 1984; Roberts, 1982; Wersig & Windel, 1985). The concept information, therefore, is often treated as an explanatory concept that is useful, simultaneously, for both the natural and social sciences. However, despite the confidence displayed by Ursul and others that the concept information explains physical and social reality in a way that other scientific concepts do not, there remains no agreed conceptual framework for information and communication within the disciplinary or national and international policy discourses. The disciplinary and policy fields are unclear in terms of scope, objectives, and methodology (More, 1987: 16). "In fact, there is not even agreement on what we are talking about: there is neither an agreed terminology, nor a basic taxonomy" (Ploman & Hamilton, 1980: 214).

In this chapter the authors will explore key historical accounts and discourses in the disciplines of electronic engineering and language to show that the major debates about the nature of information in the key information and communication disciplines always take the same form—those who think of information as an object that has temporal extension (and can be measured and quantified as a result) and those who do not.

Do not panic, however, when you see algorithms about information. The authors present these to show what they mean, not to frighten you if you have a dislike of algorithms. Electronic engineering in particular started theorists thinking about information as a quantity and that thinking extended beyond signal states to questions about information and the human mind. These disciplinary debates matter because issues of agency affect how we design our Internet systems for the social distribution of knowledge. If information determines who we are and what we do, then information is a social actor in its own right. If computers become intentional beings, then how we interact with computers becomes a moral and not only a procedural matter. If the Internet is a social actor in its own right, capable of making decisions and acting on them, then what effects will this have?

As you will see in this chapter, it is not only electronic engineering that has taken an interest in information as an intermediary in human affairs. Language and human communication theorists have taken an interest in the idea of information as a physical code and humans as encoders-decoders. In practice, though each discipline has its own theoretic framework and fundamental concepts associated with the concept 'information'. Usage of the terms 'information' and 'communication' varies widely. For example:

Data: "Information...is essentially raw data. Knowledge is interpreted data." (Kochen, 1970: 49)

Decision-making: "The information contained in a decision-state is related to the mean square variance of the expected values of the courses of action." (Yovits & Abilock, 1974: 166)

Information transfer: "Inherent in at least one set of definitions of the words 'knowledge' and 'information' is the concept that an item of knowledge becomes an item of information, when it is set in motion." (Murdock & Liston, 1967: 197)

Perception: Information is "the experience arising from the direction of attention through the gestures of others to objects and their characteristics and cannot be called 'knowledge'.... Perception is not itself to be distinguished from information." (Mead, 1938: 54–55)

Propositions: "Ontologically information is propositions." (Fox, 1983: 12)

Resource: (where no formal definition has been supplied): "This information decade will be the effort to bridge the widening information gap between supply and demand and to curb the technically speaking high under consumption of information." (Coltoff, 1984)

State-change: "The information of *s* is the amount of uncertainty we are relieved of when we come to know that *s* is true" (Hintikka, 1968: 312). Information is "the alteration of the Image which occurs when it receives a message. Information is thus an event which occurs at some unique point in time and space to some particular individual.... [It is] that-which-occurs-within-the-mind-upon-absorption-of-a-message." (Pratt, 1977: 215)

Conventionally, information carries with it a variety of meanings ranging from news to acts of informing or conveying. The Latin word *forma* is derived from the Sanskrit word *dhar*. *Forma* means shape, figure or contour. The verb *formo* means to give form to something, to form an idea of a thing, to sketch or represent (Lewis & Short, 1900: 768). Modern meanings of information tend to be more discipline dependent. Levitan (1980) identified the following contexts of information: channel capacity; changed behaviour; communication; documents; decision-making; entropy and negative entropy; goal-seeking; information-transfer; information flow; information processing; information storage and retrieval; learning; libraries; medium; message; organisation; problem solving; recorded knowledge; relevance; representation; semiotics; subjective knowledge; subject-matter specialities; selective information; stimuli; uncertainty; variety; word frequencies. According to Levitan (1980: 244) information is infinitely variable in that it characterises every different subject one is able to recognise and "it is ubiquitous in that it pertains to everything." Such a term is of primary importance to all disciplines.

The term 'communication' shares this importance and this ubiquity. Dance (1970) identified fifteen major definitions of communication.

Communication is the verbal interchange of thought or idea. (Hoben, 1954: 77)

Communication is the process by which we understand others and in turn endeavor to be understood by them. It is dynamic, constantly changing and shifting in response to the total situation. (Andersen, 1959: 5)

Interaction, even on the biological level, is a kind of communication; otherwise common acts could not occur. (Mead, 1963: 107)

Communication arises out of the need to reduce uncertainty, to act effectively, to defend or strengthen the ego. (Barnlund, 1964: 200)

Communication: the transmission of information, ideas, emotions, skills, etc., by the use of symbols—words, pictures, figures, graphs, etc. It is the act or process of transmission that is usually called communication. (Berelson & Steiner, 1964: 254)

The connecting thread appears to be the idea of something's being transferred from one thing, or person, to another. We use the word 'communication' sometimes to refer to what is so transferred, sometimes to the means by which it is transferred, sometimes to the whole process. In many cases, what is transferred in this way continues to be shared; if I convey information to another person, it does not leave my own possession through coming into his [sic]. Accordingly, the word 'communication' acquires also the sense of participation. It is in this sense, for example, that religious worshippers are said to communicate. (Ayer, 1955: 12)

Communication is the process that links discontinuous parts of the living world to one another. (Ruesch, 1957: 462)

It (communication) is a process that makes common to two or several what was the monopoly of one or some. (Gode, 1959: 5)

(pl.) ... the means of sending military messages, orders, etc. as by telephone, telegraph, radio, couriers. (American College Dictionary, 1964: 244)

Communication is the process of conducting the attention of another person for the purpose of replicating memories. (Cartier & Harwood, 1953: 73)

Communication is the discriminatory response of an organism to a stimulus. (Stevens, 1950: 689)

Every communication act is viewed as a transmission of information consisting of a discriminative stimulus, from a source to a recipient. (Newcomb, 1953: 66)

In the main, communication has as its central interest those behavioral situations in which a source transmits a message to a receiver(s) with conscious intent to affect the latter's behavior. (Miller, 1951: 191)

The communication process is one of transition from one structured situation-as-a-whole to another, in preferred design. (Sondel, 1956: 148)

Communication is the mechanism by which power is exerted. (Schacter, 1951: 191)

These various usages suggest that the terms 'information' and 'communication' are often considered together and that an analysis of either term should include an analysis of the other. In the following analysis, the authors explore the *reductions* of 'information'—the phenomena to which the terms actually refer; to what is in fact signified in the discourse.

The *Machina Ratiocinatrix*—The Reasoning Machine

Electronic engineering produced a theory of information that encapsulates well the dichotomy between those who hold information to have temporal extension and those who do not. Information theory has become associated not only with the coding and transmission of signals, but also with the "reduction of uncertainty" or "curtailment of variance" of a human's mind or cognitive state, that is, for the human receiver of a message. Campbell (1982: 61) said, for example, that a message conveys no information unless some prior uncertainty exists in the mind of the receiver about what the message will contain. Similarly, according to Sampson, "it seems intuitively plausible that receipt of a less likely message conveys more information" (1976: 9). As Shannon and Weaver (1964: 19) note,

> that would certainly lead one to say that the received message exhibits, because of the effects of the noise, an increased uncertainty. But if the uncertainty is increased the information is increased, and this sounds as though the noises were beneficial! It is generally true that when there is noise, the received signal exhibits greater information.

Ritchie (1986) argued that Shannon defined the information capacity of a channel in terms of entropy minus noise. He called Weaver's statement a serious contradiction. Ritchie did not take into account, however, Weaver's qualification that "uncertainty which arises by virtue of freedom of choice on the part of the sender is desirable uncertainty. Uncertainty which arises because of errors or because of the influence of noise is undesirable uncertainty" (Shannon & Weaver, 1964: 19). The point for our purposes though is clear: Both Shannon and Weaver are open to serious misinterpretation. In order to reduce some uncertainty surrounding Shannon's theory, it is worth outlining basic details of signal transmission.

Imagine that there is a head office in Melbourne, Australia, and a branch office in Sydney connected by a simple telegraph line. Along this line, every second, a signal travels from Melbourne to Sydney. The signals repeat exactly the same pattern and we are unable to stop and start the stream of signals. From an engineering point of view no information has been sent on this channel because it is impossible to vary the pattern of the signal: Where there is a variation of the pattern, there is information. In Shannon's mathematics, information is measured, for the source, by the number of alternative messages at the source's disposal. For the receiver, information is measured by the degree of initial uncertainty as to which of several alternative messages will be sent. The greater the number of messages available to the transmitter, the greater the initial uncertainty for the receiver.

Lathi provided the following example. In a morning paper there are three headlines: (1) Tomorrow the sun will rise in the east; (2) United States invades Cuba; and, (3) Cuba invades the United States. "If we look at the probabilities of occurrence of these three events we find that the probability of occurrence of the first event is unity (a certain event), that of the second is very low (an event of small but finite probability), and that of the third is practically zero (an almost impossible event)" (Lathi, 1983: 608). Information is, in this context, connected with the element of surprise, which is the result of uncertainty or unexpectedness. If p is the probability of the occurrence of a message and I is the information gained from the message it is evident from the above discussion that when $p \to 1$, $I \to 0$, and when $p \to 0$, $I \to \infty$. That is to say, as the probability of the occurrence of a message increases, so does the amount of information decrease. This suggests the following model: $I \sim \log 1/p$ (Lathi, 1983: 608).

Shannon, in introducing entropy as $H = -\sum_{i-1}^{n} p_i \log_2 p_i$ bits/symbol (where i stands for any alternative), formulated the concept of average information. One bit/symbol is the average information contained by a choice between two equally probable alternatives, that is, the value of the equation is unity when exactly two alternatives are considered, each has the probability 0.5, and the log2 is used. Take the example of a person who awakens from a coma and asks "What day is it?" The seven possible outcomes are equiprobable, thus $I = \log 27$ bits $= 2.81$ bits. When all values of p are equal—in any case of equiprobable alternatives—the formula simplifies to $\log 1/p$. The negative sign occurs in the Shannon measure of information because one of the rules for manipulating logarithms is that $\log 1/x = -\log x$ (see also Attneave, 1959).

One useful application of this concept is source encoding. In a discussion of source entropy, Lathi wrote that, from the engineering point of view:

> [The] information content of any message is equal to the minimum number of digits required to encode the message, and, therefore, the entropy H(m) is equal to the minimum number of digits per message required, on the average, for encoding. From the intuitive standpoint, on the other hand, information is thought of as being synonymous with the amount of surprise, or uncertainty, associated with the event (or message). (1983: 612)

Lathi's position is not unlike that of Campbell (1982: 61) who argued that probability measures both knowledge and ignorance, just as Shannon's entropy does. If entropy is a maximum, that is to say, if all the possible messages are equally probable, then his or her ignorance is also a maximum (Campbell, 1982: 63). The engineering and common-sense viewpoints converge, says Lathi, on the notion of source choice. In the ideal system, where source and destination begin from the same set of presumptions, the receiver's uncertainty about the transmitted message is equal to the source's freedom of choice in constructing the message.

However, amount of meaning and amount of information are not equivalent in this context. For example, the statement "Tom is a mammal" is less probable in normal conversational English than the statement "Tom is a man". Yet it is not reasonable to assume that because the statement "Tom is a mammal" is less probable in conversation it is, therefore, more informative. Nonsense sequences or structures require as much information as do those that carry functional meaning (Wicken, 1987). Let us look at a problem Lathi (1983: 656) posed.

> A television picture is composed of approximately 300,000 basic picture elements (about 600 picture elements in a horizontal line and 500 horizontal lines per frame). Each of these elements can assume 10 distinguishable brightness levels (such as black and shades of gray) with equal probabilities. Find the information content of a television picture frame.

The total number of possible pictures is $10^{300,000}$. If all pictures are equally likely the probability of any one picture is: $p = 1/10^{300,000}$

The information content of one picture is: $I = \log_2 10^{300,000}$ or 10^6 bits.

Figure 1: Maximum physical information

Figure 1 provides a graphic view of what maximum information is physically in Shannon's theorem. The picture shows random television signals on a television screen.

If we return to the newspaper headline example, we may say that the semantic content of each proposition or headline is not equivalent to the average information carried by each proposition. There may, indeed, be a relationship between the probability of an occurrence of an event or state of affairs and my interest in that event. The information carried by a signal depends, in part, on what one already knows about the alternative possibilities.

However, preoccupation with entropy does not allow us to deal with the semantic content of particular messages in Shannon's theory. According to Shannon, the fundamental problem of communication from an engineer's point of view is the reproduction at one point, either exactly or approximately, of a message selected at another point. The semantic aspects of this communication are "irrelevant to the engineering problem" (Shannon & Weaver, 1964: 31). Information theory is not associated with the meaning of the message, or the message itself, but rather with the probabilities associated with the message. Tribus related a discussion with Shannon:

> I had asked Shannon what his personal reaction had been when he realized he had identified a measure of uncertainty. Shannon said that he had been puzzled and wondered what to call his function. Information seemed to him to be a good candidate as a name, but it was already overworked. Shannon said he sought the advice of John von Neumann, whose response was direct, 'You should call it "entropy"'. (1983: 476)

This suggests that Shannon reduced information to entropy, and in some senses that is true. Wicken (1987: 184), alternatively, said that Shannon's formula measures the complexity of structural relationships. But Shannon is concerned with a method of calculation for the coding or transmission of accurate messages. Entropy represents the measure of information, rather than information itself.

In his work, Weaver attempted to extend the mathematical theory of information *to issues of human communication in general*. When Weaver defined communication, he said the word 'communication' would be used in a very broad sense to include all of the procedures by which one mind may affect another.

> This, of course, involves not only written and oral speech, but also music, the pictorial arts, the theatre, the ballet, and in fact all human behaviour. In some connections it may be desirable to use a still broader definition of communication, namely, one

which would include the procedures by means of which one...affects another mechanism. (Shannon & Weaver, 1964: 3)

Weaver said that there are three problems associated with the broad subject of communication.

Level A. How accurately can the symbols of communication be transmitted (the technical problem);

Level B. How precisely do the transmitted symbols convey the desired meaning (the
semantic problem);

Level C. How effectively does the received meaning affect conduct in the desired way
(the effectiveness problem). (Shannon & Weaver, 1964: 4)

Weaver argued that the communication paradigm outlined by Shannon
should be considered an expression of that which constitutes human communication.

One can imagine, as an addition to the diagram, another box labelled 'Semantic Receiver' interposed between the engineering receiver (which changes signals to messages) and the destination.... Similarly one can imagine another box in the diagram
which, inserted between the information source and the transmitter, would be labelled 'semantic noise', the box previously labelled as simply 'noise' now being labelled 'engineering noise'. (Shannon & Weaver, 1964: 26)

Weaver's importance to the understanding of reduction of communication and information in this book is in the introduction of 'mind', a word not
found in a reading of Shannon's work. In his conception of communication,
Weaver shifts us from the discourse of engineering to that of social theory and
philosophy. Instead of an engineering channel, he imagined a knowledge
channel.

The concept of the information to be associated with a source leads directly, as we
have seen, to a study of the statistical structure of language; and this study reveals
about the English language, as an example, information which seems surely significant to students of every phase of language and communication.... [Entropy] not only
speaks the language of arithmetic; it also speaks the language of language. (Shannon
& Weaver, 1964: 27–28)

Weaver stressed the fact that in his discussion of Shannon's entropy theory, he is talking about the amount of freedom of choice: "Information is, we
must steadily remember, a measure of one's freedom of choice, and hence the
greater the information, the greater is the uncertainty that the message actually

selected is some particular one. Thus greater freedom of choice, greater uncertainty, greater information go hand in hand" (Shannon & Weaver, 1964: 18).

Weaver's introduction of the knowing subject is clear. Choice and uncertainty are related to the amount of organisation or disorganisation that characterises the knowing subject at any one time (Shannon & Weaver, 1964: 12) In doing so, Weaver translated the parts of the engineering communication system to the problem of knowing. "Thus one says, in general, that the function of the transmitter is to encode, and that of the receiver to decode, the message. The theory provides for very sophisticated transmitters and receivers—such, for example, as possess 'memories'" (Shannon & Weaver, 1964: 17). This means, of course, in Weaver's sense, not only computers but also the knowing subject, who is simultaneously source/transmitter and receiver/destination. If this is not the case, then Weaver's point about the importance of entropy to every phase of language and communication is lost. We use language.

For Weaver, knowledge cannot be exhaustively defined. However, it is possible to reduce it to its basic parameters—to construct its model. Entropy in Weaver's model constitutes the logical principle of transformation of knowledge. Learning, life and knowledge are subordinate to the principle of entropy. This may sound like an exaggeration of Weaver's position. However, he helped provide the basis on which authors (such as Campbell who was cited earlier) develop Shannon's second theorem into a universal principle at work in human affairs. Weaver's paper is not about mechanical cognition, nor the operation of the engineering communication system. It is about human cognition. The knowing subject, information source/transmitter or receiver/destination, is bound to the same laws as Shannon's source. "Information theory" in Weaver's sense, then, becomes associated with the general limitations of human cognition and with the relative degree of our lack of organisation.

Weaver called communication all the procedures by which one mind may affect the other. A sympathetic reading would suggest that Weaver meant that communication is all those procedures outside the mind that involve signal transmission. If this is the case, then Weaver, like Shannon, reduced communication to the "transfer of accurate signals." Weaver's intervention of "semantic receiver," however, would suggest that this was not his contention. We may substitute the phrase "human interactive behaviour" for "communication" in Weaver's analysis.

Discovering what Weaver meant by entropy is not a simple task. At one moment in the text it is said that "information is measured by entropy," specifying a difference between the concepts, then it is said that "entropy is related to 'missing information,'" and finally, that "entropy and information" are equivalent concepts (Shannon & Weaver, 1964). Weaver maintained the inverse relation between information and meaning introduced by Shannon. However, his speculations alter the discipline-dependent nature of Shannon's theory.

Weaver suggested that human choice and uncertainty are constrained in the same way that source choice and receiver uncertainty are constrained in cryptography. Choice, in this instance, does not refer to freely chosen ends. It means that the more likely it is that a particular statement will be made in normal conversational English, the less informative it will be. The greater the cognitive uncertainty associated with a statement, the greater my cognitive organisation as a result. A source's freedom of choice in selection of a message is equivalent to a receiver's uncertainty about that selection. Information reduces to two concepts in Weaver's analysis. We may substitute the phrase "measure of choice" for "information," where reference is made to the source of a message. We may substitute the phrase "measure of uncertainty" for "information," where reference is made to the receiver of a message.

Choice and uncertainty, in both cases, are put in inverse relation to the meaning of a message. Uncertainty and choice, in this context, do not refer to attitudes taken by someone towards the meaning of a message, but the occurrence of a particular message in an ensemble of messages. The 'measure' refers to the degree of order which characterises our cognitive architecture at any moment in time.

When we attempt to understand Shannon's entropy measure or Weaver's gloss on that measure, we encounter difficulty. As Machlup and Mansfield have pointed out, the terms measure, rate and relation refer to some specified object or objects, but it is not clear just what the object, misnamed information, is meant to be. We still have to be told what is being measured (1983: 659). Machlup, in his well-balanced criticism of information theorists, said that their system is a sad misuse of the language. "Appropriate words to use in the context would be signal transmission, actuation or activating impulses" (Machlup & Mansfield, 1983: 661).

Shannon's functional definition of information is transposed by Weaver to general discussion of mind. Machlup's criticism of use of a particular disciplinary language, in areas that are not appropriate for that language, is important. Wiener also claimed to provide a theory of rational behaviour based on information theory. In the study of society his cybernetic epistemology has been influential, even where theorists have claimed to use the cybernetic thesis in a purely metaphorical way (Bateson, 1972). It is necessary therefore to investigate how Wiener conceived of information and communication.

In order to do this, a brief explanation of the way an invention—the flyball governor—works is necessary. James Watt patented the flyball governor for the steam engine in 1782. The governor consists of two balls linked to a vertical spindle that is rotated by the engine. The weight of the balls keeps them down against the spindle. However, centrifugal force of rotation makes the balls fly out and up. In moving up and down as the centrifugal force varies, the governor operates a throttle valve between boiler and engine. This valve is closed when the speed of the engine exceeds normal value and opens when the speed is below normal value (Jonas, 1953). There are two important aspects of this self-regulating mechanism: 1) a part of the energy output is redirected to the controlling apparatus further back in the causal order of the system; that is, feedback; and, 2) this feedback counteracts the machine's action (it is corrective not reinforcing); that is, negative feedback. Servo-mechanisms of a much more complex kind are now common.

Wiener called the science of servo-mechanisms cybernetics. Servo-mechanisms include things like target-seeking torpedoes and electronic computers. Wiener (1950; 1951), in his popular works, attempted to interpret human functions in terms of the mechanisms that take their place and those mechanisms in terms of the replaced functions. In a joint paper with Rosenblueth and Bigelow, Wiener posited that some machines are, like rational beings, intrinsically purposeful. "A torpedo with a target-seeking mechanism is an example. The term servo-mechanism has been coined precisely to designate machines with intrinsic purposeful behaviour" (Rosenblueth, Wiener & Bigelow, 1943: 19).

According to Wiener, rational behaviour is goal-directed behaviour: "The term purposeful is meant to denote that the act or behaviour may be interpreted as directed to the attainment of a goal—i.e. to a final condition in which the behaving object reaches a definite correlation in time or in space with respect to another object or event" (Rosenblueth, Wiener & Bigelow, 1943: 18). What condition is final? It is not the one in which the goal is reached because the finality of the condition defines the goal. Final condition may be taken to mean the condition in which the action ends; in the relativistic sense, a condition of rest. Death for the organism is the most definite correlation to the environment reachable by an organism. This is the goal of the total motion of life as one sequence of active behaviour. Increase of entropy, the move towards disorganisation, defines the direction of all natural processes. In this context, the most important mechanisms of organisation for Wiener were information and communication. These mechanisms proceed beyond the individual into the community (Wiener, 1951: 27).

The cybernetic thesis is that the functioning rational being, like the servo-mechanism, attempts to control entropy, or the trend toward disorganisation, through feedback. It is the tendency of rational beings to produce a temporary and local reversal of the normal direction of entropy (Wiener, 1950: 36). Feedback is the property of being able to adjust future conduct by past performance. "When we desire a motion to follow a given pattern, the difference between this pattern and the actually performed motion is used as a new input to cause the part regulated to move in such a way as to bring its motion closer to that given by the pattern" (Wiener, 1951: 13). Wiener classed communication and control together:

> Why did I do this? When I communicate with another person, I impart a message to him [sic], and when he communicates back with me he returns a related message which contains information primarily accessible to him and not to me. When I control the actions of another person, I communicate a message to him (1950: 24).

This process is regarded as the essence of the rational being's life (Wiener, 1950: 27). The structure of the human mind, following the principle of feedback, is an index of the performance expected from it. Wiener (1950: 141) argued that society can be understood only through a study of the messages and the communicative means which belong to it.

The fundamental idea of communication, for Weiner, is that of transmission of messages. A message, in cybernetic epistemology, is form or organisation and sets of messages that have entropy-like sets of states in the external world. Just as entropy is a measure of disorganisation, the information carried by a set of messages is a measure of organisation. It is possible, therefore, to interpret the information carried by a message as, essentially, the negative of its entropy, and the negative logarithm of its probability (Wiener, 1950: 131). One might still ask of Wiener, as one would perhaps of Weaver, what is information? Wiener explains that,

> It emerges through effector organs, generally [our] muscles. These in turn act on the external world, and also react on the central nervous system through receptor organs such as the end organs of kinaesthesia; and the information received by the kinaesthetic organs is combined with [our] already accumulated store of information to influence future action. (Wiener, 1950: 26)

A kinaesthetic sense is a record of the positions and tensions of muscles (Wiener, 1950: 35). In the afterword of *The Human Use of Human Beings*, Rosenblith said that there is little point in "deriving here the mathematical formula in the manner of information theorists" (Wiener, 1950: 277). The "'commodity' that circulates in a communication system, no matter what its physical form, is information" (Wiener, 1950: 277). Information is, on this view, the content of that which is exchanged with the outer world as we adjust to that world and make our adjustments felt upon it. "The process of using information is the process of our adjusting to the contingencies of the outer environment, and of living with that environment.... To live adequately is to have adequate information" (Wiener, 1950: 26-27). The amount of information held by an individual is not to be equated with the amount of information held by the community. "Whatever means of communication the race may have, it is possible to define and to measure the amount of information available to the race, and to distinguish it from the amount of information available to the individual.... Certainly, no information available to the individual is also available to the race, unless it modifies the behaviour of one individual to another" (Wiener, 1951: 183). Indeed, a community tends to have less information than any one individual. "In connection with the effective amount of communal information, one of the most surprising facts about the body politic is its extreme lack of efficient homeostatic processes" (Wiener, 1951: 185). Homeostatic processes of society are not efficient compared with those of the individual.

Wiener's work, like Weaver's, is highly suggestive. Any pattern or form may be transmitted. For example, it is feasible to send a person by telegraph (Wiener, 1950: 139–140). "The distinction between material transportation and message transportation is not in any sense permanent and unbridgeable" (Wiener, 1950: 133–144). In cybernetic philosophy, therefore, it is not at all a question of conservation of simple content or substance that is of concern. Rather we are concerned with perpetuation of form or pattern; the preservation of the idea; the maintenance of the genotype. Deviations from form must be corrected; this is the function of feedback. Feedback is a mechanism of equilibrium between a structure and its environment. The equilibrium represents a play of opposing forces, just as the flyball governor entails opposing movements of compensation with regard to exterior influences. Without feedback, communication and information are incomplete. Feedback implies that each pattern sent produces a pattern in return.

Wiener argued that information is not a commodity in any sense.

What makes a thing a commodity? Essentially, that it can pass from hand to hand with the substantial retention of its value and that the pieces of this commodity should combine additively in the same way as the money paid for them. (1950: 158)

A given amount of electrical energy may be the same at both ends of a transmission line and a price may be placed on electrical energy in kilowatt hours. The power to conserve itself is a helpful property for a commodity.

> Information, on the other hand, cannot be conserved as easily, for as we have already seen the amount of information communicated is related to the non-additive quantity known as entropy.... Just as entropy is a measurement of disorder, so information is a measure of order. Information and entropy are not conserved, and are equally unsuited to being commodities. (Wiener, 1950: 158–159)

The message is information in Wiener's theory, where the message is form, where that form is a local enclave in the general stream of increasing entropy. What then did Wiener mean by information as the content we exchange with the world as we act and react on that world? He meant nothing static. "Information is more a matter of process than of storage" (Wiener, 1950: 166). Information may be a message consisting of the interception of a beam of light in a photoelectric door. Any performed action, rather than intended action, is always a sign of information. A signal or code is not to be equated with information under Wiener's analysis. The odours perceived by an ant may appear to lead to standardised conduct, "but the value of a simple stimulus...for conveying information depends, not only on the information conveyed by the stimulus itself, but in the whole nervous constitution of the sender and the receiver of the stimulus" (Wiener, 1951: 183). Without a code of sign language all I need to do is to be alert to those moments when another shows signs of interest or emotion; that is to say, a signal does not require intrinsic content (Wiener, 1951: 183). In Wiener's analysis, we may substitute the phrase "negative entropic messages" for "information." However, information can be used in three senses in this context:

1.   primary perception or sensation;
2.   messages or patterns;
3.   negative entropy.

The three senses form an unbreakable trinity in Wiener's work. It is not surprising, therefore, that Wiener cited Leibniz as the patron saint of cybernetics. "The *calculus ratiocinator* of Leibniz contains the germs of the *machina ratiocinatrix*; the reasoning machine" (1951: 20). Communication is "feedback (error correction)" in cybernetic epistemology, and its purpose is control. Purpose, for Wiener, lies in wholes, receptors plus effectors plus the coupling in the form of the multiple system. Intrinsic purpose in the rational being therefore is not unlike that of target-seeking torpedoes—the torpedo adjusts itself in relation to other entities in relation to its target. In the case of humans, all our conduct is related to adjustments in relation to the final condition which defines our goal.

In the cybernetic epistemology we have examined, negative entropic messages have nothing to do with knowledge or the acquisition of knowledge in the process of informing. Information need is not a thirst for knowledge. Communication need is not a requirement for loving human company. The sole purpose of human communication is control, and information provides the means to that control through the reduction of uncertainty and by providing the basis for action. Thus, Wiener was concerned with the basics of behaviour control in the organism.

Weiner's argument, by no means simple, has been incorporated in relational message theory. According to Bateson, for example, the elementary unit of information "is a difference which makes a difference, and it is able to make a difference because the neural pathways along which it travels and is continually transformed are themselves provided by energy" (1972: 459). Information, in Bateson's theory, as in Wiener's, is not possessed or processed by minds; it is processed by wholes, by systems.

> The cybernetic epistemology which I have offered you would suggest a new approach. The individual mind is immanent but not only in the body. It is immanent also in pathways and messages outside the body; and there is a larger Mind of which the individual mind is only a sub-system. This larger Mind is comparable to God and is perhaps what some people mean by 'God,' but it is still immanent in the total interconnected social system and planetary ecology. (Bateson, 1972: 130)

Here, Wiener's functional definition of information in cybernetics is transposed to a general discussion of human society and human action. It cannot be doubted that cybernetic theory plays a role in analysis of physical consequences of human action, like raising a glass of water to the mouth. However, "From analogy to metaphor is only a short step and users of a metaphor may become so used to it that they adopt the term as the genuine designation of the phenomena or processes they wish to describe" (Machlup & Mansfield, 1983: 652). Wiener does not intend his definition to be metaphoric. His argument is that information is the move towards order or form and that equilibrium is both a personal and social goal.

What we can conclude from the analysis of Shannon, Weaver and Weiner is that there are two ways that we can look at information. The first is nominalist. We use Shannon's calculations to measure signal states. This is a simple reduction of the concept information to signal states. There is no need to talk about the nature of mind in such a reduction. The second way to look at information is through realist eyes. Information is an object with temporal extension that has special properties in its own right. This dichotomous way of looking at information, as we will see in Chapter Three, occurs in a range of information and communication disciplines and has consequences for how we think about humans and how they communicate. This in turn has consequences for how we think of, how we design, and how we use information and communication technologies such as the Internet.

Shannon's theorem has, historically, been translated into other domains, including studies of human communication generally. This has included incorporating theories of encoding and decoding into the theorization of natural language. In turn, this has led to the idea that there is a gap to be bridged in any human communication and that that gap is met by code.

Humans as Encoders and Decoders

According to Wilbur Schramm, communication research in the United States is concerned with all the ways in which ideas are exchanged and shared: "Thus we are talking about both mass and interpersonal communication. We are talking about the spoken word, signal, gesture, picture, visual display, print, broadcast, film—all the signs and symbols by which humans try to convey meaning and value to one another" (1963: 6). Schramm's description of the process of human communication is interesting. In its simplest form, he said, the communication process consists of a sender, a message, and a receiver. The sender and the receiver may even be the same person, "as happens when an individual thinks, or talks to himself. But the message is at some stage in the process separate from either sender or receiver. There comes a time when whatever we communicate is merely a sign that stands for some meaning to the sender and that stands to the receiver for whatever meaning he reads into it" (Schramm, 1963: 7).

Some internal activity precedes the offering of signals or signs or messages. "One must feel a reason for communicating in the first place" (Schramm, 1973: 48). That internal activity involves information processing and results in message encoding and "giving orders to the musculators of the body that produce the signs" (Schramm, 1973: 48). According to Schramm, this is a Type A communication act. When someone makes use of the signs or signals, this is a Type B communication act. "That is, someone must direct his [sic] attention to them, extract certain information from them through his sensory channels and (in his black box) process that information" (Schramm, 1973: 48).

Signals have the capacity to represent. These signals, at some point in the process, fall out of our control.

> For a moment it may seem strange to think of the signs as being separate. Yet if we re-call one of our own common experiences with communication—mailing a letter or a manuscript and then wishing one had it back to make some changes or perhaps to re-consider whether to send it at all—we can understand this situation. (Schramm, 1973: 49)

Schramm (1973: 38) wrote that information is the stuff of human communication. By information, he did not mean facts or truth nor did he mean instruction or the kind of knowledge we find in an encyclopaedia. Instead he referred back to Shannon and Weaver's use of the term, arguing that "We are using the term in a way not unlike that in which Shannon and Wiener used it when they wrote about information theory and cybernetics: anything that reduces the uncertainty of a situation" (1973: 38). But Schramm's interpretation of Shannon is suspect. For example, for Shannon, a bit is a useful device for calculation; for Schramm a bit is that which resolves uncertainty.

The influence of the uncertainty, or negative entropy, thesis should not be underestimated. In China, social scientists have adopted the conception with vigour (Li Ming, 1985). Schramm is not alone in his interpretation of information theory, the notion is replicated by a range of authors. Krippendorf, for example, wrote:

> The second concept in the title of this paper is information. By this I do not mean a statement of fact (as opposed to entertainment or pleasure), knowledge about the world, or the content a message conveys. Although facts, knowledge, and message content involve information in some way, I find it useful to regard information as a change in an observer's state of uncertainty caused by some event in this world. This conception of information is not new, although its process nature is rarely realized. By way of explanation, let me compare information with the more acceptable concept of energy: I would suggest that information is related to uncertainty as energy is related to matter. (1984: 49)

And J.R. Pierce has suggested that:

> The need for communication arises because something unguessable must be imparted concerning our understanding or actions. A little must be added to what we already know or as a basis for modifying what we would otherwise do. It is this element of the unguessable that Shannon measures as entropy. And it is the unguessable, the surpris-ing, that is an essential part of communication, as opposed to the mere repetitions of gestures, incantations, or prayers. (1961: 8)

For Schramm (1973: 57, 64) there is no way that a message can directly cause overt behaviour. It is the sign that is shared rather than the meaning. A sign (a sound, a gesture, a written word, a picture) is a cognitive intermediary in mass communication theory that stands for information. A sign represents things like ideas and thoughts or "hidden information such as the name of the person occupying an office" (Schramm, 1973: 61). But Schramm, according to his earlier definition of information, excluded things like knowledge or meaning. To reconcile this apparent conflict, he suggested that there are other kinds of information and a contemporary, Cherry (1959), took this up. Cherry differentiated between syntactic, semantic, and pragmatic information.

Syntactic information is no less than Shannon's information theory. The probabilities concerned are relative frequencies of signs or their estimates, that is, statistical probabilities (Cherry, 1959: 242). Semantic information refers to the meta-language of an external observer. The natural human language is the object language and the scientific language that describes it is the meta-language. Meta-language is abstracted from all human sign users and concerns the rules associated with declarative sentences, that is, propositions.

> We may regard the signal ("symbol") s as one of the set employed in the communication channel A->B, being watched and described by an external observer; then the statement 'The symbol s is transmitted' is made by this observer in his [sic] meta-language, whereas s is in the object-language and its 'meaning' is quite irrelevant to the semantic information content of this statement. (Cherry, 1959: 241)

An external observer operates at the level of syntactic and semantic information and is, in Cherry's theory, limited in what it is possible to report on. An external observer can observe "the transmission of signs between the communicators, and assess their probabilities objectively, as frequencies.... Thoughts, beliefs, judgements, emotions are all private; they cannot be observed and described in an external observer's meta-language" (Cherry, 1959: 243). The final kind of information is pragmatic information.

> As we have presented our argument here, a sign sets up two kinds of reaction in a recipient—overt responses and other internal changes in the state of his [sic] nervous system correlating with a changed 'state of mind'. The receipt of the sign causes him to make some overt response and at the same time adds to his accumulation of experiences; for that instant he is no longer the same man. (Cherry, 1959: 264–265)

By 'mind', Cherry did not mean some unknown entity but a specific ensemble of experiences (inborn factors, environmental influences). His thesis is that we rank-order beliefs; that there are degrees of intensity of belief just as there are degrees of freedom of choice in Weaver's theory. Pragmatic information is a change from a prior to a posterior state of belief. The hearing of an utterance, for example, has two results: "it has changed your state of belief, and it has selected an overt response in you" (Cherry, 1959: 248).

Human communication, we are told, actually takes place at the level of pragmatic information (Cherry, 1959: 242). Rational judgements are reduced to likelihood function in Cherry's analysis. "You may believe that the letter T occurs more often than Z, or that some words or phrases are more frequent than others; you have an immense store of beliefs, gathered from experience, concerning the probabilities of events of all kinds" (Cherry, 1959: 245). Therefore, if my range of hypotheses is reduced, my beliefs become more restricted and my uncertainty is made less. When I reply to you, this constitutes a selective action exerted upon me by signs, "a selection, perhaps, corresponding to your 'most intense' belief, though not necessarily" (Cherry, 1959: 248).

Cherry argued that a division between mind and matter is a false one: "Minds are not things, to be possessed" (1959: 262). But it is precisely a subject and object dichotomy that Cherry and Schramm create. The true process of human communication operates at the subjective level. "Statistical laws of human utterances [have] nothing whatever to do with free-will" (Cherry, 1959: 104). In Schramm and Cherry's work, it is "signs" or "codes" or "messages" that bridge a "gap" between two individuals, or between one thought and another, in the process of communication.

Malmberg (1963) presented an account as a specialist in linguistics that appears to be representative of this view. He started from what he called a very simple case of communication between two individuals. One, the sender, conveys a message to another, the receiver. In principle, he can do that in many different ways. He may use cries, or gesture, or mimic. He may attract another person's attention by shouting, whistling. The receiver may or may not interpret the message correctly (in accordance with the sender's intention).

> If, or to what extent he will 'understand' depends on the number of possibilities he [sic] has at his disposal of interpreting the other person's behaviour, and this number will be determined by the context and by the receiver's previous experiences and personal capacity. The interpretation is guesswork, the success of which is a question of probability. The degree of understanding is to a very large extent correlated to the degree of predictability of the elements communicated (i.e. to the amount of redundancy) (Malmberg, 1963: 17–18).

Malmberg said that this is a simple case of communication between two individuals. He exemplified the mechanics of this communication with "a 'normal' linguistic contact, i.e., a situation where a sender chooses to encode his [sic] message into a linguistic form" (Malmberg, 1963: 18). That is to say, any occasion when one person talks to another. The example includes a scene where a person comes across a murder and screams "Murder!" On Malmberg's analysis the message communicated by the scream is that a person has been or is being murdered. A message is encoded into the sign "Murder!" by a sender and transmitted to the ears of a receiver. The message is decoded by a receiver who interprets the sign.

Communication and information may well be processes, but is Malmberg's description of the process correct? Do we code and decode when we simply talk to one another? Or do we, in fact, resort to conveying or communicating messages only when we cannot directly say what we wish? For example, if a mother says she cannot communicate with her daughters she does not mean she has lost the faculty of speech. The gap to be bridged is the generation gap and not a communications gap. Where is the communications gap in natural linguistic contacts? We do not bridge a gap by talking to each other. It can be argued that it is a fundamental error to suppose that a person comes to understand what another says by the way it is said unless the person does not understand what the other is saying (Seidensticker, 1974).

According to Malmberg, there are three sub-coding processes involved in the translation of linguistic messages. A receiver recognises an acoustic stimulus "i.e. those of them which are picked out as important according to the code" (1963: 27). Reference is made in this instance to a set of codes stored in the brain (first sub-code). Phonome sequences are then translated into signs or words by reference to rules of a code (second sub-code). The relationships among these signs or words are in turn recognised by reference to distributional rules, sentences and sentence sequences, of the code (third sub-code).

Malmberg (1963: 31) argued that there are two kinds of information. The first kind deals with meaning. The second kind he called distinctive information,

> i.e. the distinctive characteristics which make it possible for the receiver to identify the signs—or more exactly their expression level, for this identification does not necessarily imply understanding of the message. Information in this sense has consequently nothing to do with meaning and has no reference to the outside 'facts' about which a receiver may be informed through the linguistic message.

Malmberg is referring here to information theory. He placed his discussion about information in the context of Wiener, Cherry and others (1963: 32, 33).

Malmberg said that it is important to understand that the encoding of a message into a linguistic form concerns the content itself and that "it is of no, or little, use talking about 'the same content' or the same ideas or concepts differently expressed on different occasions or in different languages" (1963: 19). By this, he meant that the amount of information, the probabilities associated with the reception of a message, are bound by particular sender-receiver contexts. Messages and codes are not transferable directly "with the same amount of information—not more and not less—into any other language" (1963: 20). For example, if I screamed the English word "murder" in a Russian city, I would increase the amount of information associated with the message and decrease the amount of order. "Order favours predictability and consequently reduces the information capacity of each item of a pattern. Disorder on the contrary increases the amount of information of each unit of a pattern, since disorder excludes predictability. Chaos implies chance" (1963: 32). Malmberg's thesis is that language is probabilistic in nature and leads to either order or chaos. "The amount of information (WIENER's term) consequently also becomes a measure of the degree of order—associated with those patterns which are distributed as messages in time" (1963: 32). Sounds have an identity and the way we make those sounds has an effect on the a priori probabilities associated with their reception.

Malmberg said that a thorough knowledge of a code is necessary on the part of the sender and the receiver. This knowledge "is one of the indispensable conditions for language to function, another condition must be that the code remains identical with itself from one moment to another" (1963: 178). There need not be perfect identity between one person's code and another person's code; "quasi-identity is enough...and even a considerable amount of so-called semantic noise is perfectly tolerable" (1963: 179).

Let us return to Malmberg's example of the person who screams "Murder!" We are asked to believe that the message communicated by the scream is that someone is being, or has been, murdered. The message is encoded in the English language sign "Murder!" by a sender and transmitted by the sound of a scream to a receiver. The message is deciphered by a receiver capable of interpreting the sign. The example entails, therefore, all three sub-coding principles outlined by Malmberg.

Malmberg wrote that auditory stimuli are received during speech as *gestalts* (1963: 25). This would suggest that Malmberg was not advocating a conscious or semi-conscious process of encoding and decoding of signals, signs, and relationships between words and sentences. However, in his description of a "natural linguistic contact" Malmberg uses many of the elements of the theory of encoding and decoding found in the works of Shannon, Wiener and Cherry. Indeed, Malmberg, in his explanation of how language comes to be acquired, set up an opposition between the chaos of chance, on the one hand,

and the order of language, on the other hand. Our choices in the use of language conform to the kinds of choices outlined in the mathematical theory of information. That is to say, we come to understand what someone is saying by the way it is said. The question for the sender in Malmberg's murder example, therefore, is which a priori probabilities might attach themselves to the reception of a particular sound and which sign choices, "Killing", "Manslaughter", "Violent robbery", convey the least "distinctive information". The more the "distinctive information," the greater the chaos.

Figure 2 below provides a visual representation of what the authors think that the encoding-decoding thesis look like. It gives the impression that we are bound in a system.

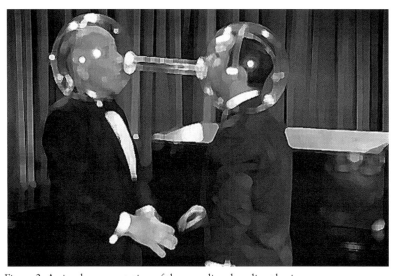

Figure 2: A visual representation of the encoding-decoding thesis.

Seidensticker (1974) agreed that the idea of encoding and decoding has been influential in the study of language and human communication, but that it was not necessarily an accurate description of a language act.

> It should be obvious that the scream "Murder!" in Malmberg's example is not a sign encoding the message that someone has been, or is being, murdered. Somehow Malmberg was led to misconstrue the obvious. He set about to show us how language functions as a communications system without the slightest attention to the question: what would ever make us think that anything is communicated by means of language? He finds it possible to discuss a 'natural linguistic contact' as if it were a genuine case of communication, talking about signs, messages, transmissions, interpretations, senders and receivers, only because he is already captured by the view of language as a medium of communication. (Seidensticker, 1974: 35–36)

Seidensticker's last point about "language as a medium" is an important one. The murder witness does not have to resort to encoding and decoding processes because it is possible to say "Murder!" directly. If a person did not understand what the murder witness was saying, then it is highly likely that the murder witness would have to resort to processes of encoding and decoding in order to convey a message.

> Compare the following two examples: (I) A miner is trapped by a cave-in. He is completely cut off from the outside world. He must communicate to those on the ground that he is alive and where he is trapped. He begins tapping on the wall with a stone in a steady, repetitive pattern. The tapping is heard. His rescuers know that he is alive and what they must do to free him. (II) I sit down to dinner with my family. As I do I say 'I'm hungry.' Do I communicate with my family in a manner parallel to the trapped miner's communication with his rescuer's? Are the sounds I make by saying 'I'm hungry' analogous to his tapping? Does my saying 'I'm hungry' convey a message (that I'm hungry) in the way that his tapping does (that he is alive and where he is trapped?). The analogy does not hold. The miner makes sounds to indicate his presence. I do not make sounds to say 'I'm hungry.' (Seidensticker, 1974: 38).

Similar considerations apply to Malmberg's "Murder!" example. Are codes and messages cognitive intermediaries or do we only use codes in situations where we cannot directly say what we wish? Is knowledge of codes a prerequisite for the use of language? Certainly, the miner must make sounds and messages to inform rescuers of his presence. The way he makes those sounds will have an important effect on how he is to be understood. But it does not follow that use of a language is use of a code, and even less so that the way we make sounds is the way I come to be understood, unless someone does not understand what I am saying.

Malmberg differs from Cherry in his treatment of human communication in important respects. Following Cherry, Malmberg characterised codes and messages as triadic in nature and human communication and language as an encoding and decoding process. However, Malmberg also argued that language is an expression of a particular social structure (1963: 179).

The difficulty with Malmberg's theory is that language is viewed as a medium. The a priori probabilities assigned to signals, words and word sequences may differ from one situation to another and from one culture to another, but if we all made sounds in the same way we would all be understood.

The authors' point here is not to say that Malmberg is wrong in all his explanations of how language works, but rather to indicate how widespread have become the effects of the idea of a language act as achieved by encoding and decoding. It has been pointed out also that, perhaps, absence of codes may be a characteristic of normal conversations and that use of codes may only be a special case. Schramm and Cherry presented us with what appear to be common sense examples of human communication. But when the mechanics of that communication are described we discover examples that contradict common sense. Schramm (1963: 7) suggested that thinking is a form of communication, and that a sender-receiver relation operates in processes of deliberation. A working assumption of Schramm and Cherry is that a gap has to be bridged to communicate or to think. In a trivial sense this is true. A community can be spatially isolated. But this is to miss the point. A community can never be socially isolated.

In the work of Schramm and Cherry, it is the sign or code or message that bridges a gap between people or thoughts. A code is a fundamental intermediary that requires decoding. Information, in this context, does not reduce to a single concept, but to three.

The first reduction is to coded messages (signs). There are three functions of a code when transmitted: statistical, propositional and representational. A coded message is an external manifestation of information.

The second reduction is to picture (image). There is, supposedly, a correspondence between a thought encoded into a particular signal (Murder!) and a picture in the mind of the receiver of a signal (Murder!). The image is an internal manifestation of information.

The third reduction relates to both external and internal aspects of information. Schramm and Cherry reduce information to reduction of uncertainty.

Human communication, similarly, has its external and internal aspects. The first reduction is to transmission of codes (motion): Language is a channel along which codes are transmitted. The second reduction is to picture (image) alteration: On receipt of a coded message the picture in a person's head is changed. Schramm warned us not to take Shannon's diagram, and its derivatives too literally: "No thoughts are transported or transferred. On the contrary, a source, drawing upon his [sic] internal resources, encodes something that becomes separate from him, and a destination decodes some or all of those signs to be interpreted and added to the destination's internal resources" (Schramm, 1973: 298). However, the encoding-decoding model of human communication appears to be none other than what Reddy (1979: 7) called a conduit metaphor which leads to the "bizarre assertion that words have insides and outsides." The notion that thoughts themselves are encoded into signals is a powerful one. Many of our statements about knowledge imply the movement of knowledge along some form of conduit.

Schramm and Cherry lead us to misconstrue the obvious. It is true that I cannot speak without making sounds but it does not follow that speaking is nothing more than making sounds. It can be argued that it is precisely when I cannot say something directly that I resort to encoding, decoding and transmitting messages. If language is a form of code, then the use of language is the use of a code. Does it follow that when you speak you carry out encoding, and that when you listen you decode? In some sense this must be true. When we speak we exercise our vocal apparatus to produce pressure waves in the air about us, which a listener translates as speech. But this is not to say that the use of language is an act of encoding or decoding. When we use language we influence the understanding or actions of others. We act and react to language and we do not generally go through an additional act of encoding or decoding unless we fail to understand one another (for example, if we speak to a French person and do not understand the language well). A similar point applies to codes in general. Take the case of red/amber/green traffic lights. In most of our driving we do not decode these to 'I am being commanded to stop', 'I am being warned that I am going to be commanded to stop' and so on. Rather, we simply stop for red, go for green and slow for amber. We respond to the signal itself, not to a translation of it. Equally, we generally respond to speech, not to a decoding of it. A language act is executed by an encoding process (into air vibrations) but a language act need not be an act of encoding.

Take the example of a smuggler at night on the Welsh shore who has the choice of placing one lantern on a post to tell smugglers at sea that "all is safe" or two lanterns to tell them that "the police are coming." The amount of uncertainty of the smugglers at sea is not unlike that of Shannon's measure with the unit information the choice between equally probable alternatives. The smuggler on shore decides one night to send a written note to the colleagues at sea. On the note is written "Two lanterns on the post." If the note were intercepted by police, the constable would not be puzzling about how to interpret the language sign "Two lanterns on the post." The constable would be attempting to interpret the sign to decode the message. If a smuggler sends a note telling his or her colleagues at sea that "The police are coming" this is hardly a sign that needs to be interpreted in order to decode the message.

The problem relates to need. The smuggler, when on shore, needs to send coded messages to the smugglers at sea. However, it might be argued that I do not create the English language sign "I love you" in order for you to interpret the sign to decode the message. I do not make sounds to say "I love you." I may communicate my love to others by a show of affection under particular circumstances. People may correctly interpret my behaviour. But when I say something, it is not a sign of what I intended to say. If I say I will no longer communicate with you, I do not mean that I have abrogated the conventions of interpreting language signs.

Take, as another example, the notion of telepathy. It is not necessary for the purpose of the example that telepathy actually exist. The point is that the notion is not nonsensical. It is logically possible to posit the fulfilment of the conditions of human communication without codes, signs or signals or their transmission, as defining characteristics of human communication. If my intentions are made known to another, as long as those intentions are recognised, I have communicated with another. Human communication is a purposeful activity involving intentions. Since human communication centrally involves recognition of intentions, then its important operations become those to do with intention. Thus it is that people can truly be said to be communicating although they have not the least interest in the code, sign, signal or mode of transportation of codes, signs or signals—these are merely means. Since human communication is indifferent to actual motion or the means by which human communication is executed, the conception of human communication can survive where no means or motion exist. Human communication takes as its premise that one may communicate without traversing the space between, thus breaking the fundamental conditions of motion, signal and code, but satisfying the conditions of human communication since these are indifferent as to how human communication is accomplished (Figure 3).

Figure 3: Language is not an encoding-decoding channel.

These are not minor theoretical issues. "If theoretical language inevitably carries with it implications for action, then the scientist can no longer take refuge in the Shangri-la of 'pure description'" (Gergen, 1982: 205). The encoding-decoding model of communication, when misapplied, carries with it consequences for our conceptions of the nature of language and the formation of meaning. Some considerations arise immediately. Our ability to interpret and explain, according to the encoding-decoding thesis, is not dependent upon the practices of justification that obtain between you and me, but upon pre-culturally determined codes. As suggested earlier, there is a difference to be made between a language act and encoding and decoding. But this difference is not accepted by the code theorists. We must unpack a natural language sign to recover a message. This unpacking requires an underlying code.

Human language is extensible, able to talk about itself, and allows the flexible creation of new speech structures by the application of syntactic rules (for example, sentence creation). If use of human language is dependent on an underlying code—one that we are not responsible for so to speak—then meaning is not formed through social practice and justification, but by some other means. The local rules of a given language are a result of an underlying code to which we consciously or unconsciously refer when we encode and decode. The notion that coded messages are cognitive intermediaries that 'bridge a gap' gives the impression that messages exist independently of the language into which they are encoded. What fills the 'gap' is language, regarded as a channel along which codes travel. The meaning of a message is fixed because a cognitive representation has been encoded into a natural language sign. The recovery of that message therefore is dependent on the encoding-decoding apparatus of the individual, that is, the procedural competence of the hearer. Interpretation may be a matter of guesswork, but the code is reliable.

Our ability to think creatively is dependent upon language. We think not in complete abstractions but most commonly in words (Schauer, 1982: 54). If human communication is stifled, the development of language is restricted. The problem with the encoding-decoding thesis is that it narrows the scope of inquiry in human communication. It assumes that procedures involved in making sounds are human communication. The authors have argued the opposite. Our ability to explain and interpret is not determined by the sounds we make or by the codes we use even though we make sounds and use codes. We have argued that the encoding-decoding model confuses language acts with their method of execution.

The reduction of information to reduction of uncertainty may be considered independently of the coding issue. Cherry (1959: 104) argued that we have free will, not bonded to statistical probabilities associated with messages. If knowledge is not a well-defined and stable statistical ensemble, then what use is the peculiar alteration of Shannon's theory? If the effect of information is reduction of uncertainty, then what would amount of information mean?

As an analogy, consider the problem of amount of pain. Is there, can there be, more pain in the world than the pain suffered by one individual? You cannot add together the pain of individuals to get a total of suffering. Can you add together the information of individuals if information is reduction of uncertainty? According to the argument promoted by Schramm and others, information is not facts, knowledge or meaning, but it does reduce uncertainty. A consequence of this reduction is to construe all information as of value if and only if it reduces uncertainty. Something, of whatever nature, that puts me in doubt (does she love me?) would not be information. Of course, what is of value for Schramm and Cherry are those things where there is a determinate answer: hypothesis testing and decision-making.

Summary

There can be little doubt that the mathematical theory of information did two things. Firstly, it introduced to the world the idea of information as a quantity and the idea of channels and networks required to deliver that quantity. Secondly, it provided the basis for theorizing information as a causal agent in and of itself—an agent that has special effects. In 2010, these key assumptions about information remain, with the resulting confusion over what information as a causal agent in fact is. Hjorland (2007) for example says that the key questions are:

- Is information in the author/sender of the information?
- Is information in the texts/symbols/messages?
- Is information in the receiver understood as a biological being?
- Is information in the receiver understood as a social/cultural/specialized being?

Hjorland (2007) however, misses the fact that each discipline has two positions on information. The first is nominalist—in name only. In Shannon's theory, information refers to signal states and these signals may be more or less organised. The term 'entropy' in this context does not relate to the human mind but to the physical dynamics of signal states in electronic transmission. The second position is realist—information is an actor in its own right, as something that determines order or disorder in the human mind, certainty or uncertainty. A reduction of this type is to something real, occupying the place of other objects yet not identical with them. The encoding-decoding thesis draws on a realist view of information.

The impact of the idea of information as a quantity has had a direct effect on theories of information value. In the 1980s it was assumed that the study of information was an exact science and that research would lead "to insights about its nature and properties" (Kochen, 1984: 198). This is despite arguments to the contrary that "as every library science student knows, no sound theoretical or practical means have been found to establish the value of information for an individual or an organization" (Lyttle, 1986: 319). For the *United States National Commission on Libraries and Information Science* (NCLIS) task force report on public sector/private sector interaction in providing information services, for example, the concept of information "appeared and was generally understood to refer to the content or symbolic substance of a communication, as separate from the physical form in which the communication occurred. But despite the appearance of a general understanding of the term, it simply eluded definition" (NCLIS, 1982: 16). One resolution of this dilemma, adopted by task force members, was to treat information "as a commodity, as a tool for better management of tangible resources, as an economic resource in and of itself" (NCLIS, 1982: 26). By the middle of the 1980s the idea of information as a resource was well established. "In 1985 one can state that 'information is a valuable resource' without attracting much attention. In 1980 that statement would have been regarded as odd" (Lytle, 1986: 310).

In ordinary discourse we use the notion of 'resource' in many ways. For instance, we might call our family a resource because we get advice from family members. Equally, we might say that our friends have great resources of will. But the resource conception of information is not of this kind. According to Paulsen (1980: vi), for example, the adage 'information is power' properly refers to the role of information in social power. Perspectives on information power can be examined as "control of information and communications technology, information as a resource to control other resources, information as cybernetic control, and information as a power/work transformation variable" (Paulsen, 1980: v). This is a realist position on information.

The resource conception of information carries with it explicit assumptions about rationality. Information economists, for example, require an epistemology of decision-making behaviour. "The epistemological theory of decision-making is, of course, pretty empty unless we can specify ways in which the inputs of the past determine the present images of the future" (Boulding,

1971: 29). "One should hardly have to tell academicians that information is a valuable resource: knowledge *is* power" (Stigler, 1971: 61).

Proponents of the resource doctrine of information do not support reductions of information to documents, signals or data structures. The NCLIS report is a paradigm example. It specifically avoided identifying information with the media that convey it.

> That definition (in identifying 'information' with the media that convey it, and with a limited set of such media at that) is irreconcilable with the usage in the Task Force. (NCLIS, 1982: 16)

For the NCLIS (1982: 16) task force, rather: "Information is an intangible which can be made available in many media."

The suggestion that information is an intangible, yet an entity of some kind, is not a new one. Stonier (1986: 278) in his new theory of information for information policy, supported the proposition that "'information' is as much a part of the physical universe as are matter and energy and that, like matter and energy, 'information' may be considered a physical entity in its own right." But, by information, Stonier (1989) did not mean documents, signals or data structures.

Arguments about the value of information and its ontology are—as we have seen—related. Kochen (1983: 278) suggested that in the 1950s information meant the reduction of uncertainty whereas in "the 1980s it means decision-relevant data." It is in cognitive science and artificial intelligence that we encounter notions of information bound to effort of cognitive processing and value in decision-making. Relevance of information, in this context, is determined by utility. In the resource doctrine of information, it is the intellectual worker, the "brain worker," that is the resource. Information economists are not interested in what it is to be informed, but in decision relevance. The adages "information is power" and "information is a resource" are, in many ways, unintended consequences of an epistemology of decision-making behaviour. It is for this reason that theorists like Blaise Cronin (1986: 128) said that information activity "is cerebral activity (be it at a low or high level). Inputs and outputs are 'soft.'" And it is information that "has all the hallmarks of the new capital" (Cronin, 1986: 129).

In Chapter Three the authors will explore ideas of information in computing, artificial intelligence and information retrieval. Each of these disciplines tackles information as a phenomenon and each has a direct bearing on what future Internet networks will look like.

Networks and Relevance (Intention, Knowledge Representation and the Theoretical Index of Mind)

We tend to think of knowledge as good in itself, but knowledge is useful only when we can exploit it to help us reach our goals.

—Marvin Minsky (1987: 57)

In Chapters One and Two the authors argued that how information is construed is important to understanding how information networks, codes, or the human mind are thought to work. For theorists like Shannon, signals are intended to provide an adequate indication that the signal sent is the signal received. For theorists like Wiener, signals are more than this: They are a part of an entropic network that defines what happens to the human mind. How the value of information is decided upon will have, and does have, a direct effect on how relevance is embedded in modern computer networks. Minsky's quote above highlights one view of information value. For this understanding, only information that is related to decision-making, problem-solving or the pursuit of goals is seen as relevant; information and relevance are intimately related. In this chapter, the authors look at information and relevance within cognitive psychology, artificial intelligence and information retrieval. These disciplines have immediate and influential links to how our information retrieval systems are designed and how knowledge is represented.

Intentionality

From the cognitive science point of view, computation, information processing, and rule-governed behaviour all depend on the existence of physically instantiated codes or symbols that refer to or represent things and properties outside a behaving system.

> In all these instances, the behaviour of the systems in question (be they minds, computers, or social systems) is explained, not in terms of intrinsic properties of the system itself, but in terms of rules and processes that operate on representations of extrinsic things. (Pylyshyn, 1983: 70)

In order to capture the regularities in a system's behaviour we must mention the content of the representations (Pylyshyn, 1987: 102). Sperber and Wilson (1986) attempted to account for the nature of the mind's representations and the nature of the processes which operate over those representations. They were also concerned with human communication which involves direct evidence of one's intent. Language pairs phonetics with the semantic representation of sentences. However, there is a gap between the semantic representations of sentences and the thoughts actually communicated by sentences. Sperber and Wilson (1986: 9) have suggested that this gap is filled not by more coding but by inference. For example, Peter asks Mary, "How are you feeling today?" Mary responds by pulling a bottle of aspirin out of her bag and showing it to him. Her behaviour is not coded. There is no rule or convention which says that displaying a bottle of aspirin means that one is feeling sick (Sperber & Wilson, 1986: 25). What is involved in bringing about a result intentionally? Peter has to be able to distinguish between mere happenings and deliberate actions. Mary performs her action not only with the intention that Peter should think that Mary intends to obtain a certain response from Peter, but also with the intention that Peter should recognise that Mary has the intention just mentioned. The inference is one from the phenomenon to its cause.

In the case of the Peter-Mary example, we are faced with meaning given to an action on occasion. According to the theory of Sperber and Wilson, Peter must be able to recognise three forms of sign: informative intent, communicative intent, and an assumption or set of assumptions. Mary wants Peter to recognise and fully understand an idea in the propositional form "I'm not feeling well." The process is something like this: Mary performs an act in a certain way and Peter sees the action and infers that Mary made the action with the object that an audience (Peter) should have reason to believe that Mary believes (that Mary is not feeling well). Sperber and Wilson have provided examples that appeal to common sense, but underlying the simplicity is a complex theory of inference processes.

Within the framework of the encoding-decoding model, mutual knowledge is a necessity. If the only way to communicate a message is by encoding and decoding, and if inference plays a role in verbal communication, then the context in which an utterance is understood must be strictly limited to mutual knowledge (Sperber & Wilson, 1986: 18). Shannon required statistical regularity in source and receiver for the selection, transmission and reception of messages. Sperber and Wilson (1986: 15) argued that the set of premises used in interpretation of an utterance constitutes the context. They suggested it is reasonable to assume that people within the same linguistic community converge on the same language and on the same inferential abilities, but this is not true to the same degree of their assumptions about the world. In the mutual knowledge hypothesis, the assertion is that if the hearer of an utterance is to be sure of recovering the correct interpretation, the one intended by the speaker, every item of contextual information used in interpreting the utterance must be not only known by the speaker and hearer, but mutually known (Sperber & Wilson, 1986: 18). Such a hypothesis leads to an infinite regress. It is necessary not only for X to know what Y is, but for X to know that hearer Z knows what Y is, and so on.

Sperber and Wilson (1986: 38) agreed that any account of human communication must incorporate some notion of shared information. But, instead of mutual knowledge, they suggested that cognitive environments intersect now and then. The cognitive environment of an individual is the set of facts manifest to that individual. A fact is manifest to an individual at a given time if and only if he or she is capable at that time of representing it mentally and accepting its representation as true or probably true (Sperber & Wilson, 1986: 39). To be manifest is to be inferable or perceptible. Information, on this view, is facts, but 'facts' includes all assumptions: "From a cognitive point of view, mistaken assumptions can be indistinguishable from genuine factual knowledge" (Sperber & Wilson, 1986: 39). There may be degrees of manifestness. For example, in an environment where the doorbell has just rung, it will normally be strongly manifest that there is someone at the door, less strongly so that whoever is at the door is tall enough to reach the bell, and less strongly still that the bell has been stolen (Sperber & Wilson, 1986: 40). The same information may be manifest in the cognitive environments of two different people. The intersection of cognitive environments constitutes the information two people share.

A communicator produces a stimulus which makes it mutually manifest to communicator and audience that the communicator intends, by means of that stimulus, to make manifest to the audience a set of assumptions (Sperber & Wilson, 1986: 155). Ostensive communication is explained by the principle of relevance. Relevance applies only to ostensive communication and not to coded communication. For example, a telegraph employee who communicates messages by encoding them is expected to be accurate in his or her encoding:

he or she is "not expected to produce particularly relevant stimuli" (Sperber & Wilson, 1986: 158). He or she is engaging in coded communication: The conveying of a message whose content in many ways is irrelevant to the sender (the operator) of the message. However, for the person who provides the original message (which the telegraph operator encodes and later decodes), the message content is relevant and also presumed to be relevant to the final recipient of the message. The relevance of an assumption is assessed in terms of the improvements it brings to an individual's representation of the world. A representation of the world is a stock of factual assumptions with some internal organisation. Many words cannot be defined in terms of, or decomposed into, more primitive concepts. "Take 'yellow'; assume that it can be defined in terms of more primitive concepts: one of the concepts would undoubtedly be colour; what would be the other(s)?" (Sperber & Wilson, 1986: 91).

An assumption is a structured set of concepts. Concepts are contained in logical forms. A logical form is a structured set of constituents, which undergoes formal logical operations determined by its structure (Sperber & Wilson, 1986: 72). Information is stored in memory at certain conceptual addresses: logical, encyclopaedic and lexical. The logical entry in memory, for example, consists of deductive rules which apply to logical forms, that is, a set of premises and conclusions. The encyclopaedic entry contains details about a concept's extension or denotation, that is, the objects, events or properties which instantiate a concept. A lexical entry in memory contains details about natural language that can be used to express a concept (Sperber & Wilson, 1986: 86).

> The whole framework of current cognitive psychology rests on a distinction between representation and computation, of which our distinction between encyclopaedic assumptions and deductive rules is a special case. The information in encyclopaedic entries is representational: it consists of a set of assumptions, which may undergo deductive rules. The information in logical entries, by contrast, is computational: it consists of a set of deductive rules which apply to assumptions in which the associated concept appears. (Sperber & Wilson, 1986: 89)

In order to understand the claim that assumptions are processed in context, and that the relevance of an assumption is analysed in terms of the modification that it brings to the context, Sperber and Wilson (1986: 89) suggested that it is possible to make a distinction between the content of a representation and its context: "The distinction between logical and encyclopaedic entries is thus quite fundamental to our framework." Sperber and Wilson built on the work of Fodor (1981: 26) where propositional attitudes are relational and among the relata are mental representations which are symbols with formal and semantic properties. Mental representations have a causal role because of their formal properties and propositional attitudes inherit their semantic properties from mental representations that function as their objects. The adjustment Sperber made in his earlier work was thus:

> Just as it would be mistaken to define 'speaking' as 'uttering sentences', it is mistaken, I suggest, to define thinking in terms of attitudes to propositions: many of our utterances do not match sentences but semi-grammatical strings; similarly, many of our thoughts are what we might call semi-propositional, they approximate but do not achieve propositionality. (1985: 51)

In the Peter-Mary example, communicative and informative intentions, and all assumptions, are representations. When interconnected, new and old representations are used together as premises in an inference process and further new representations can be derived. When processing of new representations gives rise to such a multiplication effect, the representations are relevant (Sperber & Wilson, 1986: 48). An individual's particular cognitive goal at any given moment "is always an instance of a more general goal: maximising the relevance of the information processed" (Sperber & Wilson, 1986: 49).

Sperber and Wilson were concerned about the nature of operations by which representations are selected, transported, utilised and stored. Cognitive processes may involve transfer of representations (fully formed propositions or otherwise) from one structure to another or from one form to another within the same structure. The problem of intersubjectivity is reduced to the problem of representational and propositional content. Gergen (1982) made a distinction between "exogenic" and "endogenic" views of knowledge. The exogenic view emphasises the role of the external world in the generation of knowledge. The endogenic view holds processes of mind as preeminent. The epistemology of Sperber and Wilson is "endogenic." They take it as basic that we live in a world of things which have some sort of extra-linguistic identity. Pearson, a science writer at the end of last century, provided an account of mind not unlike that of Sperber and Wilson.

> We are like the clerk in the central telephone exchange who cannot get nearer to his [sic] customers than his end of the telephone wires. We are indeed worse off than the clerk, for to carry out the analogy properly we must suppose him never to have been outside the telephone exchange, never to have seen a customer or any one like a customer—in short, never, except through the telephone wire, to have come in contact with the outside universe. Of that 'real' universe outside himself he would be able to form no direct impression. The real universe for him would be the aggregate of his constructs from the messages which were caused by the telephone wires in his office. (1892: 56-58)

The identification of information with sentences and propositions is not new. Fox (1983: 212) argued that, ontologically, information is propositions. There are no well-established theories of either a realist or nominalist bent, but, according to Fox (1983: 18), ordinary discourse dictates the realist position. "For this reason, an information realist position is adopted here. Thus a fundamental premise of this work is that...there is an entity or kind of entity, to which we refer when we use the term information." Fox (1983: 84) rejected such conceptions of information as spatio-temporal entity (process or event), structure, reduction of uncertainty, change of an individual's cognitive state, or Shannon's information theory. His position was that the information carried by a sentence S is a proposition appropriately associated with S. "We characterise information-that as information to the effect that some state of affairs obtains. In other words, our concern in this essay is to investigate the sort of information that embodies claims about what is the case" (Fox, 1983: 84–85). Derr (1985) agreed with Fox that the use of the term 'information' in ordinary discourse provided the clue to the ontological nature of information. He said that information is an abstract, meaningful representation of determinations made of objects. By objects, Derr (1985: 491) meant individuals, groups, situations, linguistic expressions, abstract entities, physical things and "other existents."

The way information and communication are reduced in cognitive psychology is now reasonably clear. We can substitute the phrase "sentence (propositional form)" for "information" in Sperber and Wilson's analysis. This includes representations in encyclopaedic entry in memory and inference rules in logical memory. Inference rules transform representations of the world. The linking concept is propositional form. We can substitute the phrase "intersection of cognitive environments" for the term "communication" because there is, supposedly, sentence (propositional form) equivalence when two cognitive environments intersect.

Sperber and Wilson place the human agent in computational relation to representational or propositional entities. The conditions governing the validity of communicative discourses are the conditions governing formal inference or propositional processes. Sentences (propositional forms) are the result of effort of processing. Each person's goal is to improve that person's representation of the world. All information is directed towards this goal. Effort of processing is a guide to the material value of the sentences (propositional forms) obtained. Sperber and Wilson are at complete odds with those like Gergen (1982: 207) who place "the locus of knowledge not in the minds of single individuals, but in the collectivity."

There are numerous theorists who make a content-relation distinction in human communication theory:

> Communication functions not only to transmit information, but to define the nature of the relationship binding symbol users. (Hawes, 1973: 15)

Communication is a form of action by which persons collectively create and manage social reality. (Pearce & Cronen, 1980: 305)

Human communication is a patterned, spatio-temporal circuit of concatenous events involving two or more persons who are within each other's perceptual field. (Penman, 1980: 14)

It is true that cognitive scientists argue that human communication has more functions than simply information transfer and that society must be taken as a further abstraction to the collective identification. But there is a basic difference between relevance of information determined among people and relevance of information determined by one person's cognitive device. Inference processes do not establish the relevance of information to society. (Indeed you cannot use inference processes to define relevance.) Arguments about the creation of meaning in intersubjectivity are now well established (see for example, Wittgenstein, 1953). *It is important to realise that the emphasis of cognitive science is on decision-making and that information is assessed solely in terms of utility to the cognitive device.*

Intelligent Machines

The interest taken by artificial intelligence scholars in cognitive psychology during the 1950s signalled a fundamental change in computer science. "The key to the change was the concept of information" (Cohen & Feigenbaum, 1982: 5). Research into short-term memory indicated that measurements of memory are best made in terms of "semantic chunks—meaningful units of information—not abstract bits" (Cohen & Feigenbaum, 1982: 5). The result of this shift in emphasis was that Shannon's mathematical formulation "has been largely abandoned" (Cohen & Feigenbaum, 1982: 5).

Minsky (1979: 400), one of the founders of artificial intelligence research, said that computer science attempts to understand ways in which information processes act and interact. Information processes means the processes involved in knowledge representation. Levesque characterised the knowledge representation hypothesis as follows: "Just as there is a calculus of arithmetic, where numerical expressions are formally manipulated in a value-preserving way, so might there be a calculus of thought, where propositional expressions could be formally manipulated in a truth-preserving way" (1986: 257). There are, of course, echoes of Leibniz, whose influence on information retrieval has been mentioned.

Artificial intelligence research is concerned with writing descriptions of a world in which an intelligent machine might come to new conclusions about the world by manipulating symbolic representations. Newell (1982: 90) conceded that though we have programs that search, "we do not have programs that determine their own representations or invent new representations." However, Bobrow and Hayes assessed the state of the art of artificial intelligence research in 1985 and cited a comment by Newell as the best expression of the intention of the discipline:

> One of the world's deepest mysteries—the nature of mind—is at the centre of AI. It is our holy grail. Its discovery...will be a major chapter in the scientific advance of mankind.... There will be a coherent account of the nature of intelligence, knowledge, intention, desire, etc., and how it is possible for the phenomena that cluster under these names to occur in our physical universe. (1985: 388)

There is no theory of knowledge representation (Barr & Feigenbaum, 1981: 147). However, as Newell's comments indicated, there are basic theoretical assumptions at work. Let us look at his principle of rationality. According to Newell, the behavioural law that governs an intelligent system or agent is the principle that knowledge will be used in the service of goals: "If an agent has knowledge that one of its actions will lead to one of its goals, then the agent will select that action" (1982: 102). There exists a distinct computer systems level, lying immediately above the symbol level, "which is characterized by knowledge as the medium and the principle of rationality as the law of behaviour" (Newell, 1982: 99), thus "Knowledge is intimately linked with rationality" (Newell, 1982: 100). Representations exist at the symbol level (data structures and processes) that realise a body of knowledge.

Newell (1982: 90) argued that if a system has and can use a data structure which can be said to represent something (a procedure, an object, for example), then the system itself can also be said to have knowledge—the knowledge embodied in that representation about that thing.

> [When] we talk, as we often do during the design of a program, about a proposed data structure having or holding knowledge K (e.g., 'this table holds the knowledge of coarticulation effects'), we imply that some processes must exist that takes that data structure as input and make selections of which we can say, 'The program did action A because it knew K'. (Newell, 1982: 116)

A representation therefore provides a means of access to a body of knowledge that can be used to make selections of actions in the service of goals. It is a "system for delivering the knowledge encoded in a data structure that can be used by the larger system that represents the knowledge about goals, actions etc" (Newell, 1982: 114).

Newell's principle of rationality can also be found in the work of Minsky which linked knowledge and usefulness together (1987: 57). Minsky's understanding of free will exemplified his epistemology: Whenever a regularity is observed in our behaviour, "its representation is transferred to the deterministic rule region" (Minsky, 1968: 431). What we call consciousness consists of little more than "menu lists that flash, from time to time, on mental screen displays that other systems use" (Minsky, 1987: 57).

In Minsky's theory, our thoughts are largely shaped or framed by things which seem most similar. Standardised situations are frames: "Each type of knowledge needs some form of 'representation' and a body of skills adapted to using that style of representation" (Minsky, 1987: 72). A frame is a skeleton, like an application form, with many blanks or slots to be filled. Minsky referred to these blanks as terminals suggesting that they are used as "connection points to which we can attach other kinds of information" (Minsky, 1987: 245). For example, a frame that represents a table might have terminals to represent the top, legs, and so on.

Mind is made up of agents who turn other agents on and off in a society of mind. Agents form into agencies.

> When you drive a car, you regard the steering wheel as an agency that you can use to change the car's direction. You don't care how it works. But when something goes wrong with the steering, and you want to understand what's happening, it's better to regard the steering wheel as just one agent in a larger agency. (Minsky, 1987: 23)

Different kinds of agent can be attached to the terminals, such as polyneme agents that arouse different activities, at the same time, in different agencies. A polyneme associated with an orange, for example, sets your agencies for colour, shape and size into unrelated states that represent being orange, round, and orange-sized. Polynemes (which should strictly be polymnemes since its root is said to indicate a connection with memory) are connected to frames. A pronome is a type of agent that has a particular role or aspect of a representation, "corresponding for example, to the Actor, Trajectory, or Cause of some motion" (Minsky, 1987: 330). A travel frame may contain the pronomes for Actor-Origin-Trajectory-Destination-Vehicle. When you think of the sentence, "Jack drove from Boston to New York on the turnpike with Mary," you think of New York, "the polyneme for New York is attached to an AND-agent with two inputs; one of them represents the arousal of the travel-frame itself, and the other represents the arousal of the Destination pronome" (Minsky, 1987: 246).

The process of creating meaning, on Minsky's analysis, involves the re-creation of a representation by an agent. To learn to use a new or unfamiliar word, for example, you start by taking it to be a sign that there exists, inside another person's mind, a structure you could use (Minsky, 1987: 131). This position is, unsurprisingly, not unlike that of Sperber and Wilson. Meanings do not correspond to particular structures but to connections among and across fragments of interlocking networks among agencies. Thus it is that Minsky (1987: 429) concluded that mental processes resemble, "the kinds of processes found in computer programs: arbitrary symbol associations, treelike storage schemes, conditional transfer, and the like."

When computer scientists refer to data or to transformed data, they refer to those data as information. Reference to data structures, however, does not inform us of the nature of human experience, or indeed, the meaning an individual may assign to data. It would appear strange to suggest that in computing, in general, the goal of the science is to develop theories of motivation. Yet the principle of rationality suggested by Newell and the self-maintaining engines of Minsky reveal theories of motivation.

General motivational statements do enable us to predict that, in a given situation, a person is likely to act in a certain way because he or she will likely be motivated by such-and-such a factor. However, according to the dispositional laws of Minsky and Newell, we *must* act in a certain way because we *must* be motivated by such-and-such a factor. This is what Newell means by knowledge as the medium and the principle of rationality as the law of behaviour. Information is always in the service of goals and problem solving.

> Each of us has an 'estate'—the collection of possessions we control. And this 'realm of estate' is more important than it might seem, because it lies between the realms of objects and ideas. In order to carry out our plans, it is not enough only to know what things or ideas are required and how to adapt them to our purposes. We must also be able to take possession of those objects or ideas, either by right or might. (Minsky, 1987: 293)

Minsky does not assess the psychological status of a frame. (As mentioned earlier, a frame is a standardised situation). As Williams (1987: 34) asked, do we come to acquire it because we have been exposed to English sentences, and have in effect abstracted it from them? And how could we understand them, at least on Minsky's account of the matter, unless we already possessed the frame?

However, our interest here is with information. Is information a stimulus input into the mind? If the input is a face, or a tune, or a shape, then the job is already done. What Minsky and Newell mean is that inputs are organised or integrated into meaningful chunks. Information is the meaningful chunks. It would seem that we can substitute the phrase "representation (meaningful chunk)" for "information" in the analyses of Minsky and Newell. This is, not surprisingly, similar to the reduction we encountered in analysis of Sperber and Wilson.

In traditional computing theory, information is reduced to data structures. When artificial intelligence theorists discuss the concept of communication, it is with reference to intelligent agents. Communication occurs when one intelligent agent is able to re-create in his or her own mind a representation occurring in the mind of another agent. Communication may be said to reduce to isomorphic representations in artificial intelligence theory. This is one of the understandings underpinning the ideas behind the semantic web. The vision of the semantic web, for Tim Berners-Lee (the so-called father of the World Wide Web), is to design systems that can present chunks of data or information on the web in such a way that it is meaningful to the computers that 'read' it, and thus these computers and their applications and programs will be able to understand, act on, and be able to communicate this information across various technologies and contexts in a rational and predictable manner (Berners-Lee, 2001).

The concept of communication is usually used in conjunction with other concepts like system or network. In the context of database technology we return to the concept of entropy or the reduction of uncertainty or disorder. A computer is a complex recording device where every state of its memory is represented by a specific configuration of distinct physical states (currents, voltages, fields). A data processing operation, for example, may include copying of signals from one device into another. Communication systems are "usually studied with Shannon's model in mind" (*Dictionary of Computing*, 1986: 68). We can substitute the phrase "data transmission" for "communication" in traditional computing theory.

Computers are not means but ends in the theory of Minsky and Newell. Minsky's theory of motivation has its counterpart in the work of Hobbes. The race has no other goal, no other garland, but being foremost, and in it, "continually to be out-gone, is misery. Continually to out-go the next before, is felicity. And to foresake the course, is to die" (Hobbes, 1839-45: 53). Minsky and Newell have represented the non-instrumental as instrumental. However,

> To make a creative step is not simply to produce something new or unpredictable, but to produce something new that we find interesting or significant; and the fact that we do see some innovation in that light is, first of all, a cultural and not merely a psychological matter, and, inasmuch as it is a psychological matter, it is not in the first place a question of the heuristics of problem-solving. (Williams, 1987: 35)

Are scientists being misled into thinking that computers communicate? In the case of human beings, we normally speak of communication as an interpersonal relation. One person communicates with another. We sometimes speak as if communication takes place between people and machines. "The computer says that you are enrolled in this tutorial." However, this use of the concept of communication, or more appropriately the word "says," is deviant. The temptation to take such cases as instances of communication stems from the fact that computers are sophisticated devices and we request answers in natural language. But the sentence "the computer says..." no more implies that the computer has communicated with me than the sentence "the watch says...." Neither case actually is an instance of communication (Levy, 1974).

Suppose, for example, that Mary and Peter, both on different shifts, work in an office where there is a computer. Both have agreed to a system of leaving messages for one another. One morning Mary feeds in the message "Peter: Smith telephoned this morning at 9 am from Paris and wants you to call him back at 3 pm today." Reading the message, Peter believes that Smith phoned him that morning. Peter's reasoning in this example includes such propositions as, "The computer printed out this sentence because Mary fed it into the computer", "Mary is reliable and generally correct," "Mary has no reason to deceive me," and so on. It is clear that the message that Smith phoned was communicated to Peter. But is it the case that the sign in question (the printed message) comes from a person capable of intentions? The sign comes from the computer. The computer is not a communicator but merely a vehicle of communication. The computer has no intentionality; it is purely a mediator or means of communication. The computer can be programmed to behave in creative ways and the technological systems can appear to interpret and react intelligently, but this is a function of the ways these systems are designed and used by people, and the understandings of information and of communication that these people hold.

Adequate Indication versus Theoretical Index of the Mind

Disciplines of a more developmental character (that is to say, rather less concerned with pure theory than those considered up to now) may be subsumed for convenience under the title of information management. They include librarianship. In librarianship we are dealing with the creation of systems that serve human inquiry. The concept of index, considered by theorists to be relevant to the construction of information systems, will be investigated here. There can be little doubt that information retrieval and computer systems, perhaps more than any other kind of system, tend to be associated with an information revolution

The expression 'information retrieval' was coined in 1950 by Calvin Mooers (Sharp, 1965: 1). In 1965, Sharp expressed the view that there was "no recognisable or accepted body of theory" for information retrieval (1965: 1). This may be said to be still the case today: Except for Landry (1971), there have been few attempts to formulate a pure theory. This is not to say, though, that there exist no basic theoretical positions that underpin information retrieval.

At the core of information retrieval is the concept of index and, as Metcalfe suggested: "The subject is important because without adequate indication books are lost or wasted" (1959: 2). Information retrieval is marked by two very different theoretical approaches. The first the authors will call the Cutter Tradition, and the second the Otlet Tradition.

Cutter (1904) published his *Rules for a Dictionary Catalog* in 1876, the same year Dewey published the Decimal Classification. Cutter's basic rule or principle 172 exemplifies his approach: "Enter books under the word which best expresses their subject, whether it occurs in the title or not" (Cutter, 1904: 55). This is called specific entry. Metcalfe (1959) distinguished between subject specificity and document specificity. It is worthwhile quoting him at length on the issue.

> The idea of entering each document under a representation of its peculiar subject in all its aspects and relations, in what Otlet called 'toutes les nuances d'analyse idealogico-bibliographique' has had little or no influence on alphabetical subject indexing; it came in with Otlet's UDC but has been rejected by at least its British editors. Later schools of 'synthetic' classification, and particularly the Ranganathanite school of 'analytico-synthetic' classification still appear to assume that for classified cataloguing there must be synthetic or compound class numbers 'co-extensive with the subjects of the works catalogued'. But subject cataloguing is the indexing of information in documents, and not the cataloguing of documents by their peculiar subjects, each in what Ranganathan has called 'all its foci, all its criss-cross of subjects and forms and all its interlacings—fully and literally....'. (Metcalfe, 1959: 278)

For Cutter and Metcalfe, a book about 'influence of the moon on tides' would require two separate subject headings 'moon' and 'tides.' Alternately, for Otlet, Ranganathan, Austin and others (as we shall see later) it would instead require a single, complex heading such as 'tides:influence:moon.' The essence of class-making is that things are related. However, as Sharp (1965: 25) pointed out, in information retrieval, logic, though it can provide for class-making by rigorous methods for its own purposes, cannot provide us with a universal method for generating classes which will give us an hierarchical arrangement of the subject matter of even a comparatively narrow field. Metcalfe (1959) suggested that in bibliographic classification there is, of course, class-making, because subjects are assigned to documents. But these classes are not derived from a genus by a principle belonging to logic. The retrieval theorist need not be concerned with logic as a philosophical tool of analysis.

> Subject cataloguing or bibliography, or documentation, or information retrieval, whatever its fashionable name for the moment, must be logical, whether it is alphabetical or classified, and no less so than any other art or science. But this does not mean that it must become involved in the art or science of logic, with the difficulties

and subtleties of logic as a philosophical discipline, even for those with aptitude for logic and long training in it. (Metcalfe, 1959: 231)

In order to clarify the distinction between the Cutter and Otlet Traditions in more detail we need to explore the concepts of pre-coordinate and post-coordinate indexing, controlled and uncontrolled vocabularies, and precision and recall. Lancaster (1968) pointed out that nearly all retrieval systems introduce a measure of control over terms, that is to say, a controlled vocabulary is used. An indexing language consists of a vocabulary and syntax. If terms are used as they appear in a document without modification then we use a natural language in the index. But authors may use different words to denote the same idea (synonyms) or the same term may label two or more different classes of document (homograph). It may be necessary, therefore, to structure the language in some way. Foskett (1969: 48), in the Otlet Tradition, gave the notation of a classification scheme as an extreme example: for heat treatment of aluminium we may use the code 669:71.04.

To exemplify the nature of vocabulary control, Lancaster provided the following description. We may have a particular document that deals with aircraft engine noise. We may index the document under the headings 'aircraft' 'engine' and 'noise.' However, the document also relates to the specific topic 'aircraft engine noise.' There are two ways we can use a system vocabulary to index and retrieve documents of this nature. It is possible to create a label specifying the intersection of the three classes. This vocabulary is pre-coordinate: "the term AIRCRAFT ENGINE NOISE is a pre-coordination of the terms AIRCRAFT, ENGINES, AND NOISE" (Lancaster, 1972: 5). Post-coordination, on the other hand, involves manipulation of terms at the time of search.

As Lancaster (1972: 6) suggested, the distinction between pre-coordinate and post-coordinate systems is an important one. Also important is the related distinction between enumerative and synthetic vocabularies. Post-coordinate systems are, by definition, synthetic; but pre-coordinate systems may be fully enumerative or partly enumerative and partly synthetic. This use of the terms is related to, but significantly different from, their use in relation to synthetic and enumerative classification schemes. Let us suppose we have two different vocabularies, both lists of terms, used to index documents. In one the rules of vocabulary use allow the indexer only to employ terms independently and do not allow a combination of terms to express something more complex. This vocabulary is enumerative. The second vocabulary does list terms used in indexing but rules of vocabulary use also allow terms to be combined to form new terms. This vocabulary is synthetic.

In indexing and search formulation the object is to gain high precision, through specificity, and high recall through exhaustivity. An index is a filter and reduces the number of document surrogates we need to look at. It is easy to gain 100 per cent recall by retrieving everything in a database, for example, but that gives us close to zero percent precision. The effectiveness of a retrieval system depends primarily upon the size and composition of the document classes existing in the system, "and upon which classes are consulted when a search is undertaken (i.e., the search strategy used). In general, if we create large classes we make it easier to find all the documents on a particular topic (i.e., achieve a high recall) but more difficult to retrieve only relevant documents (i.e., achieve a high precision)" (Lancaster, 1972: 1).

Otlet and La Fontaine conceived of a "universal index to recorded knowledge" in 1894, that resulted in the Universal Decimal Classification, first published in English in 1936 (Foskett, 1969: 238). The phrase "universal index to recorded knowledge" encapsulates Otlet's approach. In order to understand what adequate indication might mean in such a context, we must look backwards to Leibniz. Leibniz argued that if all the complex and apparently disconnected ideas which make up our knowledge could be analysed into their simple elements, and these elements in turn represented by a definite sign, then we could have an alphabet of thought. As Latta (1898: 85) wrote: "By the combination of these signs (letters of the alphabet of thought) a system of true knowledge would be built up, in which reality would be more and more adequately represented or symbolised."

> I feel...that controversies can never be finished, nor silence imposed upon the Sects, unless we give up complicated reasonings in favour of simple calculating, words of unique and uncertain meanings in favour of fixed symbols.... When controversies arise, there will be no more necessity to disputation between two philosophers than between two accountants. Nothing will be needed but that they should take pen in hand, sit down with their counting tables, and (having summoned a friend, if they like) say to one another: let us calculate. (Leibniz, cited in Latta, 1898: 85–86)

Leibniz's point is that the progress of knowledge consists in moving from obscure to clear ideas, from clear ideas to distinct, and from distinct to adequate. Ideas are adequate when they are complete, and when all the elements of the clear and distinct ideas are themselves clear and distinct. Thus, for Leibniz, it is possible to sit down and work out, from any position, all knowledge, since analysis moves to the most accurate representation, or the most adequate indication, of reality.

Ranganathan (1966) posited the existence of five "fundamental categories" that underlie all thought: Personality, Matter, Energy, Space and Time (PMEST). These categories are fundamental because, according to Ranganathan, all subjects must be manifestations of one, or more, of them. Ranganathan's citation order is embodied in his Colon Classification. For example, in the Personality facet of Medicine we may have listed Eyelid as 18511 and in the Energy facet Inflammation as 415. This would be combined in the expression L18511:415. According to Ranganathan (1966: 205) the fundamental categories are the "stable rock-bottom" of facet analysis. Ranganathan has been influential among those in the Otlet Tradition.

Austin's PRECIS (PREserved Context Indexing) is a more contemporary example of the tradition. Austin (1974: 58), in his presentation of the theoretical groundings of PRECIS, tells us that the Classification Research Group in London, of which he was a member, aimed to "establish a system of categories which should be capable of accommodating any of the concepts likely to be encountered in current and future literature."

In his discussion of PRECIS, Austin said little about information itself. However, his statements about information science are revealing. He argued that the concern of information scientists should not be with the surface structure of language, but rather with the a priori structure that underpins all human discourse. Traditional grammar, we are told, deals with whether or not words or strings constitute well formed sentences according to the rules and precepts that apply within a given language (surface structure). "The principal question which then concerns us as documentalists or information scientists is: What form does the deep structure take?" (Austin, 1976: 43).

The purpose of PRECIS was to create a string of terms specific to a document. The indexer examines a document and formulates a title-like phrase. One of Austin's examples is the phrase "the recruitment of teachers in American Library schools." The construction of the string is determined by which term denotes the action. In this case that term would be "recruitment," coded as '2.' The term "teachers" is coded as 'p,' indicating a part or property of "Library schools" which, as the object of the action, is coded '1.' "American" is translated into its substantive form, "United States," and coded '0.' The object of the role operators (codes) is to retain the syntactical context of the terms. This is why it is called a context dependent system. Each word in turn can be placed in the lead of the string and shunted, for example:

United States.
Library schools. Teachers. Recruitment.

Library Schools. United States.
Teachers. Recruitment.

Teachers. Library Schools. United States.
Recruitment.

Recruitment. Teachers. Library Schools. United States.

Note that in each shunting the context of each term is preserved, and that the final shunting is very like the natural language expression of the subject of the document. Austin notes that, "These various entries were generated by the computer out of a single string, they were not written by the indexer" (1974: 51). Austin clearly belongs in the Otlet Tradition. An indexer faced by a subject such as "the applications of computers in the payroll accounting of professional salaries in universities" should be able to write as an ordered string of bits of machine-readable notation which uniquely identify the separate elements (computers, payroll, accounting, salaries, and so on) "the subject as a whole being represented by the aggregate of symbols so formed" (Austin, 1976: 19). That is what Otlet meant by "toutes les nuances d'analyse ideologico-bibliographique" (Metcalfe, 1959: 278).

Exhaustivity and specificity govern precision and recall. Exhaustivity is the measure of the extent that distinct subjects in a document are recognised in the indexing operation. Specificity is the ability of the index language to describe topics precisely. A high level of exhaustivity of indexing makes for high recall and low precision. A high level of specificity of indexing makes for low recall and high precision (Lancaster, 1968: 67). What then is information, if precision and recall are the measure of the effectiveness of information retrieval systems? Is information only the relevant documents retrieved? According to Lancaster (1968: 121), relevance assessment is a "value judgement on a retrieved document." But an index is essentially a matching device. Information cannot be both "all documents retrieved" in a given search and "all relevant documents retrieved" (unless all documents retrieved are relevant, which is highly improbable).

Weaver, discussing the generality of Shannon's mathematical theory of communication, made a number of suggestions related to the theory of meaning and communication in general. He said that he had the "vague feeling that information and meaning may prove to be something like a pair of canonically conjugate variables in quantum theory, they being subject to some joint restriction that condemns a person to the sacrifice of one as he [sic] insists on having much of the other" (Shannon & Weaver, 1964: 28).

The concepts of precision and recall developed quite independently of Shannon and Weaver. They had their origin in Cleverdon's research project in 1962 (Cleverdon 1962). Recall, as stated, is the ability of a system to produce wanted documents. Precision is the ability of a system to hold back un-wanted documents. Weaver's suggestion that there may be an inverse relation between meaning and information seems to apply here. Recall has an obvious, though hitherto unnoticed, relation to information, in Weaver's sense, and precision has a similarly unnoticed relation to meaning, in Weaver's sense. And it turns out, empirically, that there is an inverse relation between preci-sion and recall. The more documents you retrieve in a given search, the higher the probability that some of them will be irrelevant, which is not unlike saying that some of it will be meaningless to you.

This, combined with the fact, mentioned above, that search formulation deals not with documents but with information needs, might be taken to im-ply that, in this area of information retrieval, information is not reducible to documents. Foskett (1966: 77-78), in the Otlet Tradition, for example, argued that the term information rather than documents has been used quite deliber-ately in information retrieval.

> Very few readers are interested in books—or any other kind of document—for their own sake; a white-on-blue fiche is unlikely to arouse the agonies of artistic argument excited by a Blue Poles. Readers are interested in documents for what they contain. It is convenient to measure the success or failure of information retrieval systems in terms of wanted and unwanted documents; recall and relevance are normally geared to documents found or not found. But information retrieval is what is being talked about.

For Foskett, information is something retrieved from the document, not unlike beer from a bottle, and it is made to appear that the creator of adequate indicators is involved in such a process. Foskett's conceptual distinction is sig-nificant. It distinguishes information from documents, and has echoes of Ot-let's notion of an encyclopaedia of knowledge. But analysis reveals that a search formulation is nothing more nor less than a description of a document which, if it exists, will meet the needs of the enquirer. Mention was made of classification above, in discussion of Ranganathan's Colon Classification. A brief discussion of classification is necessary to develop further the relation be-tween information and documents in information retrieval theory.

Some classificationists have believed that classification schemes are de-rived from a real and discoverable order of nature. Bliss (1966: 169) for exam-ple, claimed that his scheme was consistent with the order of nature as discovered through the educational and scientific consensus. Such theorists tend to develop an a priori scheme and fit documents into it. Other classifica-tionists have argued that classification schemes merely organise literature that actually exists. If there is no literature there is no subject to be classified. Wyndham Hulme (1966: 119) developed a theory of literary warrant which, in part, extends beyond classification to indexing generally. Such theorists tend to organise documents according to their empirically observed characteristics.

It is clear that for Hulme, as for others in the Cutter Tradition, there is no distinction between information and documents. Lancaster (1968: 2) distinguished between data or look-up retrieval systems (where sentences, words or numbers are retrieved, for example an answer to the query, 'How many parts in stock?'); document retrieval systems (where full document text is retrieved); and, reference retrieval systems (where citations are retrieved). In discussion of "question-answering" and "fact related" retrieval systems, Lancaster affirmed that they "do not answer questions directly, nor do they retrieve 'facts' or 'knowledge'. They retrieve textual statements which may or may not be factual. They may usefully be regarded as sub-document retrieval systems" (1968: 2). Similarly, for Metcalfe, adequate indication does not consist in the creation of a universal language, a universal code, or a universal encyclopaedia of knowledge, from which all classes derive and from which all relationships among classes may be specified. Information, for Metcalfe, is the thing that is pointed-to, labelled, identified, or indicated: that is to say, a document or a document surrogate.

Document, in this context, is intended as any recorded communication, no matter what the medium or physical form, whether visual, auditory, tactile or conceivably even gustatory or olfactory. That is to say, not only the codex book in all its forms, but also microfilm or fiche, audio and video-tapes, computer tapes and discs, Braille books—in fact, any recorded message can be understood as a document. But, for the purposes of information retrieval, what is not recorded in some way is not seen as information: A private discussion, a public lecture, a cry for help do not become information unless they are recorded in some way. A document surrogate is something that for some but not all purposes stands for the document itself. The most common example is a citation, but an abstract is another (and more useful) example.

It has become popular to talk of information in information retrieval as that which changes the knowledge state of a receiver (with emphasis on cognitive psychology). According to Galvin, for example, "of greater importance to librarians, I believe, is the research which centres on the behavioural and cognitive aspects of human information processing.... The new science of information science centres on the study of the user of information" (1984: 85).

Landry, like Galvin, separated information from documents: "The indexing system cannot assume that all (or any) statements in a document contain information—indeed, a document is just an author-assembled collection of data elements. We infer that the data elements of the document become information when they are assimilated or put to use by the receiver" (1971: 97).

Landry regarded information as data elements of value in decision making (1971: 100).

For Lancaster, on the other hand, an information retrieval system "does not inform (i.e., change the knowledge of) the user on the subject of his [sic] inquiry. It merely informs him of the existence (or nonexistence) and whereabouts of documents relating to his request" (1968: 1). This distinction is of fundamental importance. As Metcalfe (1959) has argued, it would be a mistake to suggest that information retrieval systems, through manipulation, create new knowledge. To illustrate his argument, Metcalf notes the suggestion that there would have been much earlier discovery of DDT as an insecticide if there had been co-ordinate indexing of documents on DDT and on insecticides. But he counters, "[T]his is utter nonsense. Until there was an experiment about 1939 in which DDT was rediscovered and found for the first time to be insecticidal, and until there was a document stating this, information on it could not be retrieved because it had not been put into a document and didn't even exist as knowledge" (Metcalfe, 1959: 203).

Van Rijsbergen (1975: 1), on the computer side of information retrieval, accorded with the view that one can adequately describe information in information retrieval by simply substituting document for information. He also took the view that information retrieval systems do not inform, but rather locate documents that are relevant to a request. But the reason for distinguishing the concepts of information and documents in information retrieval theory has to do with the desire of authors to create a meta-language that goes far beyond Metcalfe's notion of adequate indication. Metcalfe, like Cutter, wished to keep adequate indication as close as possible to the natural usage of language based in the social context. This is not to say that an index is not artificial. But the conventions of language use, for Metcalfe, for all intents and purposes, govern adequate indication. Austin, on the other hand, goes much further. One would be flummoxed by Austin's attempts to seek "deep structures" unless he is understood in the context of the Otlet Tradition.

It is interesting to note that, for the most part, work in the field of information retrieval has been able to progress without explicitly stating, in a theoretical sense, what information is. Information retrieval research and practice rarely consider the problem at all. Despite Galvin, there is very little research into behavioural and cognitive aspects of information processing (Galvin, 1984: 85). Robertson (1975) introduced the concept of synthema: "Two documents, or a document and a question, are said to be synthematic if they are close in subject matter." Hillman (1973) in the design of the information retrieval system LEADERMART said that information depends on what the system user needs and the time and context of such a need. However, his situation-specific concept was not used in practice: "The user is presented with information judged by LEADERMART to be pertinent to his [sic] inquiry." User and situation specificity are now accounted for by the notions of pertinence or acceptability or relevance. With some exceptions (like Landry, 1971) there are few attempts to take information retrieval theory into the domain of the theory of problem-solving.

In the Cutter Tradition we have a clear, discipline-dependent, reduction of information to documents or document surrogates. While those in the Otlet Tradition seek to distinguish documents from information, it is difficult not to conclude that the reduction of information, in their case also, is to documents or document surrogates, because the distinction leads only to special systems of indexing designed to retrieve documents, not to any study of the behaviour of document users. Therefore, we can substitute the terms document or document surrogate for information in information retrieval. However, it must be stressed again that a document can be any kind of record.

Prior to the widespread adoption of the Internet as a means for locating, creating and sharing information, the modern student needed to, in most circumstances, walk to the appropriate shelf and remove a book in order to retrieve information. This is full-text information retrieval. However, a student may also have had access to a document surrogate, for example an abstract, that revealed something about a document. Most modern information retrieval systems are not full-text retrieval systems but retrieve only document surrogates, either citations or abstracts.

> The IS&R system user cannot know precisely which data are stored in the system.... However he [sic] must understand how the system stores, organizes and represents documents. Effective communication with the system is achieved when the system [is] known and understood by the user. (Landry, 1971: 94)

The general uptake of the Internet as an information sharing system broadens the possibilities for extensive full-text retrieval. However, while in some ways, these possibilities shift the boundaries within which debates about information retrieval have historically taken place, information retrieval and indexing still remain key to the social distribution of knowledge. This is because there are a wide range of ways in which records can be accessed online but also because the various applications and platforms are structured according to different organizing and classificatory systems. The principle of transparency, for example, can be found in some classification systems, like folksonomy, but not in others, such as Google.

Folksonomies, for example, are used within social resource sharing or social bookmarking sites such as Flickr and del.icio.us. Folksonomy is a term coined by Thomas Vander Wal to refer to the ways in which general users can apply their own classificatory keywords, or tags, to content on these sites. These tags can be individually coined and applied or chosen from the site's continually expanding, user-generated, and collectively aggregated selection. Tags are applied to all manner of documents whether they are text-based, photographic or image-based, or audio files. The tags can also be represented as clouds or clusters according to the popularity of the tag, the rates of its occurrence, and the association of other terms used in conjunction with it.

Landry, along with all information retrievalists, is concerned with the effective transmission of documents or document surrogates. Transmission of information entails the transfer or diffusion of documents. Bernal (1987), for example, discussed the problem of scientific communication. However, he was not talking about how scientists send memos to each other complaining about particular problems in the pursuit of knowledge. Bernal referred solely to the transfer, diffusion and storage of scientific documents. We can substitute the phrase transfer of documents or document surrogates for communication in information retrieval. We can do this even in the case of Landry: I am communicating when I know how to get the micro-fiche out of the system. The purpose remains recovery of documents. For the most part, by communication, information retrievalists mean transfer of documents.

The notion of index is related to that of access to documents. Those in the Cutter Tradition are fully aware that an index is a social construction based very much in the social context. However, they would not see it as the concern of indexing theory to derive a theory of knowledge or syntactics-semantics, much like the practical enactment of folksonomy noted above would indicate. When we move beyond the discipline-dependent use of information to other areas, there are consequences involved. Landry (1971) is a good example. For him, information is that which is of value in decision-making. The indexing process is cast as a mechanical, well-defined set of operations. A theory of the indexing process must also provide the means for the description of the process of the searcher/index interaction. An indexer must be able to produce a theory of the cognitive structure. "We may conclude that cognitive structure is an observational theoretical index of the perceived environment" (Landry, 1971: 177).

How does one do this? For Landry, information need is the expression of a need to provide support for a hypothesis. Negative support will create a disequilibrium in the existing collection of hypotheses and will require continued data acquisition and new hypotheses on the part of the observer. Positive support may lead to an end-state, or goal, of the ongoing process of inquiry. Information, in this context, is the "reduction of ignorance" (Landry, 1971: 173). Landry notes, "The observer's information processing and hypothesis testing activities may be explained as an attempt to reduce the uncertainty about, and the number of attributes (states) of, the system under observation which must be processed" (1971: 174).

Landry's pursuit of a theoretical index of mind, and his specification of information as the reduction of ignorance, returns us to cognitive science, Schramm and Cherry, and those concerned with efforts to predict outcomes in human communication. The semantic web approach also seems to broadly fall into the Otlet Tradition. Landry reduced information to reduction of ignorance, which is equivalent in this context to a reduction of information to reduction of uncertainty. The establishment of a theoretical index of ignorance, one assumes, would require intrusion into the lives of people.

Summary

The Web, and everything which happens on it, rest on two things: technological protocols, and social conventions. The technological protocols, like HTTP and HTML, determine how computers interact. Social conventions, such as the incentive to make links to valuable resources, or the rules of engagement in a social networking web site, are about how people like to, and are allowed to, interact. (Berners-Lee, 2007)

The Internet and organizations like Google in particular would have given those following the Otlet Tradition great hope that a universal index to recorded knowledge was, indeed, possible. The idea that the Internet creates knowledge, no doubt, is part of the modern temper and deeply rooted in Internet culture. However, as we have seen, the debate among information retrievalists is extremely important: Are information retrieval systems part of a trend to derive a universal index to recorded knowledge or, are they there to provide adequate indications to knowledge, much as Shannon held that well designed information channels are essential to adequate indication that the signal sent was the signal received?

There is also, as we have seen, an issue of intentionality. Modern artificial intelligence scholars argue that computers can indeed be intentional and that there is no difference, in fact, between computer intentionality and human intentionality. Even if we take a simple case of modern information retrieval, the computer certainly defines relevance, but this relevance is pre-programmed via algorithms that are not public. For instance, Google argues that its retrieval of information is not biased towards any organisation or product (it is defined by frequency of searches, for instance). However, if a person searches using the term coffee, Gloria Jeans is at the top of the list. It might be that Gloria Jeans' coffee is in fact the most clicked on site under 'coffee,' but because Google's definitions of relevance are not public, then it is hard to check or to know.

Figure 1: Google screenshot

In our explorations of discourses of information, we have found relevance and intentionality figure very differently according to the position that a theorist takes in terms of the phenomena information and communication information. Figure 2 is a pictorial version of the information realist perspective. Information on the realist view has temporal extension, but as a property with temporal extension that is located within another property that has temporal extension. The container below could be a book, a signal, or a datastructure, for example. Information on the realist view is **within** the containers, not the containers themselves.

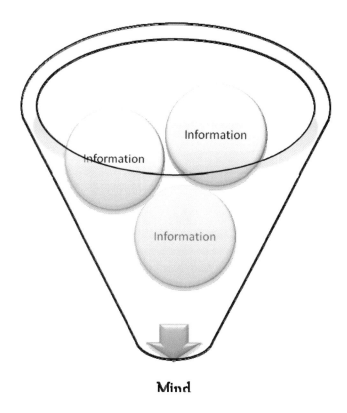

Mind

Figure 2: The elusive quantity called information

Figure 3 below puts into propositional form what we have discussed about the nature of information so far.

MORE REAL

Information as Order

At any moment we are in a particular state of uncertainty, disorder, disor-ganisation or chaos in a network defined by entropy. Information is that which reduces uncertainty, disorder, disorganisation or chaos.

Information as Reduction of Uncertainty

Hypothesis testing in the individual is an attempt to reduce uncertainty or ignorance. Information is that which is of value in reducing ignorance or resolving uncertainty.

Information as a Commodity or Resource

Information exhibits the qualities of a resource. It is a commodity.

Information as Codes

Natural language is a system of communication. People must interpret signs in order to decipher messages. Information is a code that must be decoded.

Information as Cognitions

At any moment we are in possession of certain information, cognitions, which have been thoroughly derived by induction and hypothesis. The real is that which, sooner or later, the activity of reason would result in.

Information as Adequate Indication

Information is the result of some act of recording or transmission. Information and the media that carry it are the same thing. Physical states, shapes or sounds in different places or at different times may all be similar to one another, but to be information they must be identically the same.

LESS REAL

Figure3: Superpatterns of constructions of information

There is one perspective that is missing in Figure 3. This is the perspective that holds that information does not exist. In Chapter Four the authors will explore Habermas's theory of information in detail and the theoretical context from which it is derived.

The Informed Citizen (Habermas's Theory of Information)

If there is to be a realistic application of the idea of the sovereignty of the people to highly complex society, it must be uncoupled from the concrete understanding of its embodiment in physically present, participating, and jointly deciding members of a collectivity.

—Jürgen Habermas (1992a: 462)

As we have seen, the difference between the Cutter and Otlet traditions in information retrieval exemplifies the radical differences in conception of information retrieval that can occur. For those like Metcalfe, in the Cutter Tradition, information retrieval systems do not inform or change the knowledge of the user. Information retrieval systems inform users of the existence or non-existence and whereabouts of documents or document surrogates relating to their request. Information is a record of some kind. For those like Landry in the Otlet Tradition, however, information is presumed to be a physical object that occupies the place of documents, or other physical objects, but cannot be said to be identical with them. Information is an external transformation variable that reduces the ignorance of the user or aids in decision-making.

As we have also found, there are ways of thinking about information that do not involve a reduction to a social actor that is independent of people or of citizens. Jürgen Habermas is famous for his idea of the public sphere and both the phrase and the idea are now used to describe many different things. Indeed 'public sphere' is now often used without reference to its underlying theory. But it is Habermas's and Alfred Schutz's theorizing about being informed that provides tantalizing insights into how structured subjective spaces that benefit open communication in fact work. In this chapter, the authors look at knowledge schema and their role in understanding the Internet as a mediator in the social distribution of knowledge.

The Social Distribution of Knowledge

For a while I've been using Facebook's API and Facebook Query Language (FQL) via Perl's WWW::Facebook::API module to run fairly innocent queries on my friends.... If a large number of my friends are attending an event, there's a good chance I'll find it interesting, and I'd like to know about it.... Using the example provided by Facebook, I dropped the query into my sandbox, and looked at the results which came back. The results were disturbing. I didn't just get back future events my friends were attending. I got everything they had been invited to: past and present, attending or not. I didn't sleep well that night. I didn't expect Facebook to share past event info. I didn't expect it to share info when people had declined those events. (http://pjf.id.au/blog/?order=backward&position=588&count=5)

The Frankfurt School and Second Force critical theorist Jürgen Habermas had, as their enterprise, like Hannah Arendt, the 'totalitarian proofing' of modern democracy. They had seen firsthand how communication networks could be set up, controlled, and used to destroy humans. As the Internet is not controlled in the same way that media were controlled in Nazi Germany, the Internet would seem to be an ideal structured communicative space. Perhaps it is not surprising then that theorists were puzzled when Habermas proclaimed that in the context of liberal regimes, "the rise of millions of fragmented chat rooms across the world tend...to lead to the fragmentation of large but politically focused mass audiences into a huge number of isolated issue publics" (Habermas, 2006: 423). The Internet, for Habermas, is good at subverting authoritarian regimes but not so good at joining people together. It is good at surveillance and the collection of individual data, as the Facebook example shows, but not necessarily so good at setting up a system for illocutionary acts on a large scale.

Habermas has not been alone in this type of comment. Robert Putman (2000) in his well-known book *Bowling Alone* mapped the decline in memberships in voluntary associations, informal socializing with neighbours and friends, religious attendance, and participation in politics and community affairs. He argued that TV, the Internet, and other media speed up our lives to the point where we no longer invest social capital in each other by means of overlapping memberships in clubs and other organizations, essential to human trust and mutual support.

We know of course that the Internet and social media can do the opposite. *Ravelry (www.ravelry.com), for* example, is a social networking site for knitters, spinners, and dyers. With over 400,000 members, the site allows for commercial as well as non-commercial exchanges and brings together learning, friendship and gifting (Humphries, 2008). *Ravelry* is a communicative space affording social networks as well as some economic value to those who participate. Within and across the Internet, there have emerged communicative spaces where the medium, the learning environments in which citizens learn to use the medium, and the social capital uses to which the medium are employed, come together in complex and seemingly contradictory arrangements (Papacharissi, 2010; Song, 2009).

The idea of the public sphere, or *Öffentlichkeit*, emerged from Jürgen Habermas's (1989) historical analysis of the emergence of communicative spaces over time. This concept of the public sphere has become influential in debates about how structures can be created and maintained to ensure that people can communicate freely. Of course, Habermas's ideas on the actual structures that affect how we communicate freely are more complex than the statement of public sphere as a guaranteed space where we can chat. In this chapter, the authors will examine Habermas's theory of information as the basis for understanding the structured subjective spaces that can enhance democracy and processes of communication. His theory of information, as the authors will show, is separate from his theory of communicative action, although related to it. Along the way, it will become clearer why understandings of information are important, how practices and understandings are intertwined and why the possibilities for an informed citizenry involves more than simply the provision of 'more information.'

Zones of Relevance

> There is no poverty worse than that of being excluded, by ignorance, by insensibility, or by a failure to master the language, from the meaningful symbols of one's culture: those forms of social deafness or blindness are truly death to the human personality. (Mumford, 1944: 9)

Lack of wealth is not the worst poverty, as Mumford suggests. Not being able to participate in one's own culture can be the greater loss. In his essay, "The Well-Informed Citizen," Alfred Schutz made a similar point when he suggested that in modern times individuals are less and less masters in their own right to define what is, and what is not, relevant to them (1946: 473). His argument was that modern transportation and communication methods bring everyone closer together but they also expose individuals to interests and relevances that are not their own and, indeed, which may be imposed upon them. The result of this process, says Schutz, is the loss of the well-informed citizen.

If autonomy, in the minimal sense, is the ability to make informed choices, then information and communication would seem to be essential to fulfilling such a basic need. That is to say, a person's capacity for practical understanding, choice and participation in a society is intimately tied to that person's ability to communicate and to become informed. For Schutz, there are four regions, or zones, of decreasing relevance of knowledge: primary; minor; relatively irrelevant and absolutely irrelevant. There is knowledge and activity of *primary relevance* within our reach that can be immediately observed by us and also at least partially dominated by us. The zone of *minor relevance* is where individuals may be acquainted with knowledge that may contain reference to our chief interests. Zones of knowledge which are *relatively irrelevant* or *absolutely irrelevant* are areas of knowledge which people take for granted, but where the 'that' and the 'how' of things are not essential. For example, no car driver is assumed to be familiar with the laws of mechanics, no radio listener with those of electronics, although there are circumstances where such knowledge might be of primary relevance, as is the case for experts or enthusiasts. We all rely on a varying combination of these forms of knowledge in our everyday lives.

'Zones of relevance' lead Schutz to identifying different types of knowledge 'holders,' broadly defined as expert, well-informed citizen, and person on the street. *Expert* knowledge is restricted to a limited field, but therein it is clear and distinct. The *well-informed* citizen has knowledge which enables him or her to arrive at reasonably founded opinions in fields that are at least mediately of concern to them. The well-informed citizen also considers her- or himself perfectly qualified to decide who is a competent expert and even to make up his or her mind after having listened to opposing expert opinions (Schutz, 1946: 466). The *person on the street*, however, holds only knowledge of recipes indicating how to bring forth in typical situations typical results by typical means. The recipes indicate procedures that may be trusted even though they are not clearly understood: By following the prescription, the desired result can be gained without questioning why.

Zones of relevance and types of knowledge are linked by Schutz to social roles and zones of interest. Social roles are the various social positions people may hold that have an effect on the types of knowledge they require and are relevant to them (e.g., aerospace engineer, mother, scout leader). Socially derived knowledge, in this context, is communicated or handed down to individuals, directly or indirectly. Socially approved knowledge is any knowledge, including socially derived knowledge, which receives corroboration from other trusted groups. For example, "If I consider my mother, my priest, my government to be authoritative, then their opinions have special weight and this weight itself has the character of an imposed relevance" (Schutz, 1946: 477).

The overall social distribution of knowledge, for Schutz, is always partly within an individual's control and partly imposed. The world within my reach, therefore, and in which I do to some extent determine my own goals, involves my intrinsic interests. Where my goals overlap with others, and I know the others, I am involved in common intrinsic interests. The more there is recip-rocal anonymity of partners in a social situation, then the more the zone of common intrinsic relevances and interests decreases and that of imposed ones increases. Schutz's point is clear: Autonomy disappears when there is no well-informed citizen in a society. The well-informed citizen can judge the compe-tencies of experts he or she deals with, but is not necessarily an expert. If most people were the person on the street, then it is doubtful that they could define what is relevant in their own social situation as this is done by others.

Schutz's model can be summarized thus:

> there is a relationship between the ability to judge the competencies of others and the social distribution of knowledge (the greater the gener-alisation of competencies, the greater the number of well-informed citizens),

> there is a relationship between autonomy and the social distribution of knowledge (the greater the imposed relevances, the less control an in-dividual has over definition of what is relevant in immediate social and psychological surroundings)

> there is a relationship between social support and the social distribution of knowledge (an increase in imposed interests leads to a decrease in common intrinsic interests).

Habermas knew Schutz's work well and used his idea of the lifeworld in his theory of communication. But Habermas felt that Schutz, a non-political man, did not understood the influences of social institutions and personalities on the social distribution of knowledge. Habermas recognised, however, that Schutz in formulating a non-realist theory of information had hit upon some-thing important. In Schutz's formulation of the social distribution of knowl-edge, information does not exist, only informed citizens exist.

Disclosure

In order to understand Habermas's non-realist theory of information and his expansion of Schutz's work, we need to understand the role of disclosure in human communication. Active participation and disclosure requires speaking agents to express themselves in ways that can be evaluated and understood by others within the community. According to Habermas (1984: 22), rationality is a disposition of speaking and acting agents expressed in modes of behaviour for which there are good reasons or grounds. All expressions, or utterances, are subject to evaluation: "We cannot achieve a consensus about experience and propositional contents without at the same time entering a meta-communicative discourse about the choice of one among a variety of possible paths of interpersonal relations" (Habermas, 1981: 365).

Habermas falls squarely within the theoretical tradition that regards the role of utterances—what people say in actual discourse—as the essence of language and meaning. He regarded logic as derivative from rhetorical considerations. The argument is complex, but Apel (1972: 10) expressed it well when he said,

> formalized languages of the logic of science, in principle, cannot be used for intersubjective communication in the full sense of that word. It is only sentences about states of affairs (not even statements about facts!) and logical connections between sentences that can be formulated in these languages, but not 'utterances' or 'speech acts' because these units of ordinary language do not get their meaning exclusively from the syntactical and semantical rules of a formal system, but only from the context of the pragmatical use of language in concrete situations of life.

There are of course echoes of Sperber and Wilson here. One such concrete situation is the individual's use of perception. Habermas never denied the validity of perceptions: "Perceptions cannot be false. When we deceive ourselves it must be that there was, not this, but some other perception than we thought; or there was no perception at all even though we thought we had perceived something" (1981, 363). Perception forms part of utterances and speech acts in ordinary language. Understanding how perception works is part of recognising ourselves as communicating subjects. All forms of communication, all dialogues develop on the basis of reciprocal recognition of subjects who "identify one another under the category of selfhood" (Habermas, 1981: 138).

It is statements about observations and not perceptions that play the decisive role in communicative spaces. The statement "the ball is red" involves no shift in orientation from observation to the statement of what has been observed (Habermas, 1981: 364). However, the same statement within discourse is subject to test at the level of propositional contents. Facts are what we state after discursive tests.

Habermas used the concept of discourse in a special way. Discourses make theoretical knowledge possible:

> Discourses help test the truth claims of opinions (and norms) which the speakers no longer take for granted. In a discourse, the 'force' of the argument is the only permissible compulsion, whereas the co-operative search for truth is the only permissible motive. Because of their communicative structure, discourses do not compel their

participants to act. Nor do they accommodate processes whereby information can be acquired. They are purged of action and experience.... Discourses produce nothing but arguments. Only states of affairs, not facts, can be discussed. (Habermas, 1981: 363)

The last two sentences in Habermas's quote here appear to be confusing, but what he is saying is that the way we use language and talk operates differently according to different domains of reality and, indeed, that validity claims will vary according to different domains of reality. In the scientific world we take an objectifying attitude but, when discussing our world, we take a conformative attitude (Habermas & Cooke, 2000: 92). States of affairs, therefore, do assume people have knowledge but acquisition is not the key thing:

The cartographic representation of a mountain range may be more or less accurate; but only the interpretations that we base on our reading of the map—that we infer from it, so to speak—are true or false, for example, that the mountain ranges are separated by wide valleys or that the highest peak lies 3,000 meters above sea level. In the same way, we can infer from the drawing of a broken crankshaft the proposition that the represented crankshaft is broken. However, only an interpreter who knows in advance what the representation of states of affairs means in general is able to understand the representation of a broken crankshaft as a designation with the propositional content that the crankshaft is broken. (Habermas & Cooke, 2000: 262)

The point here is that an interpreter could not even see that the drawing represents a state of affairs if she did not already have a command of the language and know how states of affairs are represented linguistically. Habermas's theory of truth is embodied in the expression "states of affairs." There is an objective world, rather than ideal consensus, but when we claim or argue something to be true, we draw on our linguistic resources and our beliefs about objects in the world to support that claim.

In communicative acts one aspect of human action is the activity of disclosure. Human disclosure is a principle of rational action. Rationality begins with concepts of propositional knowledge, but it is the way we use this knowledge that shapes our relationship with others.

Hannah Arendt, similarly, argues that in our relationships, human action is the only activity that goes on between people without the intermediary of things or matter. Human activity is diverse and various which is why disclosure is so important in communicative spaces. For Arendt (1958: 8) "the condition of human action" is marked by "plurality." Because even though "we are all the same," we are human "in such a way that nobody is ever the same as anyone else who ever lived, or will live" (1958: 8). To dispense with disclosure, if it could be done, "would mean to transform [people] into something they are not"; to deny "this disclosure is real and has consequences of its own is simply unrealistic" (1958: 183). Arendt's purpose was to emphasise the irreducible nature of human experience in human affairs (Arendt, 1958: 170).

Disclosure has different aims from that of cognition. Whereas cognition always has a definitive aim, when this aim is reached, "the cognitive process ends" (Arendt, 1958: 170). In the sciences, cognition reigns supreme and thought is considered to be of little value. Arendt points out that, on the contrary, thought "has neither an end nor an aim outside itself, and it does not even produce results" (Arendt, 1958: 170). But "men of action and the lovers of results in the science have never tired of pointing out how entirely useless thought is—as useless, indeed, as the works of art it inspires" (Arendt, 1958: 170). Thought cannot be measured in the same way as logical reasoning; however, that does not mean that thought does not have an important role in disclosure and perception.

Similarly, empathy is a part of knowledge produced in everyday communication spaces. Apel cited a comment by Neurath: "Empathy, understanding and the like may help the researcher, but it enters into a system of statements of science as little as does a good cup of coffee, which helped the researcher do his work" (Apel, 1972: 17). Apel, Arendt and Habermas rejected the "cup of coffee" theory of understanding and embraced empathy. Empathy contributes to developing a collective rational identity that is often foundational, for example, to the way activist forums operate. Collective rational identity for Habermas and Arendt can only be grounded in the consciousness of universal and equal chances to participate in the communication processes by which identity formation becomes a continually learning process. The use of knowledge is bound to moral conduct. It is in the use of knowledge in the everyday that its validity is tested.

The point of the discussion above is to emphasise that human disclosure is a principle of rational action. Rational action is not simply about scientific knowledge and logic. In order to talk about things that we might disagree on we can and do enter into meta-communicative discourses and our intentions in entering these discourses are themselves very important because they frame what happens next. The nature of human disclosure for Habermas has implications for our understanding about how democratic communicative spaces work.

Discourses are one of those communicative spaces that are democratic and they have a particular structure. Discourses,

> Help test the truth claims of opinions (and norms) which the speakers no longer take for granted (argument);

Have the 'force' of the argument as the only permissible compulsion (public sphere);

Have the co-operative search for truth as the only permissible motive (intentions of those participating);

Do not compel their participants to act (illocutionary aims);

Do not accommodate processes whereby information can be acquired (not a scientific enterprise);

Are purged of action and experience (emancipatory reason);

Allow only states of affairs, not facts, to be discussed (it is tests of validity that become important).

Habermas is arguing that these elements of discourse are axiomatic. When participating in communicative spaces with particular aims it is evident that empathy becomes important in discourse as distinct from 'facts.' In many contexts, none of Habermas's conditions for discourse might be met but, ultimately, they are essential to communication where we recognise each other as human beings; something he took further in his work on communicative action. Habermas's theory of information is a theory of information because he is arguing a non-realist and non-cybernetic approach to information as a phenomenon. His theory ties in with the emphasis among scholars like Arendt and Hans Jonas on informed citizens rather than on information as a 'thing.' As Jonas explains,

> It is I who let certain 'messages' count as 'information', and as such make them influence my action. The mere feedback from sense-organs does not motivate behaviour, in other words, sentience and motility alone are not enough for purposive action—not even for the original conditioning of reflexes which once set up, may then substitute for purposive action. (Jonas, 1953:185)

What Jonas is concerned about, of course, is agency. Any scientific attempt to shift agency from people to other things, for Jonas, is odd. Habermas likewise is intensely interested in agency. The private sphere and the public sphere are intimately linked for him. The "publicity of the public sphere" as he calls it will tell a person a lot about how free the 'private' person is. The public are always represented in some way or another, even in the most tyrannical of dictatorships. Tyrants will create symbols saying that they represent the public, but these tokens, or publicity of the public sphere, are not genuinely representative of the public or the opportunities to form public opinion.

In contemporary democratic societies, when human communication increases in scale, into the hundreds and thousands and indeed millions, additional factors come into play in the publicity of the public sphere, not least the types of *mediation* that can occur. Traditional print, radio, and broadcast media are intermediaries between the individual and the formation of public opinion in the public sphere. How closely those intermediaries actually represent real public opinion depends on the dynamics of the media themselves. For Alfred Schutz, any group or person claiming to represent the opinions of others should be subject to the 'postulate of adequacy'—that they submit their interpretations of other people's interpretations back to the original people for agreement or disagreement; genuine deliberative democracy. New media, like the Internet, are also intermediaries and the extent to which this mediation approximates a public sphere has been hotly debated (e.g., Poster, 1995; Dean, 2001; Rheingold, 1993; Papacharissi, 2010).

Habermas is a good example of a non-realist perspective on information. All speech acts oriented to reaching understanding are subject to validity claims: that the statement made is true; that the speech act is right with respect to the existing normative context; and that the manifest intention of the speaker is meant as it is expressed (Habermas, 1984: 99). While Habermas used the term communication to refer to interaction, he also made the concept of *intention* primary. The communicative intent of the speaker is basic to critical theory. Intentions are the basis of interaction. Illocutionary aims of speech acts are achieved when all participants "harmonize their individual plans of action with one another and thus pursue their illocutionary aims without reservation" (Habermas, 1984: 294).

Communicative competence in Habermas's analysis, therefore, is not simply the production of grammatical sentences, but the dimension within which we test the validity of what we are saying, that is, test intentions. He presented what he considered to be the ideal and minimum conditions of human existence. These entail tacit deference to the truth of one's conduct. This implicit commitment to the truth and correctness of conduct in turn implies accountability and a willingness to offer reasons in justification of one's commitment if challenged. "A speaker can pursue perlocutionary aims only when he deceives his [sic] partner concerning the fact that he is acting strategically—when, for example, he gives the command to attack in order to get his troops to rush into a trap" (Habermas, 1984: 294). We cannot substitute the term knowledge for information in this context. It is "statements of experience" that form the content of communication for Habermas. Discourses, defined by Habermas as corroboration of propositional contents, are not communicative. We can substitute the phrase "statements of experience" for "information." Siding with Strawson, Habermas argued that facts are not unrelated bits of matter, or perceptions, but rather the correlates of states of affairs that, within the world of intersubjectivity, are submitted to standards of evaluation. There can be no disinterested description on this view. Statements of experience are the explicit topic of disclosure. The importance of disclosure lies with intent and the intention of disclosure is honesty. Habermas represents a radical break from realist positions in the disciplinary literature. He is arguing that information, in fact, does not exist—informed people exist.

Knowledge Schema, Intelligibility and the Public Sense

What comes into the public sphere is a function of common intrinsic interests: things that are of primary relevance to the people concerned. These issues or interests, whether scientific or political, are often mediated through broadcasting, print or other media. The more that the mediation becomes representative of other people's interests, say private corporations, then the less those mediating organisations are operating in or contributing to the public sphere. There can be no doubt that knowledge schemes—ideal types, typifications or constructs—are embedded in the Internet as a medium. They make communication intelligible.

Theoretical discussion about constructs, and ideal types as constructs, is well established in the social theory literature (see for example, Becker, 1940; Martindale, 1959; Runciman, 1972). Weber (1949) and Schutz (1962) both provided definitions of 'construct.'

> An ideal type is formed by the one-sided *accentuation* of one or more points of view and by the synthesis of a great many diffuse, discrete, more or less present and occasionally absent *concrete individual* phenomena, which are arranged according to those one-sidedly emphasized viewpoints into a unified *analytical* construct. (Weber, 1949: 90)

> All our knowledge of the world, in common-sense as well as in scientific thinking, involves constructs, i.e., a set of abstractions, generalizations, formalizations, idealizations specified to the respective level of thought organization. Strictly speaking, there are no such things as facts, pure and simple. All facts are from the outset facts selected from a universal context by an artificial abstraction or facts considered in their particular setting. (Schutz, 1962: 5)

While these definitions of Weber and Schutz both appear to be similar, Schutz argued that Weber's concept of subjective meaning encompassed two aspects which he failed to distinguish properly. the meaning which is constituted within the consciousness of the individual and the meaning which is constituted in the process of social interaction (Schutz, 1967; Hekman, 1983). Weber failed to specify that both of these aspects of subjective meaning are, in Schutz's words, constituted intersubjectively. There is also an important characteristic of constructs in Weber's and Schutz's definition—constructs as sources of information about the social and natural world. Hempel (1965) wrote that ideal types do not represent constructs but theories and, that if those theories are to serve their purpose, they must have a character similar to that of the theory of ideal gases. To explain an individual event in natural science is to explain the occurrence of some general or repeatable characteristic in a particular case. Hempel attempted to show that alleged differences between the explanatory use of ideal types, and the method of explanation in natural science, are spurious and that ideal types must be construed as theoretical systems embodying testable general hypotheses. Ideal types, he said, are "at best an unimportant terminological aspect, rather than a methodological characteristic, of the social sciences" (Hempel, 1965: 171).

Hempel's quest was *reductionism* and questions of reducibility do arise with respect to ideal types, particularly in connection with what is called the doctrine of methodological individualism, "according to which all social phenomena should be described, analyzed and explained in terms of the situations of the individual agents involved in them and by reference to the laws and theories concerning individual behaviour" (Hempel, 1966: 100). The doctrine may be expressed in other ways:

> All social phenomena, and especially the functioning of all social institutions, should always be understood as resulting from the decisions, actions, attitudes, etc. of human individuals, and we should never be satisfied by an explanation in terms of so-called 'collectivities'. (Popper, 1962: 98)

The doctrine of methodological individualism entails the reducibility of specific constructs and laws of social science to those of psychology, biology, chemistry, and physics. The issue is predictive advantage. Those in the functionalist tradition also hold that ideal types should not be simply interpretative but rather predictive. Prediction of human behaviour entails the formulation of general laws about human action. Parsons (1967a) is a good example. He gave the instance where a wife boils a potato for a short period and then serves it to her husband. The husband declares the potato hard and adds that it was not cooked long enough. The husband's interest in the potato is only in its relative hardness in relation to palatability. It is not necessary to know the chemical changes which go on in the process of cooking the potato. It is generally known that to make a potato soft it must be boiled over 15 minutes.

> The one law is quite sufficient to make the explanation valid and adequate. It can be verified. Similarly in the field of action an inquirer may be told that the quickest way to get from Harvard Square in Cambridge to the South Station in Boston is to take the subway. All the elements in this statement can be verified in terms of generally known laws about everyday experience (to Bostonians). Without such general laws, indeed, all rational action itself would be unthinkable. However, they are strictly

comparable to scientific laws for the purpose for which they are used. (Parsons, 1967a: 625)

Parsons raises all the classic problems associated with prediction. Weber held that subjective interpretation by the researcher does not entail the complete individualisation of interpretations since there are typical patterns of meaning which can be abstracted from the individualised totality. Weber was quite right to insist that explanatory concepts be applicable to the understandable motives of individuals (Parsons, 1967b: 75). But do the typical patterns have to embody testable general hypotheses? Harre, commenting on the evidence on which Durkheim based his study of suicide, pointed out that:

> One might, unreflectingly, assume that a self-inflicted death was so unambiguous a phenomenon in most cases that official statistics for suicide rates would serve as a transparent instrument for their recording. And so Durkheim assumed. But of course 'suicide' as Douglas pointed out and Maxwell has confirmed, is not an objective quality of certain acts, but an interpretive category to which acts are assigned for certain practical purposes and as the upshot of a complex social event. (1979: 144)

Harre's point was that among people rules and meanings change and the same acts may not always have the same names. The same act may be treated differently for different reasons. Social life does not happen in spite of the reasons the agents have for their conduct. *Principles of conduct* are not general laws that we can refer to to explain social actions. Therefore, the notion of a principle of conduct and the notion of meaningful action are interwoven (Winch, 1973: 63). The very idea of a 'construct' and of 'ideal types' raise issues about prediction. Hempel argues that 'constructed types' should be scientific and cannot be trusted unless they can be verified by reference to *general laws*. Constructive typologists argue, on the other hand, that problems with prediction are inherent in the nature of social action.

> All that the constructive typologist ever says is that 'if and when' certain factors, which have been isolated as significant, recur in configurations which can be regarded as identical for the purposes in hand, then this in turn probably will ensue. He [sic] does not say in advance, nor can he *ever* say in advance, whether the factors which are essential for the results *actually* will recur in the required configuration. (Becker, 1940: 51. emphasis in original)

What is implicit in Becker's statement is that constructs always have an 'if-then' relationship, even though prediction by reference to general laws may be impossible. Indeed, the idea of anticipation is central to a social theory of constructs.

> If we see a dog we anticipate immediately his future behaviour, his typical way of eating, playing, running, jumping, etc. Actually, we do not see his teeth, but even if we

have never seen this particular dog, we know in advance what his teeth will look like—not in their individual determination, but in a typical way, since we have long ago and frequently experienced that 'suchlike' animals ('dogs') have something like teeth of this and that typical kind. (97)

Schutz, to exemplify points about anticipation, uses the example of a sole performer of a piece of music sitting at his piano before the score of a sonata by a minor master of the nineteenth century with which he is unfamiliar. We assume that the piano player is equally proficient as a technician and sight reader. Schutz asks,

> Can we really maintain that the sonata in question is *entirely* unknown to our performer? He could not be an accomplished technician and sight reader without having attained a certain level of musical culture enabling him to read offhand a piece of music of the *type* of that before him. Consequently, although this particular sonata and perhaps all the other works of this particular composer might be unknown to him, he will nevertheless have a well-founded knowledge of the type of musical form called 'sonata within the meaning of nineteenth century piano music,' of the type of themes and harmonies used in such compositions of that period, of the expressional contents he may expect to find in them—in sum, of the typical 'style' in which music of this kind is written and in which it has to be executed. Even before starting to play or to read the first chord our musician is referred to a more or less clearly organized, more or less coherent, more or less distinct set of his previous experiences, which constitute in their totality a kind of preknowledge of the piece of music at hand. To be sure, this preknowledge refers merely to the type to which this individual piece of music belongs and not to its particular and unique individuality. But the player's general preknowledge of this typicality becomes the scheme of reference for his interpretation of its particularity. This scheme of reference determines, in a general way, the player's anticipations of what he may or may not find in the composition before him. (1964, v2 167–168)

Schutz's example raises four major issues relevant to a definition of constructs. The first is anticipation of a musical construct, the second is when one type can be said to be the same as another type (or construct), the third, implicit, is the reasons for playing the sonata, and the fourth is use of musical techniques. All four are clearly relevant to any definition of construct in social theory. Constructs do not determine their own application but have to be used, and one of their most important uses is to bring a set of reasons, events, persons, or conduct into some scheme of interpretation. The self-consciousness of heroes like Oedipus and others in Greek tragedy did not involve discrimination between acts and knowledge of the acts. "On the contrary, they accepted responsibility for the whole compass of the deed" (Hegel, 1981: 81). The authors support the premise that "to act is to expose oneself to bad luck", because it is difficult to assess the *consequences* of any intended action (Hegel, 1981: 251). It is important not to trivialise the nature of 'thought reconstruction' in social analysis. For example, in Umberto Eco's novel *The Name of the Rose* (1984), Jorge, in an exchange with William of Baskerville, implied that reconstruction of evidence of a social kind is a form of telepathy. "You know that it suffices to think and to reconstruct in one's own mind the thought of the other" (1984: 465). What is missing in Jorge's account is how a *sensus communis* is achieved:

> This is done by comparing our judgement with the possible rather than the actual judgement of others, and by putting ourselves in the place of any other man [sic], by abstracting from the limitations which contingently attach to our judgements. (Kant, 1959: 40)

Actions preceded by deliberation, therefore, are paradigms of human action.

> Now, there is no question that intellectual agents act ahead of time in their intellects of the thing which they achieve through action, and their action stems from such preconception. This is what it means for intellect to be the principle of action. (Aquinas, 1956: 34–37)

Kant linked the "intellect as the principle of action" to the *sensus communis*. Kant said that, "By the name *sensus communis* is to be understood the idea of a public sense, that is a critical faculty which in its reflective act takes account (a priori) of the mode of representation of everyone else" (1959: 151). Kant argued that when we make judgements we refer them to the "collective reason of mankind." The idea of a *sensus communis*, or a public sense, suggests that each of us have the ability to make intelligible the accounts of others and that we think and act for a *reason*. Intelligibility results from the fact that we are already engaged in a more or less coherent enterprise of making sense of one another's concepts or actions. However, in some works it is assumed that to account for changes in practice we need a 'theory,' for example, to make aggregate patterns into laws or, following thinkers as diverse as Bourdieu (1977), Foucault (1977) and Shils (1981), to describe practice in terms that derive neither from the idiom of our practices nor the idiom of the subject practices, but in a theoretical vocabulary or an idiom of interpretation.

Weber spoke of the world as meaningless chaos. As Turner has suggested, in one sense, intentional language is just another frame for this chaos: "But it is also a gift, a gift of intelligibility uniquely given to the social sciences. But it is more than a gift. It is the sort of gift which one cannot refuse" (1984: 27). The problem in descriptions of everyday life is the extent to which theorists establish criteria of intelligibility which have as their consequence a suppression of questions about an agent's reasons. As Hindess (1986a; 1986b) has pointed out, agents make choices and act accordingly, but they do so on the basis of the discursive means available to them. It is possible, in principle, to demonstrate particular forms of thought without reference to general mechanisms, or laws, that supposedly determine those forms of thought. In Schutz's example of the musician there is no 'general law' that determines his choice of music, but there may be reasons for his choices.

In this book the authors have applied Schutz's idea of a construct to information as a phenomenon. We have explored disciplinary conceptions of information on their own terms, using the concept of reduction only to discriminate between different meanings. It is the actual subject practices that the authors are interested in rather than creating a separate language to describe those practices.

Social Interaction and the Internet

Before the Internet hit the public scene, theorists were clear that citizens in modern society were coming closer together in new communicative spaces and that this had implications for our capacity to define what is or is not relevant.

> We are less and less able to choose our partners in the social world and to share out social life with them. We are, so to speak, potentially subject to everybody's remote control. No spot of this globe is more distant from the place where we live than sixty airplane hours; electric waves carry messages in a fraction of a second from one end of the earth to the other; and very soon every place in this world will be the potential target of destructive weapons released at any other place. Our own social surrounding is within the reach of everyone, everywhere; an anonymous Other, whose goals are unknown to us because of his anonymity, may bring us together with our system of interests and relevances within his control. We are less and less masters in our own right to define what is, and what is not, relevant to us. (Schutz, 1970: 129)

There was also early recognition that the source of discourses and their networks are important in understanding how modern media shaped human action.

> The idea behind discourse networks was very simple at the time I developed it, even though I was later asked to write a methodological after-word to Discourse Networks, 1800/1900 in order to elucidate its importance. The concept of discourse networks is essentially a free application of Claude E. Shannon's information theory. Hence Shannon's theory, founded on information source, information channel and information receiver, that is, on informational inputs, transmission and outputs, is the engineering or technical model behind my literary experiment. Discourse Networks, 1800/1900 is, however, also deeply influenced by Michel Foucault. But at the time I was writing my book, and I do not think that this is a mistake, it occurred to me that what is wrong with Foucault's The Order of Things (1970) is that it merely describes the production of discourses. There are, for example, no descriptions in Foucault's book

of the source of these discourses, of the channels or the receivers of discourse in the form of, let's say, readers or consumers. (Kittler interviewed in Armitage, 2006: 19)

What happens to knowledge schema, to constructed types, when much of our communication operates in virtual mode—when the locus of interaction undertaken within many communities is not directly interpersonal? In the case of the Internet, a person's digital persona is itself a representation, a schema. Social interaction as a result takes a different form. Online, people are able to choose the level or degree of interaction they seek; choose when to participate; and choose their degree of involvement with others. A person through her/his digital persona or, as is more likely, personas, can create relationships and break them at any stage by simple withdrawal, leaving one to wonder at the level, depth, and type of commitment or investment held within these relationships.

People can have several digital personas within a community or within several communities, at any one time. Twitter, social and professional networking sites (such as Facebook or LinkedIn), and blogging practices are enacted at times, almost simultaneously. People therefore can flit between, conflate or transform one or another persona and community continuously. This is not altogether different from the multiple memberships, social roles, and identities that people have practiced in the past. However, the rate of transition among these types of roles was rarely as instantaneously possible as it is with the Internet and mobile technologies. This instantaneity accelerates the transformative skills needed to rapidly assimilate into each persona and may indeed have ramifications for a person's experience and means of relating to the world and to others. In 1995, Sherry Turkle discussed the schizophrenic or transformative potential of operating within multiple windows simultaneously. In 2010, it is not just the number of interfaces operational at any one time, there are now a diverse range of applications, technologies and engagements that are possible. The knowledge schemas, the types of constructs, and the skills required to enable navigation through this complex communicative terrain have also evolved.

As mentioned earlier, constructed types provide explanations and frameworks through which society understands and negotiates its daily life. Mythology, theology, and philosophy, for example, are all modes of explanation or knowledge. These modes are initiated and enacted by people when attempting to understand and navigate through their lives—their roles, positions, relations, and expectations. But these frameworks are not constructed or adopted out of a vacuum, untouched by social events and practices enacted around them; a complex interchange takes place in which practices and ideas feed mutually into one another. This is one of the reasons why the authors' earlier discussion of information and communication is so important. These under-standings are reflected in the ways technologies of the Internet and social (in-formation) practices are designed and also enacted. In turn, these practices reflect back upon and inform further theoretical consideration. Wikipedia's collaborative authoring, social bookmarking, browser possibilities and prac-tices, to name just a few articulations, are therefore not only representative of a wide variety of understandings of information and communication, the af-fordances that result also inflect upon the broader schemas and typifications that are necessary in order for the practices to work, be enacted and to make sense (to be intelligible).

Thus as social interactions become increasingly mediated by the Internet and extended further across time and space, knowledge schemas reflect, ex-plain, and situate life for the online citizen. These schemas also play a role in the possibilities of this extension in the first place. As interpersonal relations in general become more abstracted and mediated across time and space, away from direct and interpersonal interaction and integration through the em-ployment of technological media, subjective and inter-subjective relations are affected. In modern, and even more noticeably in postmodern, communities there is the perception of increased individual freedom and increased choice as actions and relations are experienced as being less constrained by particular spaces and times (Willson, 2006).

Within this type of worldview and idea of individual agency, understand-ings of information as resource and information as essential in the reduction of uncertainty become instantiated and reinforced. Without the immediate co-presence of another, information becomes to be understood, viewed and ma-nipulated as a discrete entity that may have relationships with and conse-quences for external other entities (such as people). It then becomes easy to claim that the importance of social context, and of social engagement becomes lost.

While in some ways this is true, such a claim also ignores the extensive up-take of social networking applications, the ways in which micro-blogging and mobile technologies, for example, as practices of social engagement have been incorporated within individual lives. What is needed then, is a deeper under-standing of the ways in which people make sense of these engagements, the constructs they employ and what this means for the types of relationships and possibilities for an informed citizenry that is developing, sharing and engaging with common intrinsic interests. Acts of disclosure require placing trust in both those with whom one engages as well as the environs within which the engagement takes place. Likewise, recognition of common intrinsic interests and the authenticity and reliability of the discussions that take place requires both the ability to operate without fear as well as the ability to be able to critically respond to others.

Schutz bases much of his analysis on participants' mutual ability to predict, anticipate, and respond to each other. In face-to-face interpersonal relations there are numerous signals that participants can interpret and use to guide their responses to one another. Where there are no face-to-face interpersonal interactions, participants need to rely on typifying constructs to anticipate behavior. If this is the case, then the spatial extension of relationships has important ramifications for the conceptualization of both community and relatedly, the possibilities for the informed citizen. Likewise, the ways in which the Internet is being deployed by both individuals and local communities as a way of supplementing preexisting face-to-face connections require accommodation.

Works by Calhoun, Wellman, Hampton, Haythornthwaite and many others point to the increasing importance of intermingling forms of sociality and modes of integration. Crossley (1996: 90) notes that Schutz does consider that media technologies and symbols allow for a society of contemporaries to exist. It therefore can be assumed that Schutz does recognize that some form of connection and continuity across various modes of engagement must be operating for people who may not know one another to be part of the same community. However, Crossley goes on to note that for Schutz, mediated communication "was straightforward and theoretically uninteresting in itself" (90). The authors disagree with this assessment. We argue that abstract or extended forms of interaction have particular subjective and intersubjective effects, but they overlay rather than completely transform or replace more embodied relations of integration.

Where Schutz is useful is in his recognition of different types of relations according to participants' respective positions across time and space. Schutz is also useful if we extend his analysis to include the implications of extended social relations. His position adds support to the argument that as social relations are extended across time and space so does the nature of community become more abstract and thinner (Willson, 2006). Arguably too the opportunities for the development and sharing of common intrinsic interests are diminished. Schutz writes that it

> becomes apparent that an increase in anonymity involves a decrease of fullness of content. The more anonymous the typifying construct is [e.g., postman, Australian, manufacturer], the more detached it is from the uniqueness of the individual fellow man involved and the fewer aspects of his personality and behavior pattern enter the typification as being relevant for the purpose at hand, for the sake of which the type has been constructed. (Schutz, 1962: 18)

Within the context of the Internet, the authors would argue that as these relationships are more detached from presence and mediated through time and space, the more specific and typifying a construct becomes. As the community relationship becomes more one-dimensional or specialized, the amount of exposure to the self and others diminishes or is relegated to that particular sphere of reference. As "a decrease of fullness in content" is experienced, "the more detached it [becomes] from the uniqueness of the individual fellow man [sic]." This leads to intersubjective relations that are more objectifying and/or less extensive. As the relationships or imaginings of community are stretched further across space and time, they become more abstracted or are viewed more abstractly through constructed types. The larger the community, the less possible it is to know all intimately; close relations are possible only with an intimate few, and then decreasing degrees of intimacy are manifested as the degree of contact diminishes. Typifying constructs are employed to navigate such diminishing contact. Any adequate theoretical position needs to take into account that as communities are stretched further across space and time, exposure to the face-to-face tends to be either increasingly ephemeral or fetishistically intense. The deployment of ego-centric manifestations of self such as is evident in social networking sites or personal blogs is perhaps inevitable.

The Internet as a Public Sphere or Zero Institution

Many of the early Internet analyses focused on the ability of participants to act within virtual spaces without the constraints of 'real life' (RL) prejudices and discriminations or the unequal privileges of rank and resource. The New Yorker's famous cartoon's quip that "on the Internet, nobody knows you are a dog" (Steiner, 1993) was seen as representing an innately liberating and equalising online condition: All could participate without fear or favour. A white American male CEO could debate and discuss issues with equal standing, fervour, and audience as an unemployed Hispanic youth (as long as they both had equal access to the sites and sufficient literacy skills). The bar had been shifted—now it was your knowledge of the environment, netiquette, typing speed and willingness to behave as a helpful netizen that was seen as leading to more privilege and audience (Rheingold, 1993). The Internet was therefore understood as offering a space (the rhetoric at that time was usually of *a space* rather than of *spaces*) that stood outside the purview, sight and control of the state. As cyberlibertarian John Perry Barlow famously stated in his "A Declaration of the Independence of Cyberspace,"

Governments of the Industrial World, you weary giants of flesh and steel, I come from Cyberspace, the new home of Mind. On behalf of the future, I ask you of the past to leave us alone. You are not welcome among us. You have no sovereignty where we gather....

We have no elected government, nor are we likely to have one, so I address you with no greater authority than that with which liberty itself always speaks. I declare the global social space we are building to be naturally independent of the tyrannies you seek to impose on us. You have no moral right to rule us nor do you possess any methods of enforcement we have true reason to fear....

We are creating a world that all may enter without privilege or prejudice accorded by race, economic power, military force, or station of birth....

We are creating a world where anyone, anywhere may express his or her beliefs, no matter how singular, without fear of being coerced into silence or conformity....

Those who apply Habermas's argument about the public sphere and communicative competencies within an Internet context consider predominantly the openness of the dialogic space itself (see Papacharissi, 2010 or Dean, 2001 for overview). Structural considerations are, at times, taken into account inasmuch as the openness of access to a site or online discussion, or delimiting of power relations may be considered. However, in the main, these analyses have focussed mostly upon the ability for open communication within a technological space and a utopian open space at that. Wikis, blogs and other participatory media have been lauded as offering just such open spaces. The technical affordances of easy participation, equal participatory status and the undermining of the notion of single authorship have all been celebrated.

Certainly there are parallels that can be drawn between claims about Habermas's public sphere and the claims being made about early Internet spaces in terms of intent: private individuals gathering together to discuss matters of public and personal interest. Viewed entirely as a neutral space, listservs, chat rooms, and online worlds provide avenues that seem commensurate with the intent and possibilities encapsulated in Habermas's discussion of the early public sphere. Indeed online spaces seem to more adequately address some of his later writings about multiple publics in response to critics who suggested counterpublics and critiqued the notion of a single public sphere (see for example, Papacharissi, 2010, Dean, 2001; Fraser, 1993).

However, one of Habermas's first public comments about the Internet deviated widely from these other commentators in terms of his interpretation of the possibilities of the Internet as a viable public sphere and its possibilities to enhance democratic practice. He said,

The Internet has certainly reactivated the grassroots of an egalitarian public of writers and readers. However, computer-mediated communication in the web can claim un-equivocal democratic merits only for a special context: It can undermine the censor-ship of authoritarian regimes that try to control and repress public opinion. In the context of liberal regimes, the rise of millions of fragmented chat rooms across the world tend instead to lead to the fragmentation of large but politically focused mass audiences into a huge number of isolated issue publics. Within established national public spheres, the online debates of web users only promote political communica-tion, when news groups crystallize around the focal points of the quality press, for ex-ample, national newspapers and political magazines. (Habermas, 2006: 423)

Habermas's comments about the Internet received immediate criticism. How-ard Rheingold concluded that he did not understand the Internet.

Habermas—a man whose theory of communicative action places high priority on pre-cision of communication—describes Internet discourse as 'a series of chat rooms,' which is a telltale that he doesn't understand the phenomenon he is describing. Cer-tainly, the Internet hosts chat rooms, many of which are the site of political discus-sion of varying degrees of rationality and civility. But as millions of people know, there are mailing lists, wiki talk pages, blogs and blog comments, and message boards as well. What I wish Habermas had said, since he clearly does not understand a phe-nomenon that is central to the applicability of his theory in the 21st century, is 'leave that work to younger scholars'. (Rheingold, 2007, par. 10)

Axel Bruns, a social media theorist, likewise, took aim at Habermas's ap-parent lack of understanding

of a number of factors which combine to allow quality material to emerge to public attention: such factors include both explicit social rating and tagging systems which in their aggregate serve to highlight quality and importance (whether this is in internal mechanisms like Slashdot's comment ratings, or in distributed models like del.icio.us), and implicit preference tracking systems (from Flickr's 'interestingness' score to Amazon's recommendations or finally to Google's PageRank). (Bruns, 2007, par. 10)

Habermas's theory of the public sphere attempts to explain how mediated communication can help political systems meet the normative goals of delib-erative democracy. His formal definition of a public sphere is as "an interme-diary system of communication between formally organised and informal face-to-face deliberations in arenas both at the top and at the bottom of the politi-cal system" (2006: 415). Personal, intrinsic interests become common intrinsic interests in the public sphere. Habermas is querying the extent to which the Internet as a massive system of many interests actually acts as a deliberative process generating genuine public opinion. In response, Axel Bruns argues that the aggregating mechanisms of the Internet are examples of how those interests or issues are pulled together. However, the extent to which aggregation algorithms are themselves 'deliberative' would no doubt be of concern to Habermas.

The critics of the Internet as a public sphere, like Jodi Dean (2003), go in the completely opposite direction of Rheingold and Bruns, suggesting the Internet be more accurately conceptualized as a zero institution. Dean credits the Internet with minimal influence in the deliberative democratic process.

> Unlike a notion of the public sphere, then, the zero institution makes no normative claims. Indeed, it makes no empirical claims in the sense of being recognized or acknowledged as such by those within the institution; differently put, one would expect dissonant, irreconcilable accounts of any given zero institution. Again, the concept functions simply as a placeholder to designate institutionality as such, Lévi-Strauss uses the idea of the 'zero institution' to explain how members of a tribe are able to think of themselves as members of the same tribe even when they are radically split, even when their very representations of what the tribe is are radically antagonistic to one another. Similarly, Žižek views the nation as a kind of zero institution, and he adds that sexual difference should also be understood as a zero institution. Whereas the nation is the zero institution of society's unity, sexual difference is the zero institution of society's split or fundamental antagonism. (Dean, 2003: 5)

Dean comes up with a description of the difference between the public sphere and the Internet in a neo-democratic context, summarized in Table 1.

Table 1. Dean's Internet as a Zero Institution

	Public Sphere	**Neodemocracies**
Site	Nation	Web as zero-institution
Goal	Consensus (legitimation)	Contestation
Means	Procedures (legal, rational)	Networked conflict
Norms	Inclusivity	Duration
	Equality	Hegemony
	Transparency	Decisiveness
	Rationality	Credibility
Vehicle	Actors	Issues

It is doubtful that the Internet is a zero institution. But equally it is not clear, despite Rheingold and Bruns's comments, how the Internet meets the conditions of public sphere as a deliberative process. There can be no doubts, though, that the Internet has become a key part of the social distribution of knowledge.

Summary

Habermas, Jonas and Arendt put disclosure and intention at the heart of the communicative enterprise. Information does not exist. Informed people exist. In order to become informed particular rules apply, not least a conformative attitude, when the citizen is engaged in dialogue. An informed citizen is not a person full of recipe knowledge alone but a person who can judge the competencies of those involved in dialogue. Schutz uses the phrase common intrinsic interests to describe the point at which a person's genuine interests intersect with others and where the generalization of competencies is at work. Imposed interests are more likely when a person is unable to judge the competencies of others and where recipe knowledge becomes the norm. Schutz's idea of zones of relevance becomes a good starting point for theorizing the social distribution of knowledge, the informed citizen and, indeed, the public sphere as an intersection of common intrinsic interests. Figure 1 below provides an overview of elements of the social distribution.

A public sphere is not simply an open physical or communicative space. Saddam Hussein, the Iraqi dictator, created an open space called the 'freedom wall' in his universities. Students were allowed to write anything on those walls that they wanted. The walls were always empty; not surprisingly given that the punishment for criticism of the regime was severe. A genuine public sphere has an institutional guarantee that the participant will not be subject to coercion or force or exclusion. The materiality of the Internet, its capacity to present a digital persona(s) in place of the person in interpersonal face-to-face relationships, is leading to a reliance on typifying constructs to anticipate behavior. This is new and it presents fascinating challenges for the maintenance of the public sphere. In Chapter Five, the authors will look more closely at the materiality of the Internet and the extent to which it meets the claims of the utopians and the extent to which it can be called a public sphere.

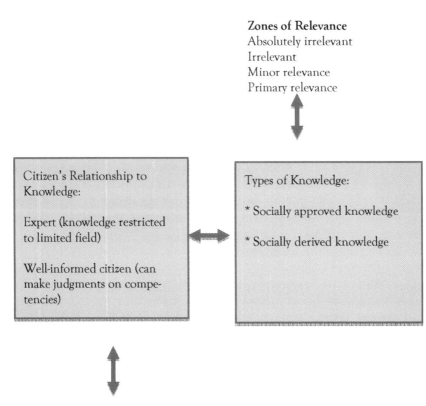

Figure 1: Model of the social distribution of knowledge

Protocol and Machinic Infrastructure (Interface, Time, Place and Space)

Facilitated by protocol, the Internet is the most highly controlled mass media hitherto known.

—Galloway (2004: 243)

In Chapter Four, the authors discussed Habermas's theory of information and briefly touched on some of the debates about whether the Internet is a public sphere. What has been missing in these debates, however, are empirical descriptions of the public sphere that are consistent with Habermas's theory of information. He held that the way we talk, walk, hear and react in communicative spaces is bounded by particular attitudes, types of discourse, rules of discourse and, indeed, limits on what can come into discourses.

Alexander Galloway and Jürgen Habermas, at first glance, do not look like conceptual partners in the public sphere. However, Galloway is sensitive to the architectures and protocols that underpin the communicative and physical spaces that we use. When we walk through a door or look through a window we are located within particular aesthetics, rules, layers, thresholds and transitions. When I use my laptop I am engaged with a physical activity requiring typing on my keypad. But I only have a certain amount of control over how this typing is presented or what the translation of this typing into a system 'does.' My screen frames things in particular ways, and my choices as to how to engage with this screen are constrained by the software program. These frames embed other frames; media within media.

Google as a window, a transition, likewise is not a neutral frame. It has its own rules for classification, search and what counts as knowledge or a record. For example, if you are interested in the preservation of indigenous culture and knowledge through a particular type of interaction, then Google is not the place to be.

Both Habermas and Galloway understood that collaborative spaces cannot escape the protocols that govern what we see, hear and do. The door, the building, the spatial arrangements and the languages that enable and constrain the public sphere are themselves important. In this chapter the authors look at how Galloway and Habermas talk about space, time and place and the empirical examples they use, including the Internet.

Strategies of Exclusion

As noted in Chapter Four, Habermas and Schutz both created models of the social distribution of knowledge. In Habermas's public sphere, any mediation of knowledge by a non-interpersonal source—for example, traditional or new media—should ultimately meet the ethos of deliberative democratic practice. In Schutz's zones of relevance, citizens should have generalized competencies and be able to judge the expertise of those who make decisions about them: At the very least, all interests should not be "imposed relevances." Information, in these contexts, is not a social actor in its own right, able to make decisions and to act on them.

The authors would argue that until now, the community's stock of knowledge has been for the most part *possessed* and *used* by the community but by legal definition not privately or publicly *owned*. Information is tied to the notion of being informed. The activity of becoming informed is a joint enterprise and this joint enterprise triggers legal principles of free speech and the freedom to publish. A right to be informed, therefore, need not be conceived as an ontological attribute of individual subjects, but rather as an ethical statement about the kinds of social conditions that might be required for a generalisation of competencies and an informed and politically aware public. Hirst (1986), for example, has pointed out that the new information and communication control technologies need not further subordinate workers to senior management decisions and supervision; "indeed, in the right social context they offer the means to decentralize a portion of decision-making and control" (1986: 11).

In a modern society, complex organisational forms are necessary for the administration of complex activities. A workable Freedom of Information Act is impossible without working practices made subject to consultation and inspection and a government made accountable not merely upward to superiors but to diverse agencies and levels within (Hirst, 1986: 20). It would seem that a generalisation of competence across the community is a natural extension of any serious attempt at popular democratic reform. If people are to have a say in how an area of activity or service is to be run or performed, even though they may not be directly involved in running a service or producing goods, then it would seem appropriate to create the right social context to enable an institutionalised representation of organised interests.

There may have been inequalities in access to or in the distribution of that knowledge, but, for the purposes of intellectual property law, it has been considered essential to treat the ideas of citizens as free. The authors are not here advocating the concept of 'freedom' as an organising principle for society. Nor are we suggesting that it does not cost money to become informed. Rather, the authors are restating the legal rules which have governed the right of access to the community's stock of knowledge and the causally necessary conditions for securing that right. The principle is well encapsulated in the role of libraries:

> I want a poor student to have the same means of indulging his [sic] learned curiosity, of following his rational pursuits, of consulting the same authorities, of following the most intricate enquiry as the richest men in the kingdom, as far as books go, and I contend that the Government is bound to give him the most liberal and unlimited assistance in this respect. (Antonio Panizzi, Keeper of Printed Books at the British Museum, 1836, cited in Thompson, 1977: 15)

When Karl Marx sought to study capitalism in 19th Century British society he went to the British Museum Library in London in order to gain access to works relevant to his pursuit. He was not denied access to those works nor asked to pay for that access. At that time, it was generally accepted that citizens should have access to what had been made publicly known (access to that which was the result of an act of publication). Marx took this right of access for granted because he, like others, did not presume that the community's stock of knowledge was the subject of proprietary rights. Marx was able to gain access to published works in the British Museum Library in order to participate in the act of publication.

Not everybody in Britain enjoyed the opportunities open to Marx to research and to write works. However, it is worthwhile repeating Wallas's (1920) comments about the effects on conditions for the acquisition and use of knowledge. If the Whig landlords who were responsible for most of the details of the glorious constitution in Britain had been also authors and inventors for profit,

> we should probably have had the strictest rights of perpetual property or even of entail in ideas; and there would now have been a Duke of Shakspere [sic] to whom we should all have had to pay two or three pounds for the privilege of reading his ancestor's works, provided that we returned the copy uninjured at the end of a fortnight. (Wallas, 1920: 146)

Max Weber said that the structure of every legal order directly influences the distribution of power, economic or otherwise, within its respective community (1953: 64). Parkin (1979: 44–46) used the notion of "exclusionary closure" to describe the attempt by one group to secure for itself a privileged position at the expense of some other group through a process of subordination. "Strategies of exclusion are the predominant mode of closure in all stratified systems" (Parkin, 1979: 45). Libraries were set up precisely to provide a physical space that enabled people to access knowledge, regardless of other contexts in which a person might be subordinated. While libraries are not theatres of conversation, in Habermas's sense, they are certainly a part of the public sphere as public representations of knowledge. The UK public broadcaster, the BBC, likewise has in its charter that there must be "room for the radical" and that it must represent diversity in society.

The Internet, however, does not represent an organization, in the sense of a library or a broadcaster with a charter like the BBC. When a citizen logs on to the Internet, they are doing so through a provider and their identity, or digital persona, becomes an important part of that process of connection. The moment that a person enters the Internet, they are part of a system that wants knowledge about them and, indeed, records that knowledge. This makes Habermas's notion of disclosure problematic for those who want to call the Internet a public sphere because the boundaries of theatres of conversations in the Internet are many times not at all clear and the underlying architectures of the Internet have their own effects.

How Can a Citizen Be(come) Informed?

At this point it seems timely to return to the informed citizen and to raise the question as to what enables or constrains the social distribution of knowledge. How can we understand the conditions of becoming an informed citizen? Once we exclude giving agency to information or information retrieval networks as a phenomenon and return agency to citizens as actors, then we can consider both the social and the material environment that might exclude or enhance people becoming informed. We can ask questions about what actual algorithms do in network contexts, for example, and the effects of those algorithms (designed and implemented by people) on people's access to knowledge and to communication with other people.

In his book, *The Structural Transformation of the Public Sphere*, Habermas (1989) points to a number of historically specific conditions that were important for both the formation and the function of the modern public sphere. Of particular relevance to this book, he notes changes in architectural spaces and places and the ways these both reflected and shaped social changes. These places—in the form of coffee houses (oft-noted by commentators in their discussion of the public sphere and its later application to the Internet), but also in salons and drawing rooms, and in the layout and orientation of houses and fences within streetscapes—facilitated the bridging or transgression of public and private domains and their functions (see for example, pp. 157-159). These architecturally structured social spaces affected the transmission of ideas, roles and cultures across spheres of action. They were also vitally important in the management of zones of relevance and the demarcation of the types of knowledge that were included within these various zones.

Thus, it was not just the physical spaces themselves that were important but the social, cultural and economic function and understanding of these spaces. The spaces enabled specific types of gatherings—the presentation of papers, the discussion of matters in the press, and so forth—with their own norms of operation. Certain etiquette evolved and accepted modes of operation were developed for within these spaces. It was therefore the combination of the physical constraints and enabling of spaces (the size of rooms, whether buildings were faced outwards to the road or inward to other houses encircling a common area), the shape, flow and function of gatherings that they enabled or constrained *and* the processes, rules and norms that were linked or attributed to the spaces (whether they were used for more privatised functions or broader ceremonial functions, how gatherings were conducted, who had access and how access was obtained, etc.) that were important. Habermas stresses therefore both the physical constraints—though these are not developed or explored in any extensive detail in his work—and the social constraints that enable and shape the informed citizen.

For Habermas, these spaces and their use were particularly important because of the role they played in enabling the creation of a between space or overlapping realm of publics and private, of the domestic and familial and the concerns of the public domain. It was in these places that the architectural space, function and positioning combined with cultural, social, political actions and relationships:

> understanding of the public use of reason was guided specifically by such private experiences as grew out of the audience-oriented (*publikumsbezogen*) subjectivity of the conjugal family's intimate domain (*Intimsphäre*). Historically, the latter was the source of privateness in the modern sense of a saturated and free interiority. (Habermas, 1989: 28)

Habermas, of course, is not the only person to note the importance of architectural spaces for enabling and constraining particular types of actions nor the first to point to changes in these as reflecting broader social, cultural, political and economic changes. Norbert Elias (1978), for example, maps in detail the ways in which the family home and its changing layout, the provision, use and demarcated functions of the home and the related development of norms, etiquette and so forth also reflects changing understandings of family structure, the nature of what is deemed private and what is public, changing understandings of sexuality, intimacy and so forth. Michel Foucault (1977) also examined the ways in which process, space and discourses interacted in institutions such as prisons, schools and the military, resulting in specific practices and understandings. His much-quoted discussions of Bentham's panopticon and the intersection of disciplinary understandings (in terms of what is deemed normal or expected behaviour in particular circumstances), architectural spaces, and modes of operation has formed the bedrock of many contemporary discussion of power, subjectivity and political systems, social forms and practices. Another example is Frederick Jameson's (1991) exploration of late capitalist understandings and their representation or articulation through architectural forms such as the Westin Bonaventure in Los Angeles, the Beaubourg in Paris, and the Eaton Centre in Toronto. However, what is useful for the purposes of the authors' investigations here is the point that it was the standardisation of the layout, space and function of these domestic-public spheres that enabled the formulation and discussion of a range of public matters through specific forms of discourse. The press too, in the form of pamphlets and weeklies, as a communication medium that carried the ideas and issues across these spaces performed a vital function and is important for our broader discussion about the Internet. At the same time, the local and public library, still one of the most visited cultural institutions in Western societies, also provided unrestricted access to books. In the process, citizens were able to be(come) informed in a way previously impossible.

Is the Internet as a material space the same as a library or a salon? The answer is no. Firstly, the scientific expertise required to set up the Internet, from computers through to government of the IP addresses far exceeds the competencies of the person on the street. Secondly, the algorithms that run on the Internet affect content in a way that stacks in a library, or a discussion within a salon, do not. The librarian will collect personal information from you only to the extent that is needed to know where the book has gone or to retrieve it if it is not returned. The host or hostess of the salon will only hold sufficient information about you to enable the decision to invite or exclude you from the occasion or discussion. The transmission of this personal information is restricted to a small number of contexts and purposes, if it 'goes' anywhere at all. The moment you enter the Internet, however, you have yourself become material code in a world of algorithms.

The Importance of Protocol

Galloway's statement about the Internet as a highly controlled medium noted at the beginning of this chapter might sound odd given the apparent access to knowledge and communication that the Internet provides to the modern citizen. But if you look at one of the author's desktops you can begin to see what he means.

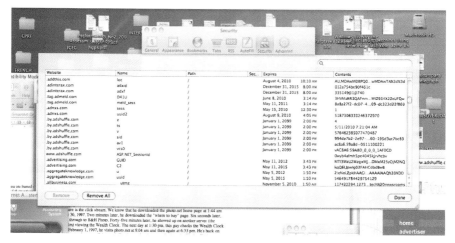

Figure 1: Screen shot of Balnaves' desktop

Figure 1 above is Mark Balnaves's, admittedly messy, desktop. This is the Internet in a work context: Mark, the employee, must log in to access the Internet via the university's network. He knows that he is under surveillance and that his work emails are, in fact, publications that can be accessed through a Freedom of Information Act or by the university management. His university restricts the kinds of sites he can visit. His work context also allows him to use the libraries' subscriptions to electronic journals regularly, without direct cost to him; something the public at large does not have access to.

At home, he subscribes to Optus, an ISP provider. This service limits him to 2GB per month, the same limit his university sets at work, but he is loathe to upgrade his access at home due to cost. He has had two major virus attacks in 2010 and about 170 social engineering attacks (false sites pretending to be his bank and inviting him to put in his password details). Balnaves is confident his ISP collects information about him from his web activities, just as he is confident there are cookies on his computer that will be doing things he does not understand or that, indeed, may be involved in severe breaches of his privacy.

Galloway's view of this is that the very material coding in modern computer networks has consequences for Mark's agency and the form of his communicative content. His information and communication practices follow structured pathways, are translated into particular communicative forms, are captured in various databases and result in specific outcomes. For Galloway,

> A distributed network is a specific network architecture characterized by equity between nodes, bi-directional links, a high degree of redundancy and general lack of internal hierarchy. Protocol refers to the technology of organization and control operating in distributed networks....Protocol exists in contemporary computer networks, but it is also at play in a variety of biological and bioinformatic networks. (Galloway, 2006: 317)

So what is protocol? Protocol means many things: it can be the set of rules or procedures that are understood and enacted between different parties to ensure effective communication is achieved; it can be the actual language used to enable communication to be enacted between different machines. For Galloway (2004; 2006), protocol is this and more. Arguing that we are in a specific historical period where computers and networks are increasingly central to our lives, he argues that we need to take computer languages and processes into account. Alongside many other commentators, he argues for the materiality and actualizing qualities of technological processes. These processes alongside the material constraints, configurations and possibilities facilitate, constrain and enable communication. As he describes it,

> *Protocol is a language that regulates flow, directs netspace, codes relationships, and connects lifeforms.* Protocol does not produce or causally effect objects, but rather is a structuring agent that appears as the result of a set of object dispositions. (Galloway, 2004, 74–75, emphasis in original)

For Galloway (2004), protocol enables communication between disparate, autonomous entities; it does this through a process that does not discriminate between content or intent except inasmuch as it might hinder communicative possibilities (p. 243); it is a language and an etiquette (p. 244). It can and indeed must change in order to be continually functional and this change is undertaken through negotiation.

In the conclusion to his book *Protocol*, Galloway outlines a non-Internet example to illustrate what he is referring to when he talks of protocol (he also uses the rather ugly term of protocological). He talks of two similar streets in two different towns that have problems with speeding drivers. In an effort to reduce or eliminate the speeding, the towns take different approaches. The two solutions are to a) install speed humps, or b) introduce speed signs, policing and fines. Both approaches are successful in reducing speeding but Galloway asks which solution is the most protocological? His answer is that while both solutions are technological (technique as device and as process), the speed hump solution is the most protocological because it induces in the driver the desire to drive more slowly (in order to protect the driver, the car and for the enjoyment of the ride) whereas the other solution of speed signs and policing is more of a request with the potential for violence or punishment. In this example, it is thus not only the introduction of a technological/structural form—the speed hump and the unavoidable need to either slow down or damage your vehicle—but also the inducement of an action or process that seems sensible, logical, easiest, unreflective This positioning of technique, logic and process is not dissimilar in its theoretical move to Foucault's discussion of disciplinary techniques: technique that is the most efficient use of a 'resource,' but one that has particular sets of outcomes. Indeed, Galloway points to both Foucault's notion of bio-power and disciplinary technique and Deleuze's

writings on control societies as being "useful for thinking about the protocological system of organization and control" (Galloway, 2006: 318).

While the way in which Galloway develops this notion of protocol is subject to some slippage and thus difficult to extract in any clear or concise form —protocol as a process, a language, a wrapping, and so on—the concept is useful for drawing attention to the ways in which the various technological layers of the Internet as well as the processes that are enacted across these bring about certain outcomes. Galloway is interested in exploring the specific physical or material constraints and affordances as well as the communicative rules and social processes that are enacted. Therefore it is the structure, process, and logic: it is the way in which communication is enabled, constrained, and interpreted that is of interest. For example, Galloway considers the various computer protocols such as TCP/IP, the DNS system and HTTP and HTML that enable communication to take place between discrete machinic entities and that direct the flow and 'behaviour' of these communications. As Flanagin et al. (2010: 182) note, "The defining characteristics of an end-to-end system is that network 'intelligence' (discrimination and processing functions) exists primarily at the periphery of the network, while the network pathways remain neutral, handling all data traffic identically."

Where technical code enables communication between differently functioning and differently purposed technological entities (e.g., DNS systems to ensure the effective management and centralisation of IP addresses and TCP/IP to facilitate information sharing and packet switching across distributed networks), Galloway employs the term protocol to describe the process by which content (and as noted above, the content of the data or information itself is irrelevant for this process) is moved through the system in an efficient and effective manner. Yet that process has particular outcomes, and it has been developed within specific social and cultural environments. Technical expediency is also coupled with social intent (the degree to which this is successfully articulated is less clear—there is considerable literature around the theme of differentiated and unintended consequences of technological developments). This point will be picked up and expanded in later sections of this chapter. However, also important to note is that while the content or intent of the data contained within these communication arrangements is in some ways irrelevant—at least in a normative sense for the discussion at hand—the ways in which the technical arrangements or protocols facilitate data sharing as well as enable possibilities for information control and surveillance have broader significance. For example, filters are technological applications devised to screen, limit and monitor exposure to particular coded content; cookies can facilitate information accessibility through the 'archiving' of information practices and pathways, reducing the time involved in accessing sites previously accessed for users but also providing opportunities for surveillance, and for data mining.

Much as Habermas has suggested that the layout of drawing rooms or the orientation of houses to streetscapes or public spaces can be linked with changing expressions of the public sphere and communicative processes, the development and practices of protocol, of technical architecture and communicative processes should also be recognised and considered within any discussions of the contemporary public sphere/s and the Internet. Habermas does not deny that a non-physical space might be required for the public sphere to reflect the increasing pluralistic, democratic and media-saturated societies within which we live. He writes in a reflective piece,

> If there still is to be a realistic application of the idea of the sovereignty of the people to highly complex societies, it must be uncoupled from the concrete understanding of its embodiment in physically present, participating, and jointly deciding members of a collectivity. (Habermas, 1992a:. 451)

While he makes space for the possibility of public sphere/s of mediated presence within online collaborative communicative spaces, as noted in Chapter Three, he pays little attention to the Internet except in terms of its potential to fracture or disperse the possibilities for public deliberation and unified political action (Habermas, 2007). Of the Internet, he suggests that it bypasses the gatekeeping function of the mainstream press and therefore also the 'staging' of particular news foci at particular times. However, his discussion does not delve much deeper than that.

This lack of attention to the vagaries and specifics of the Internet in itself is not necessarily a problem: The Internet and its possibilities are not directly the focus of Habermas's research or his writings (though an argument can easily be made that Habermas's concern with public deliberation and the public sphere would necessitate that the Internet *is* taken into account more fully). However, when the notion of the public sphere, the informed citizen or the theory of information is considered in discussions of activities on and through the Internet, then the researcher is left stumbling through any analysis without the conceptual tools to address these many layered manifestations of communicative behaviour and the environments that may constrain, shape and enable these manifestations. In order to accommodate these possibilities and constraints alongside a proclaimed increase in network forms of organisation (see for example, Castells, 2000; Galloway & Thacker, 2007), then a rethinking of the frame, language and conceptual tools is required.

Alongside Galloway's discussion of protocol, Lawrence Lessig's discussion of code is also very useful for articulating the ways in which the technological materiality of the online environment enables both social and technological constructs to shape outcomes. In an early work, *Code and Other Laws of Cyberspace*, Lessig gives a number of examples of the ways in which technical code can be used to shape practices within the Internet environment. In one example, he (1999: 8–13) describes an online community dispute between neighbours and discusses the social and technical options that are available to resolve this dispute. The story involves a dog (technical construct and outcome of program work undertaken by one neighbour) eating the next-door neighbour's poisonous flower (also a technical construct and outcome of program work undertaken by the other neighbour). The dog 'dies,' and hence the dispute over enforcement of boundaries, the right to 'grow' poisonous flowers (which are the owner's commercial enterprise) within private property and issues of theft and trespass. After a lengthy discussion of the negotiations that took place, Lessig recounts that an eventual solution is arrived at: the poisonous flowers are only poisonous while on the owner's property or when purchased. If the flowers are taken without permission, they lose their poisonous qualities and therefore can do no harm. In other words, these properties are deliberately encoded into the properties of the online flowers.

Lessig's discussion of this scenario draws attention to the fact that while it can be seen to be socially unacceptable to trespass or to poison and that this social understanding may be sufficient to prevent most people from doing so, along with the possibilities of punitive action on the part of law enforcers (offline the police and law makers, online the moderators of the online environment) and the use of physical constructs such as fences and boundary; in the online technical environment it is also possible to program specific possibilities into the environment that make it virtually impossible to trespass, steal or a multitude of another actions. There is another 'layer' of executable control that can be utilized.

Another example also proves quite useful for our discussion here: A classic tale from early cyberspace writing, "A Rape in Cyberspace" by Julian Dibble (1993), provides another illustration of technical and social possibilities. In this case it was the technical possibilities that enabled the perpetrator of the 'virtual rape' to override social and community norms as well as individual agencies. For those unfamiliar with this case, the perpetrator, represented by an online avatar called Mr Bungle, was able to take control of other people's avatars and manipulate their actions, causing considerable distress within the online community. Both social and technical measures were employed by this community to regulate the situation and to attempt to ensure that this scenario was never repeated again. The action, the ensuing community discussion, the decisions that resulted and the broader academic debates that circulated in the aftermath of Dibble's publication are a useful illustration of the argument for considering both technical materiality as well as social influence in any discussion of online publics.

On another level—or layer of engagement—Galloway (2004: 6) also talks about the RFC (Request for Comment) process that developed during the initial stages of the Internet's development, and still continues in various forms to this day. RFCs or Request for Comment documents are part of a communicative procedure that involves the formulation of an idea about a technical standard and the communication of this idea to a forum of interested individuals or groups for comments. The intent of the RFC process could be broadly summarised as a way of ensuring universality or standardisation in the technological but also normative development of the Internet so that the various parts of technologies that constitute the Internet can 'talk' to one another. RFCs were also put in place to facilitate information exchange between people—so they were a process that enabled communications amongst those individuals as well as a way of ensuring that the development of the technologies themselves could talk or communicates effectively with one another: technology to technology; human to human and human to technology communication flows were thus enabled, shaped and constrained in the process. The RFC therefore also was a type of etiquette—an evolving norm that was understood to have specific purposes, specific rules of conduct and specific modes of interpretation and application. Michael Froomkin (2003) takes the discussion of RFCs and the IETF (Internet Engineering Task Force) standard process further and explores in detail the normative, procedural and communicative processes enacted. He suggests that the ways in which this process evolved and is positioned provides an effective empirical enactment of Habermas's discourse ethics (Froomkin, 2003: 796–815).

The point of the above discussion is to flag to the reader that within a highly technological environment, consideration of the way in which processes and coding facilitate communication—for example between systems that would otherwise not be able to communicate such as the DNS system and the TCP/IP protocol, or the RFC process to ensure standardization—as well as recognition of the ways these processes and codes restrict, direct, prevent, monitor and manipulate communication—is needed. Such potentialities necessarily impact on the possibilities of an informed citizenry.

Controlling Identity on the Web

> The key question therefore is never whether control does or does not exist, but rather to ask: What is the quality of this control? Where does it come from? Is it being wielded by governments or deployed at the level of machinic infrastructure?...What is the specific character of information organization? This is the basic question of protocol. (Interview with Galloway, 2009, quesn 2)

Galloway's thesis that the push for efficiency, the easiest route, by programmers and organizations—as though it were a neutral exercise, when it is in fact not—works well as an explanation for how the materiality of algorithms intersects with citizens using structured subjective spaces and what those structured spaces are in fact like. In our earlier example, the user Mark Balnaves has no practical input into the algorithms, software, or technology that distributes his identity online. What happens to his identity-as-code when he logs into the Internet is subject to the forces that design the different algorithms that might capture it, the companies that sell the software and hardware and data, and any regulations that might protect him. He can do his best to manage his identity; for example, he tries to be anonymous in Hotmail, using the name Tiny Markham. But it does not really matter what Mark types in as his identity if the system is already able to identify him, for example, through his IP address.

Following the logic of protocol, the interface and software directs flows, induces user behaviour that seems to follow the easiest and thus the most logical approach. Coding and algorithms hide or makes less desirable alternate options. The interface that enables navigation between various 'levels' of communication, and various levels of technology also frames that communication or information exchange in certain ways. Galloway and Thacker observe that "Interface is how dissimilar data forms operate." (Galloway & Thacker, 2007: 144). As Michael Zimmer (2009) notes, interfaces are not transparent windows that simply reflect a particular situation: they change and transform one thing into a version of something else. Search engines do not simply find information: they are guided by code and algorithms that direct their searching behaviour that then present the information found in a certain order and a certain way (driven by the underlying code which in turn has been fashioned according to certain social, cultural and economic intents).

Figure 2: Tiny's Hotmail screenshot

It is interesting, as Zimmer shows, to see how different search engine companies discuss their algorithms for collecting individual information. Figure 3, by Microsoft, is partly a guess, because the actual procedures of linking personal data are not publicly available, but the figure shows that the easiest path in collecting information, from a market and a network point of view, is to collect personal information. The human language used to describe this is itself extremely interesting, as the word 'de-identification' used by Microsoft is not the same as 'anonymous'.

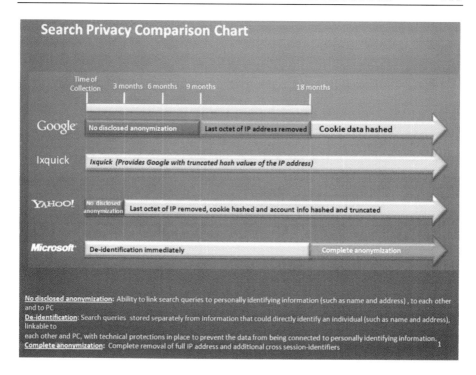

Figure 3: Microsoft's Search Privacy Comparison Chart
(http://blogs.technet.com/b/privacyimperative/archive/2009/02/10/comparing-search-data-
retention-policies-of-major-search-engines-before-the-eu.aspx)

Zimmer, whose work explores technological use, information ethics and implications for information privacy provides numerous examples of the ways in which technology can be coded to extract manipulate and repurpose information. In one incident relating to an admission by Google in May 2010 that it had breached individual privacy with its application Street View, he writes,

> Recently we learned that Google's Street View vehicles gathered people's private communications on their home WiFi networks as they drove by snapping photos. Initially, Google denied it was collecting or storing any payload data, but later admitted that it had, in fact, collected private information that it should not have, information clearly beyond what any reasonable person who expect a street mapping service to collect.

Google's explanation was that this privacy invasion was a mistake, and happened because some code inadvertently made its way into the Street View vehicles' software. ...It also reveals yet another example of how Google failed to recognize and address possible privacy issues related to the fact they are deploying an army of vehicles to harvest information about the physical (and now wireless) terrain. (Zimmer, 2010, http://michaelzimmer.org/2010/05/19/google-on-wi-fi-privacy-invasions-no-harm-no-foul/)

Marx famously wrote, "Men [sic] make their own history, but they do not make it as they please; they do not make it under self-selected circumstances, but under circumstances existing already, given and transmitted from the past." (Marx, 1852), recognizing that individuals have limited autonomy and that their behaviour, and attitudes are shaped in many ways by their historical environment. In contemporary circumstances, this could be re-phrased as...under circumstances existing already given, coded and recorded....

Work on interfaces (Galloway, 2009) and the ways in which these are framed, overlaid with various meanings that are both symbolic and practical, and the various affordances and constraints of these frames adds a further dimension to Galloway's protocol principle. For example, the ways in which graphical representations of avatars and gaming environments are framed by instructional and navigational panels make transparent to the user the various levels of engagement with the game, the software and the hardware they are navigating. The interface in this case is thus a complex site whereby there exists both transparency and opacity, where coding is both visible and invisible and layers of engagement that affect what the user can do, how they think of the space and the information that is collected about them.

This raises the question as to what type of structured subjective space Mark Balnaves, our earlier example, is operating within? It is clear that before he even gets to send an email, the online environment does not conform to Habermas's dialogic space. It is:

Surveilled: User tracking is now an established part of Internet activity;

Manipulated: Manipulation, as a theoretical concept, means that a person does not know the nature of the demand made upon them. Browsers, cookies, flash cookies, IP addresses, DNS, are all part of a system that provides at one level ease of use for the user and at another level provides systems for collecting intimate information about the user;

Invisibly directive: A person's identity-as-code is subject to whatever algorithms might grab it, whether for good or bad. What Google does with a person's activities on the web are not made clear to the user, just as other search engines do not declare publicly what the algorithms tracking users do or any additional analytics that might be applied to a person's identity.

The Internet is not a simple open dialogic space. Reading intent off the material algorithms working within the networks, for most people, is not an easy task. When people think they are anonymous they may not be; when they think that their words are not permanently archived, they may well be. When they tick a 'privacy' box they may well have done the opposite, and traded in their privacy. Indeed, companies like Acxiom, the biggest aggregator of them all, is not known by most and stands behind Google. Algorithms and code, of course, are behind aggregators and their role is growing and will continue to grow.

Material Questions for a Material Internet

The authors noted that for Habermas, information does not exist by transmission or by communication but *in* transmission and *in* communication. Therefore the mechanisms and processes through which knowledge is constrained, enabled and shaped become also of importance in enabling an informed citizenry. Habermas, as noted, recognises some of the features in the Internet: both its potential for fragmentation and for broadening communicative possibilities. He fears fragmentation through the multiplication of issues online alongside a diminished press gatekeeping and editorial capacity will result in a decline in the power of the intellectual and also applauds the possibilities for Internet information access to undermine authoritarian regimes. However, he does not deal in any depth (at least not in the English translated works) in detail with any of the technical constraints or possibilities of the Internet. Likewise he does not consider the ways in which information is presented, or framed online and how this presentation shapes the message and the interpretation of that data.

Galloway, on the other hand, is not all that useful for formulating understandings of democracy or for the facilitation of the informed citizen—though he is not unaware of critical political issues and questions. His suggestion in order to advance more progressive outcomes is to advocate hypertrophy, pushing technologies and protocols to their limits, hacking and so forth. However, coupling the normative impetus of Habermas's public sphere, the notion of the informed citizen and a social (non-realist) understanding of information with some of Galloway's notions of protocol is useful as an alternate conceptual strategy for undertaking analysis of Internet activities.

The authors wish to draw upon the evocative parts of these notions to apply to discussions of the public sphere and the Internet to ask questions about what such an analysis might bring to these discussions. How might consideration of protocol enrich or further our ability to encapsulate the workings of online deliberative communicative spaces? How might we make visible and critique the intentional and unintentional 'speed humps'; the barriers that direct the flow of online activity and encourage uncritical, instrumental navigation online? The structural conditions of the public sphere within the Internet are extraordinarily complicated and must involve tangible protocols, rules and protections. A 'conformative attitude' can only exist if there is an architecture to encourage and bound it and to allow for the informed citizen.

A loose marriage between the two approaches (of Habermas and of Galloway) does not, on first inspection, appear overly problematic. There are many similarities in both the positioning and the understanding of the concepts of public sphere and of protocol. Thus while they have different intents and foci—the public sphere on the discussion of ideas and the development of public opinion and its importance for democracy; protocol on the communicative flows, constraints, and affordances that protocol entails—both deal with communicative processes and those things that enable communication to take place. Indeed, as Table 1 below reveals, there are many similarities that can be discerned between the two approaches; similarities that might enable an argument to be made that the inclusion of Galloway's notion of protocol may be more relevant within our current historical situation.

Table 1. Comparing Habermas's public sphere and Galloway's protocol

Positioning	Habermas–public sphere	Galloway–protocol
Conceptually	Ethics	Concept tool
'Location' practiced	Outside of market and state System	Outside of corporate, institutional, governmental power.
Historically	Early capitalism; changing notions of sovereignty, human/individual rights	Network mode of organization; decentralised networks Changing notion of individual identity
Structure	Horizontal	Horizontal
Conduit	People, opinions, writing, mass media	Process, code, interoperability
Access	Open to all in defined citizen group	Negotiated
Public/s	Homogeneous originally, later to be multiple publics —universal form/process but heterogeneous content	Universal/standardised but with heterogeneity

By this the authors mean that while Habermas first situates his public sphere at a particular historical juncture which saw the separation and reformulation of the roles and understandings of the state, church and economy; Galloway is positioned within the so-called network society with a different emphasis, organising principles, notions of self, subjectivity and so forth. Habermas himself has noted about his approach to the public sphere that "The formation of a concept specific to an epoch requires that a social reality of great complexity be stylized to give prominence to its peculiar characteristics." (Habermas, 1992b: 422). A similar claim about the act of stylizing can be made about Galloway's positioning of protocol within network society and the increased dominance of networked modes of organisation; specifically decentred and distributed networks.

Habermas (1992b: 438) notes of his public sphere analysis: "My diagnosis of a unilinear development from a politically active public to one withdrawn into a bad privacy, from a 'culture-debating to a culture-consuming public,' is too simplistic." At the very least, an argument could be made that a meshing or overlay of Galloway's protocol to Habermas's public sphere considerations provides a useful additional means to consider the public sphere and the possibilities of an informed citizen in an Internet environment. Both Habermas (1989: 462) and Galloway (2004: xxii) refer to their positioning of these terms as conceptual tools that enable certain types of interrogation and analysis to be conducted. To take this a little further, the authors ask how a melding of some of Galloway's notions of protocol might meld with a discussion of the public sphere and understandings of an informed citizenry in an Internet environment. The intent here is gain a working understanding of how to practically investigate particular examples of community and citizenry behaviour online and to explore the constraints and possibilities of more grounded applications: that is, the aim is to make that difficult translation from abstract concept to empirical or grounded application.

Wikipedia is the site that says "anyone can edit." Wikipedia is a good example of the impact of protocol on collaborative knowledge building, in terms of how the processes of selection occur and how they might be much narrower than they popularly appear to be. Jim Wales, the founder of Wikipedia, at an Auburn University talk, said that while there were at the time he spoke 60 million Wikipedia users, over 50 percent of the editing is done by only 524 volunteer users. Of the more than 13 million articles on Wikipedia at the time of writing, the majority of the edits are by bots or human editors. For example, the Wikipedia article on Alan Alda has 1,700 edits but less than 100 edits actually added to the article. These volunteer editors represent a rare resource that itself is under threat. In 2009, 49,000 editors left Wikipedia's English language edition, compared with 4,900 for the same quarter in 2008. More volunteers are leaving than joining, slowing down Wikipedia. This is like the road bump example of Galloway's—a material effect that has normative consequences. As Wikipedia increases its mechanisms to ensure accuracy, so do its volunteers 'burn out' because of the excessive demands made up them, including ongoing debates about items to be posted. Users who post to Wikipedia, by extension, are more likely to be knocked back or articles removed, because the labour is not there for editing, delaying actual posting. It is ironic in some ways the Wikipedia is repeating the evolution of libraries—the creation of systematic means of classifying and verifying knowledge, with the flipside need to have people qualified to do so. The library system has Dewey classification and established means of classification in order to cope with systematic access and verification.

Collaborative knowledge building takes a number of forms on the Internet. Folksonomy is the practice of collaboratively creating and managing tags to annotate and categorize content. It is also known as collaborative tagging, social classification, social tagging and social indexing. Collaborative knowledge building is very popular and for many very useful. On the basis of our discussion of the role of machinic infrastructure, however, the informed citizen needs to know the answer to key questions associated with the material conditions of the Internet, outlined in Table 2.

Table 2. Material Questions

1. What is enabled?	The technology and software that comes into play. For example, a person with access to only very slow speed Internet has only certain possibilities enabled
2. What is prevented?	The limitations inherent in the technology, software and their management architecture. For example, not everyone can put up their names on Wikipedia.
3. How is it shaped?	The outcomes for content. Internet news aggregation for example leads to homogenization of content.
4. Where is it shaped?	The different points at which actions are taken. A drop-down menu alone, for instance, may have set classifications that affect your response. A popup page, not requested, might have to be removed.
5. Where is it directed?	Flows: The routing, movement and housing of data. Your digital persona might be located in a range of databases.

6. Is it possible to know the coding that created :	a) the frame—how it appears
	b) form—how it can be manipulated and engaged with
	c) the transmission—how it ensures functionality

| 7. The interface between all | Point of contact. |

A generalization of competence of the informed citizen with the Internet, the authors would argue, would start with at least these questions. If a citizen cannot engage the Internet at this level and relies solely on recipe knowledge, then they cannot in all honest be called 'informed'.

Summary

It is quite difficult to think about the public sphere as a physical thing. Habermas had an interest in how physical as well as intellectual spaces worked because ultimately, for the second force critical theorist, the material aspects of our relationships with capital and labour would always find themselves represented in those spaces. The public sphere he argued was physically represented in the family house. Modern private dwellings in big cities, for example, started to limit rooms used for the whole house, and made the house more of a home for each individual than the family as a whole.

> The "public" character of the extended family's parlor, in which the lady of the house at the side of its master performed the representative functions before the domestic servants and neighbors, was replaced by the conjugal family's living room into which the spouses with their smaller children retired from the personnel. Festivities for the whole house gave way to social evenings; the family room became a reception room in which private people gather to form a public. (Habermas, 1989: 45)

The private individuals of the living rooms stepped out into the salons, "but the one was strictly complementary to the other" (Habermas, 1989: 45). The private and the public spheres are thus intimately linked.

There are different types of public sphere just as there are different types of physical spaces. There is the public sphere of the salon but there is also the public sphere of letters. Sometimes the freedoms in the public spheres can be illusory or the representation of the public simply a trick. Authoritarian regimes, for instance, are always creating symbols that those in command claim represent the public. The public carries public opinion. 'The public' has always had publicity, regardless of how restricted the 'public sphere' might become. In highly totalitarian states, those in control will invariably provide publicity, or symbols, claiming to be acting on behalf of the public.

In this chapter we have seen the publicity of the public sphere, in the context of the Internet, requires an intimate understanding of the materiality of the Internet. If the private and public spheres are inextricably linked, then the question arises about the nature of the material spaces of the Internet and how they expand or restrict genuine communication and collaborative knowledge building. Lessig (2002) raises the issue of the Internet as a commons.

> It is commonplace to think about the Internet as a kind of commons. It is less commonplace to actually have an idea what a commons is. By a commons I mean a resource that is free. *Not necessarily zero cost, but if there is a cost it is a neutrally imposed, or equally imposed cost.* Central Park is a commons: an extraordinary resource of peacefulness in the center of a city that is anything but: an escape and refuge, that anyone can take and use without the permission of anyone else. The public streets are a commons: on no one's schedule but your own, you enter the public streets, and go any direction you wish. You can turn off of Broadway into Fifty-second Street at any time, without a certificate of authorization from the government. Fermat's last theorem is a commons: a challenge that anyone could pick up: and complete, as Andrew Wiles, after a lifetime of struggle, did. Open source, or free software, is a commons: the source code of Linux, for example, lies available for anyone to take, to use, to improve, to advance. No permission is necessary; no authorization may be required. These are commons because they are within the reach of members of the relevant community without the permission of anyone else. They are resources that are protected by a liability rule rather than a property rule. Professor Reichman, for example, has suggested that some innovation be protected by a liability rule rather than a property rule. The point is not that no control is present: but rather that the kind of control is different from the control we grant to property. (Lessig, 2002:1783)

In the case of the Internet of course we might find ourselves thinking that we are going in one direction and in fact are going in exactly the opposite direction. There is even in Lessig's example the problem of competence. Many of us also might not have a clue how to take open source software and to use it. And even if we do try to use Linux it is by no means a simple matter to participate in its community. In Chapter Six the authors look at this issue of collaboration and open spaces in more detail. The architecture of the Internet, as the authors have tried to show, is driven at present not by policies or regulations that want to expand a public sphere but by logics of ease in the very material creation of the Internet. These logics are not necessarily evil nor are they part of a capitalist or other conspiracies to restrict access or control people. They do have an effect, though, on how collaborative rules might be possible.

CHAPTER SIX

Trading Spaces (From Knitters and Skinners to Aggregators)

A s you have seen, the authors' interest in this book is in how actual actors within an Internet context, individual or corporate, make decisions and act on them and how those decisions affect whether or not
relevance or interests are imposed. Algorithms represent mediated agency or
alternatively could be said to enact delegated power (Brey, 2008: 82; Johnson,
1988), although the consequences of their actions may not always be seen as
intentional. The easiest, most logical route for enhanced communication in
the design of code for communication on the Internet appears to be at the
same time the easiest route to capture knowledge about citizens and their behaviour. The two often go hand in hand or, indeed, have to go hand in hand.
Privacy, an intrinsic interest, is involved in a trade-off with those who impose
the conditions under which your identity-as-code logs in.

In Chapter Four we saw that 'easy and logical' designs in codes are by no
means neutral—they reflect real intentions on the part of those who design
them. In this chapter the authors turn their attentions to the use of the structured subjective spaces themselves and how a number of different actors, including the major aggregators like Acxiom (http://www.acxiom.co.nz), are
using those spaces.

The authors provide an international picture of the different kinds of
open communicative spaces, from the big to the small, that are operating and
contrast them with spaces that look open, but where participants may be ca-
joled, manipulated, berated or, indeed, arrested and beaten.

The chapter will also look at how groups using social media have generated traditional commercial transaction economies within particular specialities and combined those transaction economies with gifting economies. What
this demonstrates is that sophisticated economic activity and the communication that underpins it are possible on the Internet. But this is not the same as
political participation. The language of 'customer' can never be the same as
the language of 'citizen' (although Papacharissi (2010) makes an interesting

argument about the ways that it can intersect). As you will see, the BBC still holds 'room for the radical' in its constitution. There is no room for the radical in most of the corporate frameworks on the Internet.

Open Spaces

For those like Habermas, learning through seeing, hearing, feeling, talking and reading is a basic birthright. Information and communication, conceived as statements of experience and disclosure respectively, are public in this sense. The concept of 'public' here is not to be equated with that of 'the public', that is, of individuals who assemble: The concept is directed at the institution and cannot be characterised simply as a crowd.

People behave as a public body when they confer in an unrestricted fashion, with the guarantee of freedom of assembly and association and the freedom to express and publish their opinions. When you talk to that interesting person across the breakfast table you engage in information and communication at zero marginal cost. In a democratic polity, when you criticise the political activity of the State you do so in public discussion with political control effectively subordinated to the democratic demand that published statements be accessible to others. If, however, your interpersonal relationships or your ability to express yourself in public discussion are controlled, for what-ever reason, then you are being denied a basic right.

What counts as an 'open space' in human affairs, therefore, depends very much on what happens in the structured subjective spaces that exist and how those spaces are theorised. If 'information' is what is in those open spaces, then it matters what information is. In the earlier chapters in this book it was shown that disciplinary conceptions of information can jump from the practical work of a discipline to generalisations about human behaviour. James Beniger, for example, supported Wiener's thesis that entropy is related to order and argued that this thesis was relevant to today. Beniger said that the subject matter of the social and behavioural sciences, if they are to complement studies of the flows of matter (input-output) economics and energy (ecology) "ought to be information: its generation, storage, processing, and communication to effect control" (Beniger, 1986: 38). This is a paradigm of course of the realist perspective: "What we recognize in the end-directedness or purpose of organization is the essential property of *control*, already defined as purposive influence toward a pre-determined goal" (Beniger, 1986: 35). Beniger, like Wiener, is concerned with human affairs. There can be little doubt that when I chop wood I need control. But the property of control in human relations cannot be other than to the advantage or disadvantage of people.

According to this understanding of information, society is a communication network and information holds it together. Nothing is said on what the information is about or why it should be relevant to have it. Indeed, the scheme allows no room for such a question even to be raised. The reason for a reduction of information to reduction of uncertainty, or reduction of ignorance, alternatively, is based on a desire to construct a theoretical index of decision-making. We are dealing with individual decision-making but information is still conceived as an external transformation variable. However, it would not be possible to derive a theoretical index of uncertainty or ignorance without intruding into people's lives.

It is difficult to find a case of purely intellectual uncertainty—one which makes no difference to anyone. An Oriental potentate, for example, declines to attend a horse race on the grounds that it is already known to him that one horse can run faster than another.

> His uncertainty as to which of several horses could outspeed the others may be said to have been purely intellectual. But also in the story nothing depended from it, no curiosity was aroused. And it is a strict truism that no one would care about *any* exclusively theoretical certainty or uncertainty. For by definition in being *exclusively* theoretical it is one which makes no difference anywhere. (Dewey, 1929: 38-39)

In order to discover what things resolve uncertainty or reduce ignorance we would require experimentation and testing. A normative ignorance calculus could not be an exclusively theoretical index. An index of uncertainty or ignorance, used for social policy, would require judgements about what resolved uncertainty or reduced ignorance. It is predictive advantage that is sought in the realist enterprise. Predictive advantage and determination of what resolves uncertainty or reduces ignorance could not be gained, on any large scale, without considerable changes and intervention in the lives of people (even if that intervention were, supposedly, to their advantage).

These confusing discourses on information trip over into the popular discourses on the Internet because the Internet is a human communication and information network. The science of information and computing gives the impression that it is at the same time a science of human affairs, which it is not. How 'open spaces' work in human society is very much a matter of how humans structure those spaces. How participation occurs on the Internet is a key aspect of open spaces, of course.

In October 2009, United States FBI agents swooped on a house in Queens and arrested a 41 year-old man for using Twitter to alert 'Group of 20' protestors in Pittsburgh about police movements; what police locally called Twerorism. Others involved in the Tweets ran for cover (Moynihan, 2009; Garrido & Halvais, 2009). Putting your name to a protest and then facing the law—your government—are two different things. Facing legal action tends to be a good test of commitment.

It is not new for people to protest against government through media. The Radical Press in Britain did exactly that and was in the end restricted by taxes. In the 1800s, the modern press—literally printing machines run by small groups of 2 to 3 people—produced "circulating libraries of the poor," printed posters the poor could put up on walls to discuss or debate contentious issues or simply to teach kids how to read and write. Wealthy residents of London and the government insisted on pulling down the posts because they looked untidy (Balnaves, Donald & Shoesmith, 2008).

E-Government and Questions of Governance

> Most government departments and parliaments now have web sites, as do individual MPs and other elected representatives. But these tend to be little more than electronic brochures: accessible via the Internet, but not conforming to the interactive ethos of online communication. (Coleman & Blumler, 2009: 90)

If we are looking at open spaces, then it is worthwhile looking at how modern governments are trying to intersect with modern citizens and enable participation. Modern governments have always been faced with a dilemma of how open they want their own governments to be. In the United States, the Open Government Directive explicitly requires government departments to explore participatory mechanics through new media (http://www.whitehouse.gov/the_press_office/TransparencyandOpenGovernment/). However, ironically, there have been calls for the very process of determining the content of the directive to be open, as 90 percent of 120 days in preparation went without consultation (http://techinsider.nextgov.com/2009/05/open_the_government_proce.php). Citizen participation, enabled by electronic means, grows, in parallel with government's apparent failure to promote it.

The use of the Internet for the transmission of government information and services is now well established in most advanced societies. Websites and services are used for all manner of interactions between the governed and their bureaucratic governors, whether it is applying for government documents; requesting particular services, or simply staying informed about what the government believes is important to know. E-government is indeed fulfilling its promise to speed up, make more efficient, regularize, and generally make the processes of government informatic (Grönlund, 2002; Gibson, Ward & Rommele, 2004). Several years ago, the United Nations reported there was a greater expansion in government online presence than in the previous five years combined. Between 1996 and 2001, the number of official government homepages grew from less than 50 to well over 50,000 official government websites. Moreover the websites have transformed from simple public affairs e-brochures to virtual information centres where the interaction between citizen users and the public sector is continuous (ASPA, 2001: 5).

The rise of e-government in this way has, however, largely blotted out and even worked against, any concomitant development of enhanced citizen participation in their own governance utilizing the Internet. The early promise of the Internet was, in part, to provide a new kind of political engagement; this engagement, enabled by clever technology, would reinvent participatory democracy so that it could be practiced in spite of the mass populations and spatial extent of contemporary societies. It would appear this early promise—despite much talk—has never been realized: e-government does not involve participation so much as compliance. There are arguments of course that political action has changed in form and expression and that Web 2.0 technologies do provide a means for the enactment of this type of engagement (Coleman & Blumler, 2009; Papacharissi, 2010). These arguments have some traction in terms of the enactment of certain types of political action (citizen journalism, blogging, online activism), however, these arguments also reinforce the demonstrated inability of governments to engage with or to accommodate this type of citizen action. Coleman and Blumler (2009: 11) suggest,

> that interactive, digital media have a potential to improve public communications and enrich democracy. That potential is vulnerable, however, mainly because an infrastructure for its proper realisation is lacking. With commerce increasingly in the driving seat of Internet development, few of its big players are out to boost citizenship. While various fragmentary and marginal exercises of online consultation, promoting informed deliberation on public policy issues, have been piloted, these have not yet been integrated into the constitutional structures and processes of liberal democracies. With suitable policies and institutional support, some of the emancipatory potential of the new media could be realised and democracy reinvigorated.

The potential of the Internet to improve civic participation has been largely ignored by policy-makers because current models of government do not engage citizens in decision-making. Put simply, government is not governance (Blomgren, Bingham, Nabatchi & O'Leary, 2005). Government is about those with the legal and policing power who are able to execute and implement activities and policies. Whereas "Governance refers to the creation, execution, and implementation of activities backed by the shared goals of citizens and organizations, who may or may not have formal authority and policing power" (Blomgren, Bingham, Nabatchi & O'Leary, 2005).

Yet the need for such engagement remains strong. Putnam (2000) famously argued that citizen engagement is a way of totalitarian proofing democracy; the inconvenience it poses to bureaucracy a sign that it is essential. The potential of the Internet to make this happen remains alluring: Thinkers and activists continue to engage with the Internet as the way of improving engagement; for example, Coleman and Norris (2005) have regularly emphasized the importance of governments seizing the opportunity of the Internet so as to make their own citizenry part of government. The distinction between government and governance became particularly marked in the 1990s with the impact of private sector networks outside public administration on policy:

> Perhaps the dominant feature of the governance model is the argument that networks have come to dominate public policy. The assertion is that these amorphous collections of actors—not formal policy-making institutions in government—control policy. State agencies may place some imprimatur on the policy, so the argument goes, but the real action occurs within the private sector. Further, in the more extreme versions of the argument, if governments attempt to impose control over policy, these networks have sufficient resiliency and capacity for self-organization. (Peters & Pierre, 1998: 225)

Before the emergence of the Internet, Peters, in *The Future of Governing* (1996, p. 47), described alternative macro-models of governance that he saw emerging. They were: (i) The Market Government Model where policy making and deliberation is achieved through internal markets and market incentives; (ii) The Participative Government Model, "almost the ideological antithesis of the market approach" where there is removal of hierarchical top-down controls and policy making is accomplished through consultation and negotiation; (iii) The Flexible Government Model where policy making is accomplished through experimentation; and (iv) The Deregulated Government Model, where policy making is achieved through entrepreneurial government. The move towards a Participatory Model of governance within an Internet context has begun, although it is only fledgling.

Definitions of e-participation do not tend to specify the exact nature of the interactions between citizens and government. For example, Andersen, Henriksen, Secher and Medaglia (2007: 29) define e-participation as "the interactions on democratic issues between citizens, politicians and officers that take place between elections, including consultation, ward representation and self organization among citizens groups." According to Torres, Pina and Royo (2005: 534) "E-governance comprises a set of technology-mediated processes that are changing both the delivery of public services and the broader interactions between citizens and government" and cite OECD good governance principles as examples of definitions used within the construct 'governance'. These are respect for the rule of law; openness, transparency, and accountability to democratic institutions; fairness and equity in dealings with citizens, including mechanisms for consultation and participation; efficient, effective services; clear, transparent and applicable laws and regulations; consistency and coherence in policy formation; and high standards of ethical behaviour. Definitions of e-participation and e-governance therefore tend to be value-laden precisely because, unlike e-government, they assumed some type of engagement with the public.

Governments have attempted to create an impression that they are engaged through the Internet with citizens and that this engagement is participative. The Citizenscape website of the Western Australian government (www.citizenscape.wa.gov.au.) for example, sought to promote citizenship related activities. Its approach is described in the following way:

> Citizen centric approach. Citizen Centric is defined as: Designing and delivering services based on the needs and delivery preferences of citizens rather than the structures and processes of an individual agency. WA Government agencies must commit to delivering information and services in a citizencentric manner. Key considerations:

- conduct user testing/market research

- allow for user consultation, participation and input

- undergo regular reviews, performance assessments and reporting

- deliver via appropriate technologies and methodologies.

Interestingly, in 2009, the West Australian government closed down its Office of E-government and is in the process of removing the terminology of e-government altogether. David Coursey (Coursey, 2005; Coursey & Norris, 2009) has provided interesting insights into what has in practice happened within e-government in terms of adoption of technologies and techniques and expectations of transformation of government practices internally and outwardly. Table 1 is an adaptation of Coursey and Norris's (2009) summary of expectations about transformation of government because of e-government. As you can see, the universal expectation was transformation of government practice from the adoption of technologies for the delivery of government services online toward participatory government of some kind.

Table 1. Assumptions about transformation of e-government over time

Step 1	Emerging presence; email and internal networks
Step 2	Catalogue, presence, enhance presence, information dissemination

Step 3   Transaction, interaction, interactive, two-way communication

Step 4   Vertical integration, transaction, transactional government,
             integration, exchange of value

Step 5   Horizontal integration, transformation, seamless, transaction,
             digital democracy

Step 5   Participation, joined up government

Source: Adapted from Coursey & Norris (2009)

However, Coursey and Norris in their empirical work found that there was in fact little transformation. Indeed, the adoption of e-government services has slowed considerably and, in some areas, seems to have halted.

The findings support the models in that most local governments have adopted e-government, at least at the basic level predicted by models, and have done so in a very short period of time. The findings also raise questions about the models in that they are clearly at odds with the models' predictions that governments will move stepwise toward the adoption of more sophisticated e-government offerings, moving from information to transactions to integration and ultimately to transformation. This predicted movement is not happening, or if it is, the movement is glacial in its speed. Another important finding from these data is that few governments reported any changes that are attributable to e-government, especially changes involving cost impacts. And not all the reported changes were positive, even though positive change is an important part of the mantra surrounding e-government and is clearly expected by the models. (Coursey & Norris, 2009).

If we turn to the United States Government policy and actions, then we can see how the discursive practices in contemporary government have changed on e-government and how those practices are likely to shape the future. The US Office of Management and Budget (2009) FY 2008 Report to Congress on Implementation of The E-Government Act of 2002 demonstrates the parameters that governments are putting on e-government:

> Effective management of information resources requires programs designed to disseminate and provide the public with access to government information. The Federal Government continues to improve the methods by which government information is disseminated and made available to the public. By utilizing Federal agency public websites and partnership agreements to complement effective Freedom of Information Act (FOIA) operations, agencies can maximize the usefulness of their information while minimizing the costs for the American taxpayer.

This is a definition of e-government that focuses on the provision of information to the public, not the engagement of the public with public administration through technology. The Office of Management and Budget points out that the United States has embraced the usefulness of USA.gov and in 2008, it received 116 million visits during the year, or 2.2 million visits per week. USA.gov, the Office also says, received national recognition for the quality and effectiveness in providing government information to the public, including *Time Magazine* listing it as one of the "25 Sites We Can't Live Without." Examples of information provision include:

- The Veterans Benefits Administration (VBA) allowing public access to resource materials relative to VBA. (http://www.vba.va.gov/);

- The Small Business Administration (SBA) providing the news media and the general public with access to information regarding SBA programs and activities through the SBA Newsroom online portal. (http://www.sba.gov/news/); and

- The Department of Education with a one-stop system for ordering Department publications provided at no cost. (http://edpubs.ed.gov/webstore/Content/search.asp).

More complex provision of public information comes through US sites like data.gov with its motto "Discover, Participate, Engage." It provides what it calls high value, machine-readable datasets generated by the Executive Branch of the Federal Government. Mash-ups are possible from these datasets: for example, citizens can take data about recreations sites and modify them for customised use in holiday planning.

The authors do not doubt that efficient provision of information to citizens is important. However, what has emerged within public administration is sophisticated use of technology for provision of information and services, with citizen engagement in public policy separated out, conceptually and practically, from that exercise. Barack Obama came to the presidency on the back of highly motivated Internet users organized by Obama's team in complex use of the fans in promoting the presidential campaign. Table 2 shows the extent of the Obama social media use, compared with his competitor, John McCain.

Table 2. Obama versus McCain

	Obama	McCain
Post political content online	26%	15%
Engage politically on an online social network	25%	16%
Share photos, video or audio content	21%	16%
Sign up online for election updates	18%	9%
Donate money online	15%	6%
Sign up for email news alerts	12%	8%
Volunteer online	11%	4%

Source: PEW Internet and American Life Project (2009)

Harnessing citizen votes for a political cause, however, is different from providing citizen engagement with actual policy decisions during a term of office. The US Federal government in the Obama administration has deployed social media in a range of governmental contexts, including information about H1N1, and the Presidential Records Act was altered to cater for social media as an archival source (Schere, 2009). But, once again, this is use of social media to distribute information, not as a means of participation in public policy making. The current situation, therefore, is one where the components of modern e-government include:

- E-government as records management;

- E-government as enhancement of access to and manipulation of existing data;

Both are important. As Coleman and Blumler (2009: 12) note,

> The Internet provides relatively inexpensive public access to large stores of retrievable data that may be tapped into by users, at various levels and depths, in line with their particular informational needs. By making it easier for individuals to find and follow what concerns them personally, and by lowering the cost of obtaining information, the influence of social status on political involvement may be reduced. Citizens and groups with few resources can undertake acts of communication and monitoring that previously were the domain mainly of resource-rich organisations and individuals.

Thus there are certainly democratic potentials that are enabled with the lowering of costs of access to a wide range of information. As you might guess, though, given the authors' argument on the influence of the design of the architecture of the Internet and the various codes that might be embedded in it, if this facet of government becomes the entrenched one, then engagement as participation will not occur. The status quo will hold. Governments will consult with publics between the voting cycles through increasingly sophisticated means of information provision and feedback, but the impetus for the development and use as a tool for actual participation in decision-making will not be there.

In Europe, the Gov2u work is the best example of an attempt of governments to link to citizens through Internet platforms in the more sophisticated sense of consultation rather than engagement. The www.gov2u.org initiative attempts to link citizens to decision-making processes and provides free software to do this following the European Commission ethos of "openness in the knowledge economy." The Give Your Voice project http://www.give-your-voice.eu/, part of gov2u.org, provides Gov2DemOSS software free and has live projects running to show how citizen engagement with government representatives might work, at least in terms of consultation. One Give Your Voice platform is being implemented in Baden-Württemberg (Germany) and one in Valencia (Spain). Citizens can, according to the site, directly contact their MEPs from their local region, ask relevant questions and voice opinions. Politicians may react immediately to proposals and answer queries. "VoicE allows them to listen to their voters' concerns and learn more about their expectations of European politics" http://www.give-your-voice.eu/.

Irani, Love and Jones (2009: 162) in their evaluation of e-government concluded that "Of prime concern is the need to understand and realise the benefits that can be gained from enabling Government legislation, processes and systems outwards towards citizen groups—not merely doing so for the sake of technology change." Modern governments are certainly interested in developing processes and systems that look outwards. For example, the European Commission used an Interactive Policy Making web tool for public consultation on legislation for regulation of chemicals. Over 6,500 contributions were received over a period of 2 months and the consultation process led to the identification of key flaws in proposals, saving billions of Euros (Timmers, 2008). But Irani et al. have touched on an important issue—the creation of a legislative framework that institutionalizes links between governments and citizens. Other than the Obama administration's non-consultative development of Open Government, though, there is little in the Western world in the way of legislation that enables collaborative government using technology.

E-government as it is predominantly practiced in Western liberal democracies and thus can be assessed in terms of generalised competencies—in terms of citizen's and government's capacities to engage in consultative and participatory practices through online forums and tools—and as spaces, in the first instance constructed by government but also influenced by citizens. The success or otherwise of these spaces can be considered through assessing the degree and scope of how the spaces and activity within and through them is constrained or enabled by:

- code (what is possible);
- people (time constraints, competencies, worldviews and understandings of engagement);
- legislative frameworks (what in fact can be done institutionally);
- and finally, intent.

Obviously there are relationships between these various levels of consideration; they are not discrete factors. However, what our discussion reveals is that the introduction of technology into government-citizen engagement is not sufficient: the technology does not automatically direct interaction or communication between the various levels. More needs to be thought through in terms of the protocols—as process and as language—that need to be developed to enable communication and coherent action across and between these various 'entities.' This needs to be consolidated through incorporation into the institutional structures themselves in the form of legislative changes and in terms of a rethinking of modes and forms of government and governance (Papacharissi, 2010; Coleman & Blumler, 2009; Irani & Love, 2008). However, while introducing technology alone is not sufficient to address these issues, the introduction of various technologies enables and disables various types of engagements that need also to be taken into account.

As a tool for creating friendship, trading and gifting spaces and as a communicative tool, however, the Internet has been enormously successful. Networks like Ravelry are paradigm examples of how intrinsic interests intersect with common intrinsic interests that require niche knowledge. Ravelry, a knitting site, combines a traditional transaction economy with a gifting economy and provides the means by which knitters can debate both craft and legal issues, like copyright.

Social Network Markets

Ravelry was created by Jess and Casey Forbes in the United States to keep track of their work and stash (stash is yarn and unspun fibre that has been stored for later use). When they opened the site to the public in beta format, the Forbes had 15,000 users register on the first weekend and by 2009 had over 400,000 members. Sal Humphreys (2009), a knitter herself and an academic, provides an insightful look into how Ravelry works.

Local yarn stores and libraries are also linked to (with maps and contact details). Searches allow the user to browse photos of the multiple versions of a pattern that have been knitted by other users, thus allowing them to see how the pattern looks in different yarns, sizes, colours and variations/modifications. Sometimes there are hundreds of finished versions of a particular pattern available for viewing. Comments about patterns and yarns are made, alerting people to their pitfalls or joys, there is a 'favoriting' system which generates searchable popularity metrics in all available categories and so on. Much of the data available about the patterns and yarn has been previously available elsewhere on the net, but the aggregation of the data into one very user-friendly searchable database which draws on user-generated content has proved immensely successful.

Designers can upload patterns and sell them. Advertisers can post ads. A year after the beta site was launched in 2007, the site had 6,000 active groups with over 5 million posts covering everything from yarn, knitting and crocheting to politics, religion and special interests. As Humphreys points out, networked production online is often described in dichotomous terms as market or non-market by Benkler (2006) and others. It is beyond the scope of this book to explore the nature of these online markets, but Humphreys also touches on something directly of interest to the authors—the role of intention in networks. Ravelry users genuinely believe that there is a spirit of Ravelry and that this spirit assumes certain community norms with the commercial and non-commercial environments.

For example, the trading system on Ravelry has a trading category called "destashing and ISO (in search of)" where users can set up a payment system where they can list fibre for sale. What interested Humphreys is the work done in the network on policing acceptable commerce for one user. The destashing trading space is not open for commercial retailers to use and users are expected to sell only if they are getting rid of unwanted yarn. The moderators check frequently to determine if someone has started using the site as a retail site, given the lower fees. If the moderator identifies a user as buying cheap yarn and reselling it as a profit-making exercise, then the user is, technically, stopped. Humphreys found, however, that there were different perceptions of users as to what was allowed and the difficulties in defining what is selling for personal reasons versus commercial selling. Who draws the line?

One commenter noted:

> ...honestly it seems almost like a business for some. They pick up yarn on the cheap that they have no intention of ever using, but know they can probably offload it with a profit on Ravelry since you've got a market of tens-of-thousands of crafters and you can skip the annoying fees of eBay, etc. (Shannon)

Another asked:

So who gets to be the destash police? "Sorry you have a $600 medical bill this month, but you've reached the destash limit, so you must be selling for profit. See ya!" (Maggie)

The first poster also commented:

there were a few posters that seemed like they were running a business vs honest destashing. I know the mods are good at getting the true commercial vendors out of there, but sometimes it seems a bit like abuse of the spirit of Ravelry. It will never be a perfect system and I'm not suggesting there's a limit or anything like that; I honestly don't have a solution, just giving my point of view like many. (Shannon, From thread: Items for sale on Ravelry? http://www.ravelry.com/discuss/for-the-love-of-ravelry/221585/51-75)

The deeper issue here, of course, is the fine line between participation and commercial opportunities and action, in any social networking site, or more precisely social networking market site. Ravelry, positioned as a social networking site and facilitative structure for exchange between 'non-commercial' individuals, also operates on another level as a commercial entity itself. Ravelry explicitly collects information about each person's transactions information about financial products and services offered by its advertisers, and uses personal information for customizing advertising and content, auditing and research. The site also notes that ""We automatically receive and record information on our server logs, including your IP address, the web request, and one or more cookies which may uniquely identify your browser. These server logs may also include your browser type, browser language, the date and time of your request." (http://www.ravelry.com/about/privacy). Part of the reason for this is to enhance the experience for the user, to enable them to have easy access to the site and to also map activities online and then customize any changes that would facilitate these practices. This in turn encourages participation and ongoing engagement with the site and other users (essential to the site's success). The other, as mentioned, is to collect data that is of use for its advertisers and to enhance its revenue-generating operations. The commercial activities and the non-commercial public, gifting and social activities of individuals are intricately entwined in online spaces.

As we have seen in the history of YouTube and other sites that generate massive audiences, once they have critical mass and numbers, they become valuable in their own right and get sold. The ethos, social norms and ways of moderation, therefore, become important for the sites' longevity. It is very easy for online sites to break down because they become ungovernable. CommuniTree is the most famous early example. It was a dial-in BBS created in 1978 to improve on the limitations of previous difficult-to-navigate BBS software. The Californian CommuniTree system had message threads allowing conversations to be more easily followed. Once school children got access to modems, however, they found CommuniTree's phone number and sent constant rude messages, jamming the system. There was no means to moderate the messages and the BBS was closed. The tools for moderation have become more complex, with Slashdot as a good example of pre- and post-moderation governance.

Moderation of sites is a governance exercise and can be enacted by moderators who are human or moderators who are technological constructs. Activities can be allowed or disallowed by the simple architecture of sites or by the social norms and conventions of the users or community who 'inhabit' the space. To extend the recognition of technological affordances even further in this complex commercial/public/private interchange, the postings on some social or content networking sites can be picked up by search engines and distributed more broadly than might have been intended. Photos on Flickr—not restricted when posted to private audiences—might be picked up and used in a Google image search, tagged in Delicious (social bookmarking site), and replicated in an undergraduate essay. How do we theorise and position these types of engagements: are they exploitative, or contributing to a broader collective knowledge or commons, or both? Do they encourage an understanding of information (and in turn, people) as resource, or are they important for the cultivation of intrinsic interests and shared conversations? And to what extent do we need to consider the technical affordances, the algorithms and the material effect of these in our positioning of these (shared?) understandings?

Gamers

In terms of the social distribution of knowledge in the Internet, the nature and role of moderation, as algorithm or as direct human intervention, has a direct bearing on how transactions or knowledge proceed. There can be little doubt, though, that the Internet enables use of collective intelligence in a scale not known before. Those closest to the expert knowledge about how computers and networks work can often therefore manipulate the economy or content of the networks in a way that the person on the street cannot. Software engineers, systems designers, hardware engineers, graphic artists, and many others form themselves into knowledge communities on the web, often sharing information through forums like Whirlpool or Slashdot. Gamers in particular have taken collaboration in manipulation seriously. 'Modders' are a famous part of this professional system. As fan programmers they are a combination of fan and producer (Postigo, 2007). Postigo's (2007) research on 'modders' involved in games design provides an inside look at how they work:

- modders make modifications, mods, to a game. Mods can be changes to the way a game physically works to changes in the narrative;
- mappers design new levels for a game. These add-ons keep the same game characters and play but new virtual worlds are created by the fan programmers;
- skinners design new characters, weapons—all the tools inside the games.

What these fan programmers do is to take existing content; refashion it, often to meet their own group's needs and desires; and then redistribute the new games or add-ons to their own community. Many times of course this activity is part of the overall economy of games.

> Many companies have openly acknowledged the value of the content that fans produce. Epic Games, Valve Software, and Id Software have all recognized the value of their gaming communities. Wagner James Au...in an article for Salon.com, has interviewed industry insiders on the role of fan communities in game design. In that article, Scott Miller of 3D Realms states that 'developers watched astounded as mods "actually helped extend the life of a game by providing free additional content for players to explore."' In the same article, Cliff Bleszinski of Epic Games (maker of the popular Unreal series) estimated that '5 to 10 percent of Unreal players have tinkered with the editing tools' and that at least half of the 2 million-plus players 'have downloaded and played mods or levels for the game.' No company has done as much as Id Software and Valve Software to incorporate fan add-ons into the development process. Id Software releases the source code for all of its games; it incorporated the most successful fan-developed game levels into one of its distributions of Doom and hired fan-programmer Robert Duffy to create the development kit, QERadiant, for Quake 3. (Postigo, 2007)

Henry Jenkins (1992) noticed years ago that a fan community of textual poachers created what he called meta stories—online stories developed by fans from television shows and movies, reworked and then resent to their own communities. These stories represent, Jenkins says, an alternative form of ownership. What we see today is a range of knowledge communities emerging, like Ravelry, that take advantage of database technology and networks to enhance their everyday hobbies or work. This knowledge aggregation, though, has its upsides and downsides, because unlike public libraries or public broadcasters, it has no common legislative framework to govern it. Indeed, early modern telecommunications networks had universal service legislation to ensure that everyone, rich or poor, had access to the plain old telephone service (POTS). A geographically remote farmer in the United States who could not afford to pay for the physical line to the telephone would be cross-subsidised by the community. Australia, the United Kingdom and other countries had universal service legislation. Private knowledge aggregators, however, do not fall under any legislative regime that might resolve any tension between equity and access and use.

The Knowledge Aggregators

"Oh we do have you on our database. I guarantee you," Mr Meyer assures me. "Your name address, phone number. You have a cat. You're right handed. That sort of thing."

This is true. I'm not sure if it's a lucky guess, but I'm impressed.

Mr Meyer, a brash, confident chief executive, explains that while the company has been nervous of promoting its activities in the past, he has no fear of a higher profile.

"We're the biggest company you've never heard of," he grins, with a hint of Southern drawl. "In the past we were afraid of people knowing us, but I'm trying to get business awareness and if consumers have privacy concerns I want to know." (Mason, 2009)

Acxiom has in its database approximately 1,500 facts about half a billion people worldwide, as the *Telegraph* reporter found in his discussion above with the Acxiom CEO. Acxiom works behind the scenes for Google and many other major Internet companies. It is a first-class knowledge aggregator. Knowledge aggregation takes many forms on the Internet. User tracking is only one form. The term 'news aggregator' describes websites or search engines that select, retrieve and link news from anywhere on the Internet. *Google News* is an aggregator of news from thousands of news sources. An RSS is an aggregator as it pulls together threads relevant to the person who has subscribed to it. These aggregators argue that they are neutral in terms of their effects on the social distribution of knowledge and in terms of their effects on the "openness" or not of the Internet in general. Others disagree:

the opinions crafted by individuals (presumably after or through discourse in a small community) can be aggregated and passed to other users and communities for further discussion and subsequent aggregation. Such sites cut out the human mediation traditionally required in a social network, allowing for a seemingly direct representation of public opinion in the blogosphere. Through a system of uncoordinated coordination, collective action has become possible on a previously unimaginable scale, due to the small amount of effort required by each human in order to bring about the so-called "wisdom of crowds". (Geiger, 2009)

Modern regulators, however, are now taking a second look at the Internet: the Net Neutrality debate in the United States is an example of the clash of the titans in aggregation or Internet service provision and the state.

This is a late recognition by regulators that the Internet is not a special kind of species or a special kind of communicative space that cannot be regulated or should not be regulated or that it is a special space that escapes the normal problems with social stratification found in society—the rich and the poor, the powerful and the powerless. Certainly, many groups have recognised that alternative ways of aggregation and owning content are possible and are being experimented with, not least the spot.us initiative that started in the United States. Unlike IndyMedia, discussed in the next chapter, spot.us does not take a collective non-monetary approach to news aggregation or service. But experiments like spot.us cannot match the resources that a News Limited or an AT&T can bring to bear. The public have even less influence or knowledge about the IPV4 or IPV6 debates.

Table 3 provides a look into the ownership of IP addresses. Each address block in the table contains 16,777,214 addresses. Decisions on the ownership and distribution of these addresses is done with little or no public consultation through the entity ICANN, the Internet Corporation for Assigned Names and Numbers, incorporated in California. At one stage all IP addresses were owned by one person.

Table 3. Internet Address and Block Owner, 1989 and 2005

	1989	2005
000/8	Reserved	IANA-Reserved
001/8	Unassigned	IANA-Reserved
002/8	Unassigned	IANA-Reserved
003/8	General Electric	General Electric
004/8	Atlantic Satellite Network	BBN
005/8	Unassigned	IANA-Reserved
006/8	Yuma Proving Grounds	Army Information Systems Center
007/8	DCEC EDN	IANA - Reserved
008/8	BBN	Net BBN
009/8	IBM	IBM
010/8	ARPANET	IANA-Private Use
011/8	DoD Intel Info. Sys.	DoD Intel Info. Sys.
012/8	AT&T Bell Labs	AT&T Bell Labs
013/8	Xerox Corporation	Xerox Corporation
014/8	Public Data Net	IANA-Public Network
015/8	Hewlett-Packard	Hewlett Packard
016/8	Unassigned	Digital Equipment Corp.
017/8	Unassigned	Apple Computer
018/8	MIT	MIT
019/8	Unassigned	Ford Motor Company

020/8	Unassigned	Computer Sciences Corp.
021/8	DDN	DDN
022/8	DISNET	Defense Information Systems Agency
023/8	DDN-TestCell-Net	IANA Reserved
024/8	Unassigned	ARIN
025/8	Royal Signals and Radar	Royal Signals and Radar Establishment
026/8	MILNET	Defense Information Systems Agency
027/8	NOSC/LCCN	IANA Reserved
028/8	Wide Band Sat Net	DSI-North
029/8	MILNET X.25 Temp.	DISA

Source: http://www.icann.org/

The knowledge aggregators set the scene for the global perspective on the Internet's social distribution of knowledge. Those in control of IP addresses can decide to restrict the number of addresses that a country might have or, indeed, to commodify the IP address market altogether. The news aggregators could favour some countries in the reporting of events over others, set up paywalls for some countries but not others, and set specific news agendas.

Summary

[A]lgorithmic aggregation sites not only make the blogo/public sphere knowable, but also play a key role in its highly non-discursive construction. The issue at hand in relation to the question of the Internet as a public sphere is not the risk of fragmentation, but of integration. While individual blogs, discussion forums, chat rooms, and other 'virtual communities' may very well be ideal discursive spaces for political deliberation, the Internet as a public sphere capable of synthesizing public opinion is not unified by discourse, but algorithms. (Geiger, 2009)

While earlier writing on the potential of virtual communities (Rheingold, 1993; Poster, 1995; Licklider, 1968: 38) posited the almost inevitable emergence of community-like structures of shared interest and the semblance of a public sphere, in 2010 and looking forward, the digital landscape is becoming considerably more cluttered and complex. Tools of communication and collaboration have radically lowered the barriers to creation and participation in both media production and (explicitly and implicitly) political expression and discussion (Rettberg, 2008; Rosenberg, 2009). Digital tools have meant more people than ever before can communicate, collaborate, and create together, without ever needing to be in the same physical or even national spaces, giving rise to new and often unforeseen public activities (Shirky, 2008). At the same time, never has personal privacy ever been more under threat, often due to the very same companies and technologies which are allowing digital publics to assemble and work together (Zittrain, 2008). Picking two recent examples from major digital corporations—Google and Twitter—some of these and other complexities can be made visible.

Google, by virtue of size, complexity and global operation, has become one of the greatest curators of public information (via its different search engines) and facilitators of public conversation (via publication platforms like Blogger). However, despite its initial company motto—"Don't Be Evil"—it also poses massive challenges to existing ideas of copyright (most directly about film and television in relation to YouTube, and print copyright in relation of Google Books) and to personal privacy (with everything from search histories to Google Streetview's pictures of your house being captured and stored on Google's servers). One recent development which epitomises the political contradictions inherent in Google's continual roll-out of new tools is the October 2009 launch (via Google Labs) of Google's Social Search. When the Social Search option is selected, all the results for any given search on Google are limited to results which appear in the content created and curated by the searcher's social network. Users of Social Search do not explicitly select their social network on Google, but rather Google aggregates a user's social network based on their existing social media profiles (for example a combination of their Twitter followers, Facebook friends and websites listed on their blogroll).

While using social networks as a content filter is far from new (boyd & Ellison, 2007) the ease of limiting Google to search your social network rather than the entire Internet—achieved essentially with one click—can determine whether the web is explored as an enormous collection of different views, perspectives and information, or whether only a predefined group of friends or connections is searched. The ease of use masks the fundamental political decision being made as to whether the web in some sense acts as a faux public sphere or it is, at best, a gated community, limited to a pre-screened list of like-minded individuals and groups (Balnaves, Leaver & Willson, 2010).

Along similar lines to Social Search, the microblogging service Twitter started rolling out a new function called Twitter Lists also in October 2009. One the most notable design features of Twitter is actually its distinct lack of features, with most of the advanced Twitter functionality being implemented by third-party clients with only the most popular of these functions being grafted onto Twitter's main web-based interface. In that context, the integration of Twitter Lists into the main architecture of the platform is notable as one of the few tools universally provided to all Twitter users. At first glance, lists appear to be very simple—it allows any Twitter user to create named lists filled with different combinations of the people they follow. Each generated list can be subscribed to by other Twitter users, essentially providing one-click access to a stream of Twitter posts ('tweets') grouped in particular ways. Like Google's Social Search, the Lists are not in and of themselves good or bad in some strict technologically determinist model, but are rather tools which have very real potential to either diversify or narrow engagement with broader perspectives via a few simple, and potentially unconsidered, clicks of the mouse.

Consider, for example, a Twitter user subscribing to a friend's list which is all about being a fan of satirical news show *The Daily Show* (who might all happen to be Democrats) or a list of people who enjoy *Fox News* (who might all happen to be Conservatives). Sorting by taste on some level—of television shows watched, for example—might implicitly also sort by politics, even if that second-level of sorting isn't immediately visible from the name of the list. While this quick example might seem a little artificial, the potential of lists to provide pre-filtered and recommended content streams from like-minded individuals and groups is clear. More to the point, in an era where the overloading of available information is a key issue, not its scarcity, these extremely simple mechanisms to create bounded content, often with bounded politics and thus incomplete access to a public sphere, are so easy to use that they will often preclude critical consideration of their broader and more lasting political effects (Balnaves, Leaver & Willson, 2010).

Twitter Lists and Google's Social Search use social networks as a key mechanism to filter content, thereby also filtering the viewpoints and political perspectives users of these services are likely to encounter. On the one hand, these tools can be used to carefully manage and maintain a representative sample of the most relevant and broad-reaching commentary and developments on any topic or issue; on the other hand, these tools could also be used to easily and almost invisibly limit the perspectives and politics to which a user is exposed entirely to social connections who already share compatible political and cultural views. If the notion of the public sphere is reliant on differing perspectives being visible, then Social Search and Twitter Lists, when used in particular ways, are the public sphere's antithesis.

Whereas the communication tools that Habermas and his Frankfurt School contemporaries examined were largely based on broadcast models, the tools which are increasingly prevalent today are based on a more participatory model which can simultaneously facilitate enhanced engagement with the public, but conversely can also ensure users are never exposed to politics or positions at odds with views they already hold. Thus, in our networked culture, Google, Twitter and other digital corporations are simultaneously facilitating and creating more connected and conversant publics while in the same instance creating tools that for some can filter and narrow the digital plethora into streams which prevent opposing views from being visible at all, chipping away any coherent participation in a truly public sphere (Balnaves, Leaver & Willson, 2010).

Collaborative Rules (Activism, c2c and the Gift Economy)

Community is fundamentally reliant on and constituted through communication processes. These communication processes, whether of a dialogical, written, or non-verbal form, provide the means by which social institutions and social relations are instigated and maintained. It is through communication processes that we recognize ourselves as social beings; it is our means of connection to others.

—Willson (2006: 29)

There have been attempts to set up collectivist, open, community-to-community (c2c) networks on the Internet that are, on the surface, designed to encourage free speech and to limit hierarchical control. Indymedia was set up precisely for this purpose. Indymedia, though, has struggled because it is not easy to contact anyone within a network, to know them, or to interact. Not all collaborative rules, like all open communicative spaces, are equal. In this chapter the authors will look at those communicative spaces on the Internet that have established collaborative rules that best approximate the structural conditions required for a public sphere. As you will see, the vernacular surrounding those communicative spaces differs radically from the language that surrounds other spaces. The language that attaches itself to protocol is itself important: We talk about intuitive interfaces, user-friendly web pages, functionality, and so on. We even accessorise ourselves with our media. Consideration of collaborative engagement online necessarily needs to engage with this vernacular and with our every-day use of the technological. In the absence of collaborative government, some groups are setting up rules of governance that incorporate all the elements of Habermas's theory of information and Galloway's ideas on protocol.

Aggregating Public Opinion

In the previous chapters we have seen that while there are codes—and their effects can be extremely complex—the reasons for code are human. In the context of the Internet there are reasons for actions, just as there are reasons for actions in (other) interpersonal environments. 'Giving reasons' for what happens in the social world is at the heart of social science, whether psychology, sociology or communication and media studies. 'Because' statements set the scene for explanation. In order to account for 'X'—where 'X' may be poverty, religion, bureaucracy or any other social phenomenon—social researchers must show how they arrived at their answers. There are three major ways social scientists come to conclusions or answers:

1. reasons explanations, which consist of interpretations of what people say and mean. In these explanations, researchers focus on the intentional language of the people they are dealing with;
2. causal explanations, which consist exclusively of establishing relationships of causality;
3. idiom of interpretation, where researchers use a theoretical vocabulary to describe what people do and which derives neither from the "idiom of our practices nor the idiom of the subject practices" (Turner, 1984: 25).

The issue of what it is to act for a reason is well established in the literature (see, for example, Anscombe, 1968; Davidson, 1968; Davis, 1979; Hindess, 1988; MacIntyre, 1977; Nagel, 1970; Schick, 1984; Skinner, 1972; Ursom, 1968). The reasons and actions dichotomy is a familiar one. "Central to the relation between a reason and an action it explains is the idea that the agent performed the action because he [sic] had the reason" (Davidson, 1968: 85).

It is assumed that reasons make actions intelligible. MacIntyre and Winch, however, are at odds in the conception of what it is to act for a reason. MacIntyre criticised Winch for failing to distinguish between those rules which agents profess to follow and to which their actions conform, but which do not direct the actions, and those rules which guide an agent's actions by providing them with reasons and motives (MacIntyre, 1977: 118). "The question inevitably arises as to whether the possession of a given reason may not be the cause of an action in precisely the same sense in which hypnotic suggestion may be the cause of an action" (MacIntyre, 1977: 117). In the example of hypnotic suggestion it is supposed that this is a case where an agent has not acted for a reason. That is to say, the reasons that the agent gives are not identical with the actual cause of the behaviour. However, MacIntyre leads us to misconstrue the obvious. The purpose of an agent's action may well reside with someone else.

This should not surprise us. Captains of ships, for example, do not expect subordinates to make the captain's purposes their own. Captains rely on their crew to execute orders. Whatever reasons the crew may have, the captains, in their own practical accounts, can substitute for those reasons their own orders as the only effective determinant of the crew's behaviour. According to Giddens (1984: 339), the main role of social science in the critique of conceptions that people hold is the assessment of reasons in terms of knowledge either unavailable to the agents or construed by them in a fashion different from that formulated in the social inquirer's description. Giddens is correct to the extent that the purpose of conversation, or dialogue, is to identify an agent's reasons. The identification of an agent's reasons, or "reasons as good reasons," forms a primary part of fieldwork and analysis (Giddens, 1984: 339). But Giddens left open the question of what it is to act for a good reason.

Suppose it is said that person N voted for 'sonatas' at the last Musicians' Association Meeting because she thought that sonatas would be most likely to attract the biggest audience at the next performance. What kind of explanation is this? The clearest case is one in which N, prior to voting, considered the pros and cons and came to the conclusion: I will vote for sonatas because they are the best way to attract an audience. This is not to deny that in some cases it may be possible to dispute whether the reason N gives is in fact the real reason for her behaviour, for good reasons might be post hoc rationalisations or excuses for behaviour caused in some other way (Hindess, 1988: 50). "But there is very often no room for doubt; and if this were not so, the idea of a reason for an action would be in danger of completely losing its sense" (Winch, 1973: 45-46).

Our paradigm case of what it is to act for a reason carries an important feature. Suppose that observer O offers the above explanation for N's having voted for sonatas: "then it should be noted that the force of O's explanation rests on the fact that the concepts which appear in it must be grasped not merely by O and his [sic] hearers, but also by N himself" (Winch, 1973: 46). The relevant feature of Winch's account of reasons, for our purposes, is that constructs that appear in an observer's explanation of an action to be representative of the actual reasons held by the person who performed the action, should be understandable to the person observed. It should be possible to take advantage of our ability to make intelligible the accounts of others, without suppressing the original purpose of those accounts. Good reasons, as they are conceived here, help to make what is happening intelligible. As the authors have tried to demonstrate, swapping real human reasons for causes, such as 'information' or even 'networks' is wrong.

Some of our actions on the Internet, like Internet banking, betting, and shopping have fairly basic reasons embedded in them. The intentional language of social networks is much more complex, not only because there are so many different kinds of networks, but because etiquette and expectations of behaviour can differ radically. Even within the same site, code can proxy for other people's reasons, which may not be manifestly obvious to members of a network. The authors have tried to show some of the reasons actors, whether individuals or companies, act like they do on the Internet, at times through the use of code and various technological affordances.

In the Ravelry network, we saw that people had a sense of the 'spirit of Ravelry' and if the intentions of those who participated did not meet this spirit then there was discussion on why. These types of discussions, of course, are about presenting opinions and judging opinions. Up until now the authors have not touched on public opinion in the social distribution of knowledge. Public opinion is intimately tied to reasons for actions, especially political actions.

The role of media in the public sphere is not only to present news but to present what might be measured or stated as agreement or consensus on particular community views or opinions. There is a large literature on public opinion and agenda setting, but for the purposes here the concern over the traditional media, for Habermas, is to what extent the representation of public opinion by traditional media actually represents that opinion (2006). This is not surprising, because modern media have tended to become centralised, with many local community papers becoming incorporated into big companies, whether in the United States, Australia or Europe.

Traditional public opinion polling mechanisms were created by some of the most famous names in media research and, indeed, political and media theorising. George Gallup, Hans Zeisel, Paul Lazarsfeld, Archibald Crossley, to name a few, created the environment where modern statistical sampling was used to poll people's views on everything from radio ratings to political parties. Polling has become an established way of measuring public opinion over the century because of its capacity to be reliably generalised across whole populations.

Has the Internet superseded traditional media in presenting and representing public opinion? Certainly, Axel Bruns (2007) thinks so, arguing that the aggregation of opinions on the Internet through modern algorithms is becoming of high quality and reliable. But Bruns is missing Habermas's point. In the Internet context we have no equivalent metrics for opinion. This is not surprising as it is difficult to establish a sampling frame—a reliable list of people from which a statistical sample can be drawn, over time.

The longitudinal aspect of gaining public opinion through polls has also been important. What has happened, however, is that (i) people are more and more refusing to participate in modern surveys (Balnaves, 2010) and (ii) modern political polling has itself become highly politicised and tied to either corporate or political agendas (political party polling is treated in the media as equivalent to the public polls in its validity, for example). As we will see in what follows, Habermas was probably wrong in assuming that the Internet is simply a fractured world of issues publics that do not substitute for a public sphere. Quite the contrary, deliberative democracy practitioners have taken up social media tools to enhance deliberative practice. He was right, though, on the Internet as a major means of either subverting authority or for mobilising political or other audiences. The authors will start with a discussion of activist audiences because activist groups have been particularly successful in using social networking to organise everything from demonstrations to membership drives.

Changing Public Opinion—Online Activists

> The open publishing system worked well, particularly during the events that individual Indymedia sites were often created to cover. It was not long however before it became obvious that this openness was a liability afterward, where Indymedia sites became sites of flamewars, racist commentary, advertising and porn. Regular posters developed the habit of posting articles to the newswires of every available Indymedia—undermining the necessity of having geographical sites in the first place. (Saunders, 2007: 1)

Time, space, the body and knowledge are still intimately linked in the modern Internet, but the tantalizing offerings of more connections and more knowledge do not necessarily result in enhanced collaboration or democratic input. Wikinews and wikis generally have open publishing and open editing with the use of 'bots', automated or semi-automated software tools, to assist with tasks. While there is a Wiki policy on bots, it is possible for what the Wikis call 'negative editors' or vandal bots to damage a Wiki's content. Similar use of bots and automated tools are evident in many online community environs, list moderation and other sites and forums. The intermingling of technologically automated action and those of the human are often indeterminable or able to be easily critiqued. In some ways, this doesn't matter inasmuch as the technological constructs, as we have consistently asserted are programmed and instituted for human reasons. The effects or consequences are evident in the outcomes. However, an awareness of the possibilities of these constructs, of the affordances of technological environs and tools for communication, data gathering, or online moderation is important for understanding the possibility for collaborative activity and the degree to which actions, issues, and discussions can be freely and openly canvassed or enacted.

Getting into contact with one of the human members of the collective that decides on Indymedia editorial is quite difficult if not impossible unless you already know one of the people personally. This is not surprising, because scale affects organizations and selection of news. An individual volunteer at Indymedia would have difficulty dealing with thousands of emails or posts a day and small editorial teams would find it impossible to read hundreds of 'thousands of potential news posts. Not surprisingly, therefore, Indymedia as an open publishing site worldwide has had varying degrees of success at selection of news. Invariably, therefore, as it grew larger, it grew more anonymous, trialling ratings systems or software solutions for choosing news items. What might this mean for the group to be able to operate according to its proclaimed goals? In some ways it enhances these possibilities through the expansion of publishing and monitoring possibilities: the use of technology enables the group to process more information than they have human volunteer capacity to manage. In that sense, technological tools are immensely important and facilitative. However it also institutes another 'level' of engagement whose implications may not have been broadly discussed or considered by the collective except in functionalist terms: what it enables them to efficiently achieve. While the proprietary nature of the tools may have been considered—political activist groups are usually extremely attuned to these questions—and open source measures adopted, the level of knowledge of code and of possible options may not be so well understood.

The original creator of Indymedia's revolutionary open publishing software, however, worked directly with code. In 1998 Arnison was a member of Catalyst, a Sydney (Australia) activist group. The group was interested in software and spent its time trying to work out how to deal with stored streamed video footage. When Catalyst put protest rallies up on the Internet the viewers had to see it as it happened. Catalyst decided therefore to write its own code that enabled them to capture 'media nuggets', snippets of footage that could be loaded on to the site for anyone to see at any time.

While in the United States in 1999, Arnison met up with activists planning for protests against the World Trade Organisation (WTO) being held in Seattle (Martin, 2004). The activists wanted a site that could have a single point of focus for WTO protest news. Arnison offered his software for free and worked on it to provide an open publishing space. It provided streaming for video and a place where anyone could put up their reports or comments. Its success was immediate and Indymedia was a direct outcome from it. It is worthwhile hearing from Arnison in an interview in 2004 with the Australian Broadcasting Corporate (ABC):

Q: How did you know that the software was different from anything else around?

A: At first we didn't. We just figured out what we needed to cover an event on the web. We knew others were streaming live footage, but you had to watch it as it happened. We looked around and realised there was no software available out there, especially not for free. We didn't have any money so we wrote our own in a couple of weeks of frenzied bursts of action. All of it was volunteer work squeezed in edgewise around full-time jobs.

Q: How much work and planning went into getting Indymedia up and running?

A: We had one or two full-time staff. The Seattle group had been planning for a while before I arrived at the beginning of November—the Seattle event was at the end of November. I was not there long, but because of the software, my coming had a big impact on the project. The software made a huge difference because we could do so much more. The Indymedia website was going to be a one-off in Seattle, but it just exploded.

Q: How did you raise funds for the project?

A: The group involved in Sydney called Catalyst ran on the smell of a burnt out engine. One guy used to get computers out of the dumpster, fix them up and sell them. We deliberately chose to do things that didn't require money.

Q: How hard was it to get your software out there and create Indymedia?

A: One issue was having to drop everything to work on it, because the time was right. Fortunately I could do that. Also, the website got very popular very quickly in terms of audience. The computer that was trying to deal with that fell over so we had to keep shoring it up.

Q: How has Indymedia changed the world of publishing?

A: It feels too big, to think of it changing the world of publishing. What it has changed is activism. It has connected a whole bunch of people that are thinking the same way. People campaigning on global justice issues feel community connections and could get live feedback from people in other countries that they didn't have before. It can be a big inspiration to people who care about issues—it helps organise and coordinate. I guess this two-way interaction is what I feel the internet is really about. Contributions from the audience are what sets a website apart from a TV station. Indymedia kicked off during the dot-com bubble, when people thought making money on the net was all about computerised sales brochures. I think the online projects that survived and prospered are the ones that managed to involve the audience in the action and create some kind of online party. Some big examples are Google (which uses web links for rankings), Amazon (which has reader reviews), and eBay. So what impact has Indymedia had on publishing? I guess it helped demonstrate what's possible online when communication runs both ways. (Martin, 2004)

The media and culture theorist John Hartley says that the pursuit of reflective self-organisation and common purpose among voluntary co-subjects who learn about each other and about the state of play of their interests through the media produces a form of media citizenship (Hartley, 2010). Indymedia is a form of activism by media citizens. It is an attempt to use collaborative rules to collect and to publish news, regardless of whether that news harms vested interests. It relies almost entirely on the global possibilities of Internet communication and publication. But what Hartley misses is that it was actual material code that created the possibilities that we now see, not simply 'organisation' of people in a particular relationship.

The Internet has made possible other forms of media activism. Activist groups have certainly incorporated social media into their strategies. Greenpeace and PETA (People for the Ethical Treatment of Animals) are two good global examples. Greenpeace International is a non-government global environmental activist organization with over 2.9 million supporters worldwide. It was created in 1971 in Vancouver, British Columbia, Canada and is now run from Amsterdam, Netherlands. Its mission involves intervention, stopping practices it considers wrong, and persuasion, encouraging people to change their attitudes and behaviours towards the environment. The People for the Ethical Treatment of Animals (PETA), also activist, and with 2 million members is the largest animal rights organization in the world. Created in 1980 in Norwalk, Virginia, United States, its mission is to end all animal exploitation. Like Greenpeace its strategies involve intervention and persuasion. Table 1 provides a summary of their respective campaigns and use of social media in 2009.

Table 1. Greenpeace and PETA Use of Social Media

	Greenpeace	PETA
Web site	http://www.greenpeace.org/international Donate funds, sign up for e-mailing list, find out how to get involved, watch videos on Greenpeace TV, follow blog, read international Greenpeace news, shop online store, play games,	http://www.peta.org Read news headlines, watch PETA TV, become a member, find information on how to live a cruelty-free lifestyle, support specific campaigns, discover ways to help, subscribe to e-news, read news releases,

	watch ship webcams, participate in online discussion forums, access reports, discover Greenpeace career opportunities, and learn more about Greenpeace	download resources, and connect to social networking sites
Blog	"Making Waves" Est. February 2006 Nine blog contributors Updated several times weekly	"The PETA Files" Est. October 2006 12 blog contributors Updated several times daily
Facebook Page	229,713 fans	198,420 fans
MySpace	12,711 friends	39,225 friends
Twitter	5,489 followers 757 updates	14,243 followers 4,395 updates
Flickr	443 contacts 168 posted items	2,932 contacts 1,295 posted items
YouTube	Greenpeace TV channel Joined: October 13, 2006 Subscribers: 10,208 Channel Views: 218,114 185 posted videos	PETA TV channel Joined: February 07, 2009 Subscribers: 8,762 Channel Views: 200,237 238 posted videos*
Featured Campaign	GreenMyApple, 2007 Goal: Pressure Apple to improve electronic waste policies and practices via GreenMyApple.org	GoVeg 2007 Goal: Promote vegetarianism via GoVeg.com

Source: Tran 2009.

Greenpeace and PETA deploy social media for persuasion and promotions, designed to affect public policy and to increase membership. Activism can take many forms, but it presupposes a policy, doctrine or agenda that shapes or defines action. In the broadest sense, activism may be seen as both a belief in an agenda for action as well as the process of taking action. Activism therefore is not "synonymous with direct action" and there are "practices or forms of activism that are less direct action driven and operate more within the dominant political and judicial system" (Cammaerts, 2007: 217).

Cammaerts says that central to a definition of activism is agency and the possibility of remaking society. Cammaerts (2007: 217) along with Meikle (2002: 4) includes "electronic advocacy, hacktivism, and culture jamming" as well as "corporate saboteurs to established political parties" as other forms of media activism. Carroll and Hackett point to the resurgence of media activism within civil society since the mid-1990s which they see as: "organized 'grass-roots' efforts directed to creating or influencing media practices and strategies, whether as a primary objective, or as a by-product of other campaigns (for example, efforts to change public opinion or environmental issues)" (2006: 84). They found that different media activist groups used distinct "action repertories and modes of organization" as well as the kinds of interventions varied (2006: 86, 90). Their findings underline a key fact "that media activism is indeed a diverse field of collective action" (2006: 90).

Geert Lovink argues that modern movements are deeply temporary and heterogeneous experiences,

> all geared toward creating a political event as an almost metaphysical statement. It can be easy to create media events, but they are not by definition political events, since they do not necessarily make much difference. (2008b: 126)

For Lovink, the Internet generates social activism through the activities of social movements. Activists tend to use the Internet as a 'tool' and Lovink argues that to date the Internet is not transformative in the sense of movements growing out of the Internet (Lovink, 2008a; 2008b: 124). The Internet is therefore seen predominantly as a means to strengthen offline collective campaigns, to broaden and facilitate communication, to recruit, and to advertise the movement's agenda and aims. These communication processes can extend from activist outwards to the public more broadly and to the institutions or corporations to which they may be working with or against. However, communication can be accommodated from outside the collective to those within, depending upon the affordances that are enabled and the types of organizational structures in place. This can be genuinely beneficial for the activist on the ground so to speak, as well as the communicating citizen who wishes to have input into a particular political issue. In an analysis of email correspondence between activists and citizens on the single-issue campaign against e-voting in the Netherlands ('Wij vertrouwen stemcomputers niet (WVSN)' ('We do not trust voting computers')), Oostveen (2010) notes the value of this correspondence to the activist group:

> In the WVSN campaign the activists were not the sole communicators publishing information on a website and sending newsletters. The info email address they supplied allowed weak supporters and opponents to return communication and to react to the communicator at relatively minimal cost (in time and money). The result is that there were opportunities for clarification, information provision or requests, and strategy input. (Oostveen, 2010: 814)

Jenny Pickerill (2006: 274) says that one of the most important aims of Internet activist spaces is to attract participation of individuals considered to strengthen campaigns. In the anti-war movement, Gillan, Pickerill, and Webster found that most Internet use by activists is directed primarily at organising protests (2008: 36). Pickerill shows that alliances of various affinity groups—whether they are local and/or global groups—are enhanced through the use of open publishing (2004: 174). However, she also points out that alongside open publishing comes increased surveillance by the state, something activists are mindful of. As our discussion throughout this book continues to demonstrate, technological affordances of the Internet enable broader collaborative activities and data gathering and surveillance possibilities. The affordances are technical, the design and uses are human.

In Chapter Six the authors suggested that modern e-government has not advanced to participatory collaborative government on the Internet. Modern media activism does not have a formal link, therefore, with modern policy making and government activity, except in protest. This is, perhaps, not a surprise given the relative newness of online networked environments. However, Habermas's interest in the formation of public opinion was connected to the ways that these opinions were communicated across private and public spheres to influence state policy.

Some forums like Gov2u, are a form of 'suggestion box democracy'. Gov2u emphasises knowledge sharing and partnerships at the level of policy formation. Gov2u was established in 2005 by a group of professionals from the fields of Legislative Information, Communication Technology and Community Activism (Government to you. A technology NGO). The broad aim of Gov2u is the development of citizens' and governments' abilities to use the tools of Information and Communication Technologies (ICTs) for the enhancement of participatory democracy. Gov2u is an example of a new media participatory citizenship forum that establishes explicit links between effective use of ITC tools and "the process of democratic participation" (Gov2u, "About Us"). The Gov2u website homepage addresses the "citizen" and the "government" as separate components of an ongoing collaborative process (Gov2u, "About Us"). For the government, Gov2u centres on the establishment of "a more open and direct relationship with citizens" through increased access to "the communication, management and dissemination of information" and greater accessibility to elected representatives. (For the Government—Gov2u Homepage). Gov2u researches, produces and distributes open source enabling technologies for the collection and sharing of legislative information. The group also facilitates and contributes to conferences, meetings, seminars and publications, communicating knowledge and best practice.

Gov2u's projects are more likely to facilitate ongoing interaction at the interface between citizen and government or institutional organisation. For example, Gov2u explains the completed project Gov2DemOSS in the following way:

> Our most notable achievement to date has been the development of Gov2DemOSS—an open source, informative and collaborative e-participation platform. Gov2DemOSS provides an efficient channel for institutions and organizations to keep their communities informed, manage their information repositories, to interact directly with their constituents and gauge public opinion. (Gov2u, Gov2uDemOSS, 'Completed Projects').

The provision of online consultation is now well established, even if it does not count as collaborative government. The provision of sites that provide direct insight into what is happening in local or national life, whether the location of toilets or the new city plans, are also important to any move towards collaborative government. The Internet sites below represent, at the time of writing, a selection of government or community initiatives aimed at strategic policy consultation or debate that combines information provision with participation in planning.

The Planning Mosman's future: A community conversation
Mosman Council's MOSPLAN "set the direction of the Council so that the community's needs and expectations are met in a planned, co-ordinated and cost-effective manner". The site integrated an online discussion forum (the forum was open from Friday 16 January to Friday 13 February 2009) and accepted YouTube videos, blog posts, or tweets tagged "mosplan." These were aggregated via Yahoo Pipes, and forum submissions were integrated into a report "Report on Proceedings from MOSPLAN Community Conversations." (http://www.mosmanroundtable.net/mosplan/)

The Future Melbourne Wiki
The free Wiki-based program (Twiki) allowed registered citizens to directly collaborate, edit and comment on broad plans for the future development of the city. Between 17 May and 14 June 2008, the site attracted more than 30,000 visits by nearly 7,000 individuals and over 200 edits to the plans, ranging from spelling and grammatical corrections to lengthy well-considered contributions (and not one instance of spam, off-topic or offensive content). As a Wiki, users have contributed links to various sources and examples. (http://www.futuremelbourne.com.au/wiki/view/FMPlan)

Lords of the Blog
House of Lords is a word-press based collaborative Group Blog featuring 14 UK Lords discussing the workings of UK government and specific legislation currently under consideration. The blog accepts comments from the public under a simple moderation policy, and as such functions as a tool for testing concepts among constituents or publishing news, opinion, and debate that traditional media outlets may not carry. The site claims it "makes politicians and government processes more accessible to the public, creates greater openness and transparency on the part of the government and leads to increased engagement and participation in democracy by the public." The site also provides links to individual politicians' blogs. (http://lordsoftheblog.net/)

Make the Future
This is the personal blog of activist/software developer Jim Gilliam. Gilliam collaborated with filmmaker Robert Greenwald (*Uncovered: The War on Iraq* (2004), *Outfoxed: Rupert Murdoch's War on Journalism* (2004), *Wal-Mart: The High Cost of Low Price* (2005) and *Iraq for Sale: The War Profiteers* (2006)—oh, and *Xanadu* (1980)) in researching and developing innovative grassroots distribution for his films. In 2006, Gilliam, Greenwald and Rick Jacobs founded Brave New Films, an activist-based media company that produces Internet videos and campaigns. As a software developer, Gilliam has produced Act.ly, a suite of activism tools for Twitter; GovLuv an application that connects government leaders with citizens via Twitter; WhiteHouse2.org; and Nation-Builder—the open source platform behind White House 2 that is also being used by Australia 2 and Parliament 2 in Canada. (http://www.jimgilliam.com)

Australia 2 BETA
Uses Gilliam's NationBuilder—an open source platform that enables users to suggest and define what they believe to be priorities for Australia. As each users adds priorities to their own list, the overall list of priorities rise in the charts—as does user's 'influence.' The idea is that as more people join, the more political clout they will have and the more likely their priorities will be heard by government. Priorities can be searched via categories: top, rising, controversial, falling, random, and new. At present, Australia 2 has 70 priorities as defined by 139 people. 139 (now 140) users do not necessarily carry a great deal of political clout. This is reflected in the banality of some of the priorities (e.g. "Reform the machinery of government," and "Exploring alternative energy options for Australia"). Yet the more concise priorities, such as "Permissive copyright as general case for Government data," have not necessarily attracted user votes. (http://au.nationbuilder.com/)

Site: Parliament 2
Uses the same NationBuilder platform as Australia 2 (above) to enable users to suggest and define what they believe to the priorities for Canada. Like NationnBuilder, priorities can be searched via the categories of top, rising, controversial, falling, random, and new. One notable difference between the Canadian and Australian platforms is that the Canadian platform allows users to register as 'citizens,' 'politician' and 'government employees.' We can thus see which priorities are authored or supported by politicians. For example, "interest free student loans" in Canada has attracted 119 endorsements, 5 politician endorsements, 4 government employee endorsements, and 12 oppositions. For Canadian politicians (at parliment2.ca) abolishing the Penny is the 51st priority, abolishing the Monarchy is the 83rd priority. At the time of writing, Parliament 2 has 91 priorities as defined by 569 people. (http://parliament2.ca/)

Whitehouse 2
This site also uses the same NationBuilder platform as Australia 2 and Parliament 2 (above) to enable users to suggest and define what they believe to the priorities for the White House. At present, Whitehouse 2 has 2,850 priorities as defined by 10,162 people. Priorities are further divided into 'everyone's priorities' and 'Obama priorities.' The site clearly indicates which priorities have been Endorsed (e.g., Restore, Uphold, and Defend the Constitution) or Opposed (e.g., Get Government out of Healthcare) by the White House along with those that are not on the agenda (e.g., End monopolies of news outlets to restore a free press). (http://www.whitehouse2.org/)

Bang the Table
Bang the Table was an online initiative aimed at addressing citizen engagement itself. The Chief Minister's Office in the Australian Capital Territory (ACT) used Internet forums to consult with citizens regarding the levels of citizen engagement they preferred, the scope of that involvement, and the preferred methods used to consult and engage with citizens. (http://bangthetable.com/actconsultations)

Deliberative democracy has now moved from political theory into practice. This deliberative turn in institutional practice has involved practitioners in many countries devising ways to involve citizens in effective deliberation and joint decision-making. Examples include consensus conferences (invented in Denmark), citizens' juries (invented in the United States, widely used in the UK and sometimes in Australia), planning cells (Germany), participatory budgeting (Brazil), participatory technology assessment of different kinds (Denmark and NZ), deliberative polls (United States, China and Australia), citizen panels (UK), citizens' assemblies (Canada), citizens parliament (Australia) and 21st century town meetings (United States and Australia). There is now a strong record of achievement by governments and organisations using these methods to solve complex public problems, and a growing research field that evaluates and critically compares and assesses these exercises. (Abelson & Gauvin, 2006; Cornwall, 2002; Fung, 2003; Leighninger, 2008; Levine et. al., 2005; Warren & Pearce, 2008).

All of these examples range from providing citizens with knowledge about what government is doing or providing, or in gaining feedback on particular initiatives. In the case of the NationBuilder platforms it is possible to see a more complex attempt to get people together to express opinions, although it is not a government initiative. These approaches complement those groups who are setting up actual procedural rules for deliberative.

Deliberative Practices on the Internet

Carson & Hartz-Karp list what they think are the minimum conditions for setting up procedures for deliberative democracy:

> Influence: The process should have the ability to influence policy and decision-making.
> Inclusion: The process should be representative of the population and inclusive of diverse viewpoints and values, providing equal opportunity for all to participate.
> Deliberation: The process should provide open dialogue, access to information, respect, space to understand and reframe issues, and movement toward consensus. (Carson & Hartz-Karp, 2005).

AmericaSpeaks is an example where an online site tries to embed the principles of deliberative democratic practice. Large scale forums such as the 21st Century Town Meeting and the 21st Century Summit are used. These forums assist leaders of organisations to assess public opinion and to prioritise. These meetings have the advantage of drawing together considerable numbers of people—from 50 to 5, 000 per meeting—and engaging them in a processes of "strategic, outcomes-oriented discussion". (AmericaSpeaks, Topics of AmericaSpeaks Projects). Through these large-scale forums, citizens can explore and deliberate on issues of public policy and draw conclusions that potentially impact policy making. The input of citizens is of primary significance in this process—input could lead to a bigger commitment to supporting the issues.

Some of the topics around which AmericaSpeaks mobilises action include budgeting, climate change, disaster recovery and preparedness, health care, international issues, organisational strategy, national policy, planning and growth, and youth and education (AmericaSpeaks, Topics of AmericaSpeaks Projects). This range of issues is diverse and the challenge for participants in AmericaSpeaks' forums is to employ strategies that positively subvert polarising debate around complex issues.

Port Phillip Speaks was an initiative of the City of Port Phillip (Victoria) in conjunction with AmericaSpeaks. Its aim was to develop community priorities for the Port Phillip Community Plan (2007–2017). The issues for consideration were mainly drawn from a survey conducted by the City of Port Phillip in 2006 (Port Phillip Speaks, *Participant Discussion Guide*: 2). The document defines a Community Plan as "an agreed framework of priorities that helps the Council and community manage change while protecting what is valued most." Community Planning is said to be an opportunity for the Council "to learn more about local issues, weigh up options to address them, and voice and opinion" (Port Phillip Speaks, *Participant Discussion Guide*: 2).

Before the town meeting, the 750 participants were asked to read the discussion guide—to have engaged with the combination of community demographics, social trends, and policy challenges it details—to have thought about the issues and discussed them with family and friends. The discussion guide structures the discussion of issues around "Options" and asks the question "What can we do to make a difference?" It lists the pros and cons of a range of alternative possibilities on each issue, and provides space for the participant's thoughts on a series of alternative approaches to the issue.

During the Port Phillip Speaks 21st Century Town Meeting each discussion is monitored and assisted by a trained volunteer facilitator. The ideas generated by each group are sent to a coordinator who will collate results and present them back to the whole group for review and further discussion. Keypads were used by individual participants to record their opinions and preferences on individual actions. At the conclusion of the meeting, each participant receives a report outlining the agreed priorities and next steps for action. Once projects had been identified, participants developed strategies for continued action based on the achievement and implementation of priorities. As a result of this plan, citizens set priorities for the community in a variety of areas including service provision, climate change, parking, public open space and residential amenities. Neighbourhood groups then discussed ways of progressing community priorities, identifying projects that could be adopted by neighbourhood groups. (AmericaSpeaks, 21st Century Town Meetings, Port Phillip Australia). In this instance, AmericaSpeaks, provides a service via the model of the Town Meeting and even though intercreative dialogue (see

Meikle, 2002) is missing, this participatory forum is applied to a specific context for the purpose of facilitating and enabling discussion.

The *Port Phillip Speaks Final Report* summarises the results of the summit and provides a copy of the revised Community Plan. It also includes a synopsis of the deliberative process that took place. The report describes how, following the AmericaSpeaks model, responses

> from each small group were captured via a computer and transmitted to a central 'theme team' who collated responses to identify themes and collective priorities that were then voted for (or not) using individual keypad polling. During the later part of the Summit, participants were brought together in seven neighbourhood groups to discuss local issues. (*Community Plan 2007/2017*: 9)

The report also records the fact that a series of neighbourhood community meetings, involving 250 people, began in May 2007 as follow-up to the summit. In addition, a Vision Statement 2007-2017 (p.10) and a list of the overall top 10 priorities decided upon at the meeting are included. As an interesting aside, the report notes that younger people were generally underrepresented at the forum (*Community Plan 2007/2017*: 16). As a result, Council conducted "an independent post-summit quantitative analysis that weighted for age to match the city's demographics" (*Community Plan 2007/2017*: 9).

Some organisations, like GetUp!, set up in Australia in 2005, have aspects of the AmericaSpeaks model but are closer to being a pressure group. GetUp!, is an Australian not-for-profit, organisation, grassroots community advocacy organization that relies on public donations and focuses more on individual participation or action in specified campaigns. GetUp!'s aim is to build an accountable and progressive Australian Parliament and for this reason it does not support any particular political party. The campaigns are community based and coordinated mainly via email and the Internet with use of traditional broadcast, print media and YouTube to run campaigns and to promote awareness (Get Up!, Annual Report 2005-2006: 5). GetUp!'s E-Democracy Project is one example of deliberative tools—the first phase of the project facilitates opportunities to learn about the role of the Australian Senate and to become familiar with individual senators. (GetUp! Project Democracy, n.d.). The project provides a range of tools to demystify mainstream political institutions and assists the development of participatory skills. For example, a summary of the role and history of the senate is outlined on their website. A list of the Senators representing each state and territory can be accessed by clicking on individual sections of a map of Australia. The site features an interactive model of the Australian senate—by placing the cursor over the individuated seats in the model of the senate chamber this highlights a visual image and introductory details about the Senator who occupies the seat. (GetUp! Project

Democracy: Your Senate, n.d.). Information available includes Senators' Senate speeches, biographies, media reports and relevant blog posts, making it easier to contact/engage with Senators about comments made, etc. Members can share thoughts about the Senator's performance via the community blogposts or receive weekly email updates about their parliamentary statements and media appearances. A contact form is included to simplify access to individual senators for those who wish to email or write. As the process is atomized, the feature does facilitate a form of accountability from politicians. In future, their E-democracy project will be expanded to incorporate a House of Representatives section. From GetUp!'s viewpoint by informing, educating and encouraging engagement with institutional mechanisms and ideas, the organization empowers citizens and encourages participation. (GetUp! Project Democracy, n.d.).

While GetUp! accentuates the power of individual (and collective) action—namely signing a petition, contacting a member of parliament, etc.— AmericaSpeaks generally does not invite the same kind of individual interaction. Although they refer to citizen engagement in democratic processes, AmericaSpeaks facilitates projects and programs at the level of the organisation or institution. In a nutshell, they provide models and tools for engaging and implementing citizen participation. For instance, the primary function of AmericaSpeaks is the provision of information through speakers who give public lectures on deliberative issues and techniques and the facilitation of deliberative mechanisms. AmericaSpeaks state that they can assist with the organisation and running of meetings, matching "appropriate technology with the power of small group dialogue," and also ensure that isolated communities are not denied access to the meeting process (AmericaSpeaks, Innovation). Central to this vision is a range of "innovative deliberative tools" such as the 21st Century Town Meeting (AmericaSpeaks, About Us). The technology they employ includes wireless groupware computers and keypad polling which allow for the rapid collation and dissemination of information.

One measure of intercreativity (Meikle, 2002) is the extent to which individual members can decide what issues are important and what actions should be taken. The question of who ultimately decides on actions is significant. So too is the availability of levels of action and degrees of commitment that individuals can opt to make. Even though GetUp! members receive emailed updates about campaigns, GetUp! states that members are "always only ever asked to take targeted, coordinated and strategic action" such as signing petitions, contacting members of parliament, engaging with the media, attending an event or get-together, supporting the airing of an advertisement in the media etc. (About Us—FAQ). Members are free to suggest campaign issues: an email format for contributing ideas for campaigns is available in FAQ under "Can I suggest an issue to campaign on?" The website stipulates that campaign issues are identified on the basis of the "interests and input" of the membership whose ideas "help to shape GetUp's direction." The "two-way informational flow" Meikle (2002) identifies with "conversational intercreativity" does not necessarily operate at the level of deciding what issues are selected to be acted upon and actions are taken. Furthermore, despite the fact that blogs give members an opportunity to express opinions, etc., they do not necessarily facilitate a grassroots decision-making dialogue at the intercreative level. The Get-Up! website does not articulate the process or the specific selection criteria for choosing campaign issues. Selection of campaigns according to GetUp! is based on the underlying notion of "shared progressive values such as social justice, economic fairness and environmental sustainability." The organization takes the view that they need to "focus national attention and action where [their] contribution will be most effective." However members of the site are left wondering: What happens to the suggestions for campaign issues put forward by the membership once the emails are received? Do they become the concern of the GetUp! board and/or various other staff? If intercreativity, as Meikle describes it, is more than interacting with a screen, perhaps organisations like GetUp! offer an important, but, nevertheless, rather regulated form of participation which ultimately does not provide members the freedom to choose the campaigns selected for action. Even though GetUp! emphasises collaboration and community, there is a difference between personally suggesting an issue to act upon, and sharing in the decision-making process about what issues will be selected for action.

AmericaSpeaks by contrast provides a service rather than being an activist forum based on the notion of intercreative exchange. The emphasis on service is reinforced on the site via the "Services" page which includes a section entitled, "request our services." On this page visitors are invited to inform the organisation about "a particular policy issue or group of people...that could benefit from AmericaSpeaks' innovative deliberative tools." Visitors are asked to share information about a potential project and how AmericaSpeaks, the respondent and others can potentially work together. This style of inviting participation via the completion of an online form lacks the spontaneity, openness, and the grassroots generative potential of intercreative exchange.

AmericaSpeaks does assist online engagement: this was evident in the lead-up to the 2008 presidential election. Working with the National Academy of Public Administration and Deliberation, AmericaSpeaks helped facilitate a ten-day citizen-driven conversation that involved the posting of in excess of 500 ideas and comments from people all over the United States. In another online initiative in 2005, AmericaSpeaks and Ascentum ran "Voices and Choices" for residents of Northeast Ohio. Two "innovative online tools" were used to enable thousands of residents to participate in online dialogue designed to establish priorities and set goals for the region. Community centres and public libraries were enlisted to increase public accesses to online activities.

AmericaSpeaks and GetUp! offer opportunities for communication and interaction that are closest to the style of "conversational interactivity" Meikle advocates (2002:31). The emphasis GetUp! places on individual action as a way of responding to specific political issues supports this view. In contrast, AmericaSpeaks is more concerned with building connections between citizens and governments/organisations through the facilitation of a range of technologically based projects and tools designed to increase citizen involvement, disseminate information, and enable organisations to work more sustainably and effectively with citizens. It could be argued then that AmericaSpeaks is largely transmissional in nature because it provides visitors with a specific range of possibilities to choose from within a framework designed to facilitate connections between people and organisations.

What is missing in deliberative practice is a universal networked public sphere to support it. This would involve, of course, legislation at the government end and the code relevant to its operation. Arnison's work on open publishing for Indymedia is a constructive example of how code was created to solve a problem. AmericaSpeaks and Bang the Table (a commercial group) provide tools to groups to undertake deliberations on issues or topics. However, this is not the same as having a networked structure that actually intersects with policy making and real decisions by government. At best, current deliberative practices on the Internet are closer to a form of activism than to a public sphere embedded in law for participatory democracy.

The Gift Economy and Cooperatives

All of the examples above involve thousands of people spending their own time, mostly unpaid, on activities designed to enhance engagement and discussion or to take action in the modern community. This type of contribution to mutuality is traditionally called a contribution to the *gift economy*. No reward is sought although there may be benefits associated with the activity, of course, that are not monetary. The Internet is now a massive gift economy, as we saw with Ravelry. It is also, often simultaneously, a commercial economy. Modern knowledge aggregators harvest massive amounts of information about individuals with no requirement to pay the individuals for it. You receive no money from these aggregators whether you are willing give information to them or not. Modern governments, by extension, do not have to relinquish any institutional power to you by virtue of the operation of AmericaSpeaks or GetUp! but governments do get the benefit, free, of feedback on issues that are of concern to their community.

The difficulty here is that the multiplication of publics and of different techniques for engagement and deliberation are not getting rewards in the generalisation of competence that equivalent cooperatives would have received in the past. A good example of the difference between the present gift economies on the Internet and how gift economies have operated in the past is in the electrifying of America. In the early days of building electricity networks in the United States the Federal legislature created the Rural Electrification Administration (REA) to provide loans to local cooperatives overlooked by private power companies. By 1931 many urban centres were well lit, with wire running to factories, stores and homes. However, rural America was pre-electric. The process of diffusion of electricity was not a simple homogenous one but entailed three types of electrical systems that took half a century to merge.

> The first was private and serviced downtown business and a few wealthy homes. The second was a municipal plant for street lighting. The third was private and drove the streetcars, ran the amusement parks, and sold electricity to the communities along its routes. (Nye, 1992: 26).

Farmers in the cooperatives were not passive receivers of electrical technology nor passive participants in the cooperative itself. Their role was to understand the technology and of course all the construction elements involved from farm to network. Each cooperative had its own ideas on the material choices that were best for their needs. These choices were not abstract choices. There were experiments with direct and alternating current, Edison lamps and Brush arc lights, with gas and electrical lighting, with steam 'dummy' trains and electric trolleys, with district heating, metered and unmetered service, and nationally public and private utility ownership. The REA visited rural areas on road shows showing the types of appliances possible and as many as 5,000 people a day visited them.

The cooperatives hired outside contractors to build the lines and worked out what to do if specialist contractors were not available. Everyone knew the cooperatives territory. "'We used to tell people that if you wanted to know where we operated you only had to look at the roads. If the road was paved that was private power territory. If it was a dirt road, that was our own territory."(Nye, 1992: 24). The example of the cooperatives is instructive. The farmers generalised their competence in order to understand electricity networks, their technology, and the specific needs to which electricity might be applied. Unlike AmericaSpeaks they were directly involved in the construction of the networks that they were talking about; directly involved in the distribution of resources; directly involved in the designs relevant to them. This is a paradigm example of generalisation of competence, where the informed citizen is not just knowledgeable, but where the intrinsic and common intrinsic interests come together. Farmer cooperatives could have over 1,000 members and they met to make decisions and offer their services where necessary for particular tasks.

There is an irony of course that electrification helped in the depopulation of farms as urban centres grew. The gift economy, however, has always had a role in complementing private business activity and government plans. The gift economy, in this triangle, was strongly identified with the public good rather than commercial culture alone. The REA was a recognition of electricity as a public good and the voluntary efforts of farmers and members of cooperatives were explicitly understood as a transaction in this context. It is not at all clear that gift transactions on the Internet have this same clarity of purpose. Indeed, if we look closely at what look like gift economies on the Internet they are far from what they seem.

Open Source Footwear is a very good example of this (Murdock, 2010). *Open Source Footwear* offer people the opportunity to send their shoe designs to the organisation to 'get real recognition.' The site says:

> Will I be rich? Are you insane? Nobody gets paid for Open Source Footware designs because nobody owns them. That's right: once you send us your design, it becomes public domain, freely available to all. We might use the whole thing, base a design of our own on its, or just part of it. And your idea might only be for part of a shoe anyway. This keeps everything fair. Having said that, if you're chosen, we'll send you a free pair! (www.fluevog.com)

The impression is given by the company site that it is open source and that this is a public domain organisation. This is of course far from the case. *Open Source Footwear* is using voluntary labour to design footwear and pays the designers nothing. *Open Source Footwear* also has first call on the design. This is a new phenomenon because the Internet can create this type of relationship on a scale never known before. What is perceived to be a gift economy is not.

It is not only organisations like *Open Source Footwear* that are in this position. The activist and deliberative engagement sites discussed previously are *like* cooperatives but are they *are not* cooperatives. They have collaborative rules but they are not interlinked, like the farmers building electrical networks, to actual systems of formal decision-making. This means, the authors' suggest, that in the long term, the very design of modern engagement sites will evolve to be understood as enhanced engagement tools, used by governments and businesses, rather than as participatory decision-making tools. The current tools are not bad things. Online engagement tools like Bang The Table, privately owned, are hired by local government councils in Australia to engage with communities on key issues. But this is consultation rather than participation in decision-making. It is not a code for collaborative government.

There is a range of types of collaborative rules, therefore, that are emerging on the Internet. These rules are built into the governance of sites such as GetUp! and AmericaSpeaks and in the tools that they advocate. All of the discussed examples are sites set up to put pressure on governments or businesses on particular issues or, in the case of Bang The Table, provide online engagement tools for citizens and governments for consultative purposes. The Port Phillip example shows how sophisticated consultation can be. The long-term problem is whether or not democracy on the Internet approximates *Open Source Footwear*, looking like one thing but being another.

Summary

This chapter began with the authors discussing the difference between different types of 'reasons for action.' In everyday life we are interested in reasons as good reasons and we are quite capable of finding out what other people's reasons for actions are, by asking them. They might lie, but it is a human facility that we can indeed find out reasons for actions. Governments also have reasons for actions and in the contemporary world modern citizens need to be well resourced in order to engage with governments on their reasons for making the decisions that they do.

Modern analysts tend to resort to a theoretical language, or an idiom of interpretation, to describe what people do or what happens in society or, as the authors have shown, give agency to things that do not have agency. Donald MacKenzie, for example, in his *Material Markets: How Economic Agents Are Constructed* (2009) argues that inanimate things have *intentions*. In his work he has teased out for his readers how systems of technologies, cognitive frameworks, simplifying concepts, and calculative mechanisms have had hidden or unforeseen effects on the financial system. This is actor-network theory. The authors' work complements the work of material sociologists like MacKenzie but does not buy into its theory of agency. MacKenzie tries to unpack the black box of financial markets; to generalise the competencies of modern citizens. He does not, in fact, need to add agency to inanimate things to provide a good overview of the complexity of financial markets. Like Galloway's discussion of protocol, we know that every system that exists can produce content-free effects. The very mind-boggling complexity of 'collateralised debt obligations' had auditors themselves tied in knots, the very people with the supposed expertise to understand them.

The reasons people use the Internet are complex, like financial markets. Like financial markets there are also layers. The democratic tools for online engagement are on a top layer of the Internet. They are not substructural and they do not address the substructural politics of the Internet and the very black-boxes that make the Internet possible. The fate of the gift economy is one of these substructural and subpolitical issues. There is much that is positive in the mix of things happening online, but an equally worrying trend towards a change from a link between the public good-driven gift economy towards a commercial-driven gift economy.

Figure 1 provides an overview of reasons for action in the context of the Internet, commerce, the public good and the gift economy. In the case of the REA cooperatives, the arrows would have been both ways from the public good to commerce. In the current economic design, the state funds public good institutions like public broadcasting.

Public broadcasting is itself a public good because it has positive externalities (to use the economic phrase). It enhances social stability and the good when shared is not diminished. In early broadcasting there were also many listening associations that gave feedback to the BBC, at no cost to the BBC (the gift economy). The situation in the Internet is much more complex. Your voluntary labour might be co-opted by commerce and, indeed, it is as soon as you log on to the Internet. Other groups on the Internet might also co-opt your labour, such as GetUp!; in this case based on your trust that GetUp! represents your interests in some way. *Open Source Footwear*, likewise, is after your voluntary labour as an up-and-coming footwear designer, equally, with the promise that it will represent your interests in some way.

Figure 1: The Internet, Commerce, the Public Good and the Gift

The BBC timeline of history plans to take historical artefacts, like pottery, and present them to the public in an accessible, 3-D, real-life context as well as many other artefacts and historical materials. The project brings together the resources of the British Library, the British Museum, the National Maritime Museum and the Museum of Bayeux. As Murdock (2010) points out, this network of public institutions acts as a way of value-adding scarce public resources while at the same time expanding valuable historical knowledge within the public domain. This may be a guide to the future. However, as the authors argue, the informed citizen requires a generalization of competence in the world of the Internet that is still not there.

CHAPTER EIGHT

Conclusion

The type of engine used in a vast majority of the modern passenger cars and trucks operates on gasoline, and is known as an Internal Combustion Engine.

—"What makes it tick?" Automotive Principles Simply Explained (1947: 4)

It is doubtful that most modern citizens have a reference manual on their car's full mechanics with details on how to repair them. This is different from the 1940s and 1950s when many people could fix many of their problems with their cars or at least undertake basic maintenance. Nowadays, modern electronics often puts repairs out of the reach of both citizens and indeed basic motor repair services. What makes "What makes it tick?" interesting as a publication is the fact that citizens, when they have the opportunity, do seek to understand the things of immediate interest to them and that have primary relevance. In industrial society, people, when deprived of access to expertise or knowledge that was important to them, attempted to create ways to enhance the social distribution of knowledge. In the 1800s, for example, the working poor supported themselves or had support through working mens' groups. The Society for the Diffusion of Useful Knowledge is just one example:

> The Society for the Diffusion of Useful Knowledge was only one, if perhaps the most important, of the agencies which tried to assist through the supply of books and treatises the self education of people who may or may not have belonged to the Mechanics' Institutes scattered around the country. The London Mechanics' Institution could employ well-known and extremely competent tutors. Elsewhere working men often had to depend either on themselves—engage in 'the pursuit of knowledge under difficulties'—or on each other in mutual improvement classes, which were described later in the century by Samuel Smiles as 'the educational Methodism of our day.' (Briggs, 1973: 9)

Annie Beasant, by contrast, is a famous example of how slow universities were to expand their conceptions of education. In the 1870s, Beasant was a science student at Birkbeck and attended classes there. She was rated first class in inorganic chemistry, mathematics, theoretic mechanics, magnetism and electricity, botany, general biology, animal physiology and acoustics, light and heat, but she never graduated. Birkbeck omitted her name from the list of its successful candidates because members of a building committee feared that contributors would withdraw if they realised she had been at Birkbeck. She printed and published a circular showing what had happened to her, giving the issue of exclusion wide publicity.

Relevance as we have seen in this book is a complex phenomenon. The Internet is not a Society for the Diffusion of Useful Knowledge—it is a complex mediation machine made up of computers and very complex algorithms. Unlike the traditional codex book that Beasant would have read, the Internet has its own processes of selection and exclusion and its own techniques that can affect personal choice. Jacques Ellul, in his work *Technological Society*, argues that the system of techniques in a society has implications for the nature of personal choice. The singular most important characteristic of modern technique, he says, is 'the one best way'—automatism of technical choice.

> When everything has been measured and calculated mathematically so that the method which has been decided upon is satisfactory from the rational point of view, and when, from the practical point of view, the method is manifestly the most efficient of all those hitherto employed or those in competition with it, then the technical movement becomes self directing. I call the process automatism.
>
> There is no personal choice, in respect to magnitude, between, say, 3 and 4; 4 is greater than 3; this is a fact which has no personal reference. No one can change it or assert the contrary or personally escape it. Similarly, there is no choice between two technical methods. One of them asserts itself inescapably: its results are calculated, measured, obvious, and indisputable. (1964: 79–80)

In Ellul's work there is emphasis both on the nature of techniques involved in modern societies and their consequences for individual choice. Indeed, the example of 'the one best way' is close to Hacking's idea of a "style of reasoning." It is not simply a matter of technique as a way of doing things, but a style, a process of deliberation—in this case, process automatism—that matters. Techniques are also not isolated. Ellul (1964: 394) warns: "Let us not forget that every one of the human techniques is related to all other techniques."

The idea that technique has effects is, of course, not new. Harold Innis took the idea of technique further, linking it to issues in time and space. He argued that concentration on a medium of communication implies a bias in the cultural development of the civilization concerned either towards an emphasis on space and political organization or towards an emphasis on time and religious organization (1951: 216).

The dominance of parchment in the West gave a bias towards ecclesiastical organization which led to the introduction of a paper with its bias toward political organization. With printing, paper facilitated an effective development of the vernaculars and gave expression to their vitality in the growth of nationalism. The adaptability of the alphabet to large-scale machine industry became the basis of literacy, advertising, and trade. The book as a specialized product of printing, and in turn, the newspaper strengthened the position of language as a basis of nationalism. In the United States the dominance of the newspaper led to large-scale development of monopolies of communication in terms of space and implied a neglect of problems of time...the bias of paper towards an emphasis on space and its monopolies of knowledge has been checked by the development of a new medium, the radio. (Innis, 1951: 216-217)

Innis's distinction between time-biased and space-biased media is made precisely because techniques of production and distribution of knowledge appear for him to produce very different outcomes—those with rock as a means of transmitting knowledge are limited in the speed at which knowledge can be transmitted and returned; those with satellites have expanded geographic spread and speed. What is important for the authors is that Innis attempts to identify specific specialised techniques in society and then to define their effects. What cannot be doubted is that different modes of communication in a society have very different requirements for the production and distribution of knowledge. Moreover, those modes of communication affect the use of time and space.

This part of Innis's thesis—that certain logics develop around new media—seems reasonable. Writing parchment, for example, required a big labour force of scribes. "Working six hours a day the scribe produced from two to four pages and required from ten months to a year and a quarter to copy a Bible" (Innis, 1951: 169). Libraries were slowly built up around stored knowledge and uniform rules in the care of books were gradually adopted. Demand for space for upright books led to the increased construction of libraries in the 15th century.

The Internet, in Innis's terms, is a space-biased medium par excellence. In the case of the Internet, there is a requirement for hardware and software—servers, computers, telecommunications infrastructure, algorithms—that are themselves techniques that provide connection worldwide, almost instantaneously. Unlike the codex book, however, if something breaks down, then connection with what is held in the digital world online is lost. Seeking knowledge on the Internet, unlike the public library, also brings with it techniques for harvesting personal data. This contradiction of openness and personal surveillance makes the Internet a new form of mediation in the social distribution of knowledge and the generalisation of competencies changes as a result.

Galloway identifies the logic that predominates within distributed network systems such as the Internet. This logic—which he calls protocological—is evident in the development, application and deployment of protocol: the means by which communication flows are directed and shaped across the various layers of the Internet. This logic and the means by which it is enacted have been discussed by the authors in terms of its implications for the realisation of public spheres and open collaborative spaces.

Where the authors differ from those like Galloway, Ellul and Innis is in the degree of causality or agency that can be assigned to codes, techniques or inanimate objects generally. They would argue that the influence of code is in direct relationship to the generalisation of competencies in modern society. The more ignorant people become about the underlying infrastructures delivered by the Internet, then the more influential that system(s) would become.

Generalisation of Competencies

The logics around the concept of information are important to how the social distribution of knowledge is understood and acted upon. As we have seen, construing information as a quantity within a quantity has moral and practical implications. The only reason that we would want to construe information in this way is in order to provide either a monetary value against it or to assume that it has agency in its own right, or both.

The disciplinary conceptions matter because those conceptions affect how knowledge is perceived and how it is re-presented and delivered. For example, artificial intelligence theorists have their own conceptions about how mind and knowledge works. The Internet is a paradigm example of a massive communication system that could be run under AI principles of mind and knowledge representation and, indeed, already partly is. Yet, the idea that the human mind and decision-making have some rational purpose independent of the culture(s) from which they are represented in software seems odd to the authors, and indeed, dangerous.

The AI phenomenon also shows us that the capacity of the citizen to become informed about a system of algorithms in the current environment is extremely difficult. The authors presented Claude Shannon's information formula to show that the work of the algorithm with signals is different from the gloss that those like Norbert Weiner put on it. The everyday person might be hard put to understand the algorithm and would need to rely on experts to interpret it. This might be acceptable in contexts where the citizen's identity and control over personal information are irrelevant to the social distribution of knowledge. However, the current development of the Internet involves expertise that is defining the algorithms being used without public overview in the same way that the whole IP address decisions are not open to public consultation.

As the authors have attempted to demonstrate protocol sets the material context for how the social distribution of knowledge might proceed. A simple thing like a drop-down menu may have categories that define the response of users who have had no input into its design. The authors have borrowed Galloway's use of the term protocol to talk about all the layers of the Internet, from IP addresses to routers and servers. However, we recommend a minimalist use of the ideas of protocol and code. According to our understanding, code is the actual discussions or decisions around programming and the way it is then instantiated in actual practice. We can see the language in the millions of discussions around the globe. Matthew Arnison in the LyX users list posts a query "how do I get LyX to ignore LaTeX errors?" and asks "I'm getting a La-TeX warning showing up as an error box in LyX. The problem is that the error is not important. But when I press Ctrl-T to view the postscript, LyX just keeps complaining about the error. But if I got the LyX's temp folder, the .dvi is there, and if I run dvips manually, then gv, it all looks fine. How do I get Ctrl-T to ignore a LaTeX error?" (http://www.mail-archive.com/lyx-users@lists.lyx.org/msg19343.html). *WikiLeaks* founder Julian Assange (previously charged as a hacker), like Arnison, knows his code. There are millions of conversations, questions and replies, like these in the modern world involving decisions on design, error, correction, transmission, content, and so on.

Instantiated code is what people use and what they buy. You can buy fake people, for instance, and buy fake traffic for 30 cents per thousand fake people. You can also buy ways of detecting fake people. This explicit ability to manipulate the metrics of public or consumer participation has implications for public and commercial enterprise. Groups wishing to demonstrate support for their cause might use fake means to achieve their ends. In audience ratings this is called hypoing and is strictly regulated by the ratings providers. However, there is no equivalent regulation at this time on the Internet.

Internet service providers at a macro level can create limits to access, something that has not escaped the eyes of the regulators in the Net Neutrality debate·

On Tuesday morning, an AT&T-funded front group, Americans for Prosperity, announced a $1.4 million advertising blitz to try to convince Americans that the FCC [Federal Communications Commission] is plotting to "take over the Internet." Last week, the FCC simply proposed to "reclassify" aspects of broadband under Title II of the Telecommunications Act to better advance its goals of bridging the digital divide and safeguarding the free and open Internet. But AFP is spinning this into, laughably and somewhat ironically, a "government takeover." (Tady, 2010)

The FCC is concerned that companies are beginning to restrict access, prioritize their own offerings and make other critical changes to the structure to the Internet as an open platform. Comcast for example blocked legal file-sharing traffic. The Net Neutrality debate in many ways is an argument about providing a public sphere within the Internet.

The authors have suggested that the informed citizen operates in a network of interests, ranging from imposed to intrinsic. Some knowledge will be directly relevant to individuals and others not. In public sphere contexts there are common intrinsic interests where diverse views can be taken into account. AmericaSpeaks was used as an example of a site that attempts to create a deliberative environment. Even if it is not completely successful, this organization at least attempts to link intention, opinion and being informed together. The next step from the authors' point of view is to create transparent algorithms that can assist deliberative democratic process on the Internet and, perhaps more importantly, expand the capability of citizens to understand the effects of the material technology of the Internet on their decisions and their identity. If this does not happen, then the Internet will evolve into a material space that:

provides the opportunity for the individual to limit their exposure to diverse or conflicting views;
makes it impossible for a citizen's digital persona to escape surveillance;
denies the citizen the capacity to judge the competencies of those who are making decisions about them or their representation on the Internet.

The authors want to draw the reader's attention to the fact that, *different conceptions of information produce different conceptions of the public.* Historically there has been a language for talking about the public and the informed citizen. It is the language of *mutuality* and it has additional notions like 'the public interest,' 'public value,' and 'the public good,' attached to it. The language for talking about the public disappears in a world dominated by the idea of information as a quantity-within-a-quantity or as a causal agent for rationality. 'Rational decision-making,' 'goal orientation,' 'commodity,' 'uncertainty reduction,' are the *lingua franca* of those involved in the discourse of information as a special causal agent. Thinking of human beings or the public as a system, as a machine, or as a network with information binding them together brings with it a particular perspective on the social distribution of knowledge. Relevance is determined not by people themselves but by characteristics of information or the systems.

Restricting access to knowledge, for example, increases its value in a commercial world. In the traditional ideas of the public, however, the citizen needs to be well resourced to participate in the public sphere. In the Western democratic context, public libraries, museums, and other public institutions have formed the societal backbone for unrestricted access to knowledge for the public good, together with universal service legislation that guarantees access to technologies such as the telephone. There are significant differences between the language of the public, the informed citizen, and the language of information as a causal agent.

The authors reassert that, *information does not exist, only informed people exist.* It is important to stand back, take a deep breath, and reflect on any claim that inanimate objects have intentions. Human communication, conceptually, is not about the transfer of 'things' but centrally about intentions, fundamental to Habermas's theory. The Internet is one of the biggest systems of 'things' that we have ever seen and it is perhaps understandable that some people think that by virtue of this complexity that there are intentions embedded in networks. The phrase the *internet of things* for example emerged to describe the radio frequency identification chips (RFID) phenomenon. This involves any and every possible object you can think of, from your broom to your lunch box, that could be tagged with a tiny device that links all the objects in your life together; an open network of objects that would communicate with one another and their users through wireless networks. Agency, ultimately, however, is in people and even though the material objects that they use may influence the way they act, this does not make those material things intentional agents.

Open source coding is an example of an intentional attempt to take material code and ensure that it is not dominated by proprietary processes. As we have discussed in the book, however, even the groupings of experts in this area of coding may be inaccessible to the broader public. In terms of the authors' theory, open source coding brings together people with a common intrinsic interest and among these people there is a generalised competence in understanding, using and deploying open source code. Obviously this is not, again, a generalisation of competence that extends outside that particular interest.

Open source is also not just about experts coming together but about social engagement, just as it was for farmers in the pre-electrification era in the United States. There can be little doubt that the gift economy on the Internet is booming and little doubt as well that the labour involved in this economy is often harvested for commercial interests. What we are missing are formal coding systems that are directed toward public culture and not only commercial need. What you tend to find and as the authors have shown is an intricate interweaving of commercial and gift activities, public and private. For example,

YouTube is a site where people freely contribute material up for all to see and to use, but it is also a monetized audience.

The authors do not have the answer to how systematic *networked public spheres* might work or be created, as distinct from current practices. There are certainly, as this book has shown, various attempts to create democratic forums. Aggregators can also be more or less democratic and transparent. The BBC timeline history was given as an example of an attempt to network among public institutions, but how the public sphere is represented overall in a networked context is a much bigger picture. In the Global Financial Crisis, banks argued that they were too big to fail. Public cultures are harder to see but are equally as tangible and can, equally, fail. Habermas, in one of his public commentaries on the role of the quality press in Germany, reinforced this point about the importance of support for those media that are able to encapsulate public opinion, at a time when quality papers were closing. The public sphere, he said,

> mediates between institutionalised discourses and negotiations taking place in the state arenas on the one hand, and the episodic and informal daily talk of potential voters on the other. The public sphere does its part in democratically legitimatising state action by selecting objects relevant for political decision-making, forming them into issues and bundling them into competing public opinions with more or less well-informed and reasoned arguments. In this way, public communication is a force that stimulates and orients citizens' opinions and desires, while at the same time forcing the political system to adjust and become more transparent. Without the impulse of an opinion-forming press, one that informs reliably and comments diligently, the public sphere will lose this special type of energy. When gas, electricity or water are at stake, the state must guarantee the energy supply for the population. Shouldn't it do likewise when this other type of 'energy' is at risk—the absence of which will cause disruptions that harm the state? (Habermas, 2007)

Habermas had no interest in how to aggregate public opinion in an Internet context, but it seems that this might be the next step in building networked public spheres; networks of public institutions whose role it is, as it has always been, to generalize competence. Coleman and Blumler (2009) touch on the possibility of independently funding an agency to enhance participatory democracy, including expansion of funding for the BBC (176). However, apart from failing to consider the intersection of national and international domains that is the terrain of Internet activity, the broader issue is the material coding that needs to be considered. The actual networked structures that can create the public sphere within the Internet that can operationally do what the BBC ethos is intended to do, need to be coded in certain ways. The BBC using the Internet, which it does now is not the same though as a networked public sphere. The BBC has a Charter and independence to establish its operations, not only in the abstract but also in the particular. The BBC provides:

- Universal accessibility (geographic): Everyone should have access to a public broadcaster's signals, wherever they are located.

- Universal appeal (general tastes and interests): "The principle of serving the diverse interests of the public is the basis then for the presence in the schedule of programmes which serve the young as well as the elderly, those interested in local affairs as well as the national political canvas, members of diverse subcultures as well as those in the mainstream." (Tracey, 1998: 27)

- Particular attention to minorities: This can include people of different colour, language and religious beliefs. Public broadcasting has a dual role; to give access to minority groups and provide them with opportunities to voice their issues as well as to provide to the broader community knowledge about their histories and cultures. There are in Britain and in the United States, for example, large numbers of Islamic migrants. Knowledge about this religion and culture is important to the broader community.

- Contribution to a sense of national identity and community and a commitment to education: Public broadcasters enable the nation to 'speak to itself' reflecting those things that are very different between us and those that are the same. A public broadcaster also has a role to inform and to educate. (Tracey 1998: 29)

- Distance from vested interests: This is the idea that public broadcasting programming works within a structure of independence. "Programmes funded by advertising necessarily have their character influenced in some shape or form by the demand to maximize the garnering of consumers. Programmes directly funded by the government, and with no intervening structural heat shield, inevitably tend to utter the tones of their master's voice." (Tracey 1998: 31)

- Direct funding and universality of payment: The forms of finance for public broadcasting are important to it retaining independence. If commercial sources of revenue start to dominate a public service broadcaster's agenda then the principles of public service may suffer as a result.

- Competition in good programming rather than for numbers: Quality programming is expected from a public broadcaster regardless of the size of the audience or its potential to pay.

- Guidelines that liberate rather than restrict programme makers: This concept allows for experiment, innovation, quarrel and mistake in the programme making process or, as Tracey puts it, "there should always be a place for the dissenting radical." (1998: 32)

Expanding the public sphere requirements for an organization like the BBC to include digital networks and the Internet would include, the authors would suggest, creating a *public search engine*, as one important aspect of a networked public sphere. Such a search engine would need to keep transparent the coding behind it and the organizing logic and intent of the algorithms that run it—keeping the purpose and practice of these open for public deliberation and input by all. Relevance would then be determined by public, not commercial, needs (including the design of the information retrieval system). Although this would not preclude commercial activities being tailored to take advantage of such systems, if it allowed ongoing negotiation and fluidity to be accommodated, such a public search engine might find ways to navigate the blurry line that in many ways only in theory divides public and commercial needs and desires. This type of approach to a public search engine design process moves the understanding of information as a quantity or a resource that can be archived, parcelled out and mined, to one that recognizes informed citizens and a social distribution of knowledge. Coleman and Blumler (2009) have therefore, in their discussion of the BBC, touched on something interesting and important, but to be networked this discussion must also include the actual issue of code.

People are citizens in modern democracies as well as consumers. As citizens there are inbuilt expectations of the media system in which they live.

1. Citizens expect to be informed. Commercial organisations can generate content on the Internet but those media attract paying audiences and a knowledge gap between elites and the general public can occur;

2. Citizens expect a rational democracy that encourages the transfer of relevant specialist knowledge to the political and public domains, and promotes balanced debate directed towards the public good;

3. Citizens expect a public culture of shared knowledge, values and points of reference. That politicians might try to buy citizen votes and their power through the Internet, expensive campaigns or clever manipulation may occur, but it is not the expectation of a democratic citizenry.

"The argument that public institutions like public broadcasting create an informed, rational and fair democratic system is currently its single most important justification" (Curran 2002: 207).

This is the *strong* version of the informed citizen that modern society has supported. Habermas assumes in his theory of information that the citizen is well-resourced when they participate in the public sphere. In "wild public spheres," while there is of course no guarantee of institutional protection of open communication, there is still the ethos that citizens will be trying to come together with knowledge relevant to discussion (Habermas, 2007). They will be able to make reflexive, informed decisions as a result.

The generalisation of competencies is therefore essential to participation in the public sphere. Farmers in the electricity cooperatives in the United States at the beginning of electrification not only understood how electricity networks worked but could judge the competencies of those who had expert knowledge. The farmers could debate within their own cooperatives on the options available to them, from infrastructure to appliances, and could understand the implications of their actions. Citizens who are not adequately resourced cannot properly participate in a public sphere. Indeed, the electricity cooperatives are in many way exemplars of the key characteristics that Habermas put forward in his description of discourse.

The authors have expanded Habermas's theory of information by incorporating consideration of the material and technical conditions of the Internet. Protocol, the rules governing material code at various levels, sets the material context for accessibility to the social distribution of knowledge in the Internet. It is used for linking individuals, linking organisations, linking machines, and linking entities that might not otherwise connect with each other. A *weak* version of the informed citizen, the authors contest, would be monitorial where we accept that the current material codes are sufficient, fractured, and do not need to come together in any institutional way.

Michael Schudson (1998) for example writes that,

> Citizens can be 'monitorial' rather than informed. A monitorial citizen scans (rather than reads) the informational environment in a way so that he or she may be alerted on a very wide variety of issues for a very wide variety of ends and may be mobilized around those issues in a large variety of ways.... Monitorial citizens tend to be defensive rather than pro-active. They are perhaps better informed than citizens of the past in that, somewhere in their heads, they have more bits of information, but there is no assurance that they know at all what to do with what they know. They have no more virtue than citizens of the past—but not less, either.

However, this book takes a different view, proposing that the modern citizen is already proactive, though this takes different forms and uses different resources than it may have done previously. The modern citizen given the opportunity would assist in the building of networked public spheres.

In conclusion, the authors have prised open the black box of information as a phenomenon. We have investigated a range of disciplines that deal with information as a concept. These disciplines have informed the design and use of information and communication systems, including the Internet. Their conceptualizations are not purely abstract and have in many ways become cultural tropes. The authors argue that the informed citizen is at the heart of the social distribution of knowledge and that recognition is vital for a revitalization of public spheres. This book is a small contribution to that revitalization.

Bibliography

Abelson, J., & F. P. Gauvin. Assessing the Impacts of Public Participation: Concepts, Evidence and Policy Implications. Ottawa: Canadian Policy Research Networks, 2006.

American College Dictionary. New York: Random House, 1964.

Andersen, M.P. "What Is Communication?" *Journal of Communication*, 9, 1959.

Andersen, K.V., H.Z. Henriksen, C. Secher, & R. Medaglia. "Costs of Eparticipation: The Management of Challenges." *Transforming Government: People, Process and Policy*, 1(1): 294–326, 2007.

Anscombe, G.E.M.P. "Intention." *The Philosophy of Action*. E. White (Ed.). Oxford: Oxford University Press, 1968.

Apel, K.O. "'The Priori of Communication?' and the Foundation of the Humanities." *Man and World*, 5, 1972.

Aquinas, T. *Summa Contra Gentiles*, Part I. New York: Doubleday, 1956.

Arendt, H. *The Human Condition*. Chicago: University of Chicago Press, 1958.

ASPA & UNDPEPA. "Benchmarking E-Government, a Global Perspective: Assessing the Progress of the UN Member States." Report by the American Society for Public Administration (ASPA) and the United Nations Division for Public Economics and Public Administration (UNDPEPA), 2001. Retrieved from http://216.149.125.141/about/pdfs/BenchmarkingEgov.pdf

Attneave F. *Applications of Information Theory to Psychology: A Summary of Basic Concepts, Methods, and Results*. New York: Holt, Rinehart, and Winston, 1959

Austin, D. "The Development of PRECIS: A Theoretical and Technical History." *Journal of Documentation*, 30(1), 1974.

Austin, D. "Citation Order and Linguistic Structure." *The Variety of Librarianship: Essays in Honour of John Wallace Metcalfe*. B. Rayward (Ed.). Sydney, Australia: Library Association of Australia, 1976.

Australia 2 BETA. Retrieved from http://au.nationbuilder.com/

Ayer, A.J. *"What Is Communication?" Studies in Communication*. Communication Research Centre, University College. London: Martin Secker & Warburg, 1955.

Balnaves. M. "Media Measurement And Using Media Research." P.J. Kitchen (Ed). *Integrated Marketing Communications: Addressing the Challenges and How to Measure ROI*. London: Palgrave Macmillan, 2010.

Balnaves, M., S. Donald, & B. Shoesmith. *Media Theories and Approaches: A Global Perspective*,

London: Palgrave Macmillan, 2008.

Balnaves, M., T. Leaver, & M. Willson. "Habermas and the Net," *International Communications Association Conference*, Singapore, 22–26 June, http://www.allacademic.com/meta/p_mla_apa_research_citation/4/0/3/3/0/p403306_index.html, 2010.

Bang the Table. Retrieved from http://bangthetable.com/actconsultations

Barlow, J.P. A Declaration of the Independence of Cyberspace, Retrieved from http://w2.eff.org/Censorship/Internet_censorship_bills/barlow_0296.declaration

Barnlund, D.C. "Toward a Meaning-Centred Philosophy of Communication." *Journal of Communication*, 12, 1964.

Barr, A., & E.A. Feigenbaum. *The Handbook of Artificial Intelligence*, Vol. 1. A. Barr, & E.A. Feigenbaum (Ed.). Stanford, CA: Heuris Tech, 1981.

Bates, B.J. "Information as an Economic Good: Sources of Individual and Social Value." *The Political Economy of Information*. V. Mosco & J. Wasko (Ed.). Maddison, WI: University of Wisconsin Press, 1988.

Bates, M.J. "An Introduction to MetaTheories, Theories, and Models." K.E. Fisher, S. Erdelez & L. McKechnie (Eds.) *Information Today*, 2005.

Bateson, G. *Steps to an Ecology of Mind*. London: Intertext, 1972.

Bearman, T.C. "The Information Society of the 1990s: Blue Sky and Green Pastures?" *Online*, 11(1): 82–86, 1987.

Becker, H. "Constructive Typology in the Social Sciences." *American Sociological Review*, 5(1), 1940.

Bell, D. *The Coming of Post-Industrial Society*. New York: Basic, 1973.

Beniger, J.R. *The Control Revolution*. Cambridge: Harvard University Press, 1986.

Benkler, Y. *The Wealth of Nations: How Social Production Transforms Markets and Freedom*. New Haven, CT and London: Yale University Press, 2006.

Berelson, B., & G.A. Steiner. *Human Behavior*. New York: Harcourt, Brace & World, 1964.

Bernal, J.D. "Scientific Communication." *The Origins of Information Science*. A.J. Meadows (Ed.). London: Taylor Graham, 1987.

Berners-Lee, T., J. Hendler, & O. Lassila, "The Semantic Web." *Scientific American Magazine*. 2001 Retrieved from http://www.scientificamerican.com/article.cfm?id=the-semantic-web.

Testimony of Sir Timothy Berners-Lee, Before the United States House of Representatives Committee on Energy and Commerce Subcommittee on Telecommunications and the Internet Hearing on the "Digital Future of the United States: Part I – The Future of the World Wide Web."2007, Retrieved from http://dig.csail.mit.edu/2007/03/01-ushouse-future-of-the-web.

Bliss, H.E. "Theoretic Principles of Bibliographic Classifications." *Readings in Library Cataloguing* R. K. Olding (Ed.). Melbourne: F. W. Cheshire, 1966.

Blomgren B.L., T. Nabatchi, & R. O'Leary. "The New Governance: Practices and Processes for Stakeholder and Citizen Participation in the Work of Government." *Public Administration Review*, 65(5): 547, 2005.

Bobrow, D.G., & P.J. Hayes. "Artificial Intelligence: Where Are We?" *Artificial Intelligence*, 25, 1985.

Boulding, K.E. "The Economics of Knowledge and the Knowledge of Economics." *Economics of*

Information and Knowledge. D.M. Lamberton (Ed.). Harmondsworth: Penguin, 1971.

Bourdeiu, P. *Outline of a Theory of Practice.* Chicago: University of Chicago Press, 1977.

boyd, d., & N. Ellison. "Social Network Sites: Definition, History, and Scholarship." *Journal of Computer-Mediated Communication,* 13(1), 2007.

Braman, S. "Defining Information." *Telecommunications Policy,* Sept: 233–242, 1989.

Brey, P. "The Technological Construction of Social Power." *Social Epistemology,* 22(1): 71–95, 2008.

Briggs, W. *The Law of International Copyright.* London, Stevens & Haynes. 1906.

Briggs, A. *Communications and Culture 1823–1973: A Tale of Two Centuries.* The Foundation Oration Delivered at Birkbneck College, 1973.

Bruns, A. "Habermas and/against the internet." Blog post: http://snurb.info/node/621, 2007.

Cammaerts, B. "Activism and Media." *Reclaiming the Media: Communication. Rights and Democratic Media Role,* Vol. 3. B. Cammaerts & N. Carpentier (Eds.). European Communication Research and Education Association: Intellect, 2007.

Campbell, J. *Grammatical Man.* New York: Simon & Schuster, 1982.

Carey, J. "Mass Communication Research and Cultural Studies: An American View." *Mass Communication and Society.* J. Curran et al. (Eds.). London: Open University, 1977.

Carroll, W.K., & R.A. Hackett. "Democratic Media Activism through the Lens of Social Movement Theory." *Media, Culture and Society,* 28(1): 83–104, 2006.

Carson, L., & J. Hartz-Karp. "Adapting and Combining Deliberative Designs: Juries, Polls, and Forums." *The Deliberative Democracy Handbook: Strategies for Effective Civic Engagement in the Twenty-First Century.* J. Gastil & P. Levine (Eds.). San Francisco, CA: Jossey-Bass, 2005.

Cartier, F.A., & K.A. Harwood. "On Definition of Communication." *Journal of Communication,* 3, 1953.

Castells, M. *The Rise of the Network Society. The Information Age: Economy, Society and Culture,* Vol. 1. (2nd ed.). Malden, MA: Blackwell, 2000.

Castells, M. *The Internet Galaxy: Reflections on the Internet, Business, and Society,* Oxford, UK: Oxford University Press, 2001.

Cherry, C. *On Human Communication.* New York: Science Editions, 1959.

Cleverdon, C.W. *Aslib Cranfield Research Project: A Report on the Testing and Analysis of an Investigation into Comparative Efficiency of Indexing Systems.* Cranfield, UK: College of Aeronautics, 1962.

Cohen, P.R., & E.A. Feigenbaum. *The Handbook of Artificial Intelligence,* Vol. 3. Stanford, CA: Heuris Tech, 1982.

Coleman, S., & J.G. Blumler. *The Internet and Democratic Citizenship: Theory, Practice and Policy.* Cambridge: Cambridge University Press, 2009.

Coleman, S. & D. F. Norris. "A New Agenda for E-Democracy ." *International Journal of Electronic Government Research* 1(3): 69–82 . [See the full Oxford Internet Institute Forum Discussion Paper no. 4 at http://www.umbc.edu/mipar and www.oii.ox.ac.uk , 2005.]

Coltoff, H. "Transfer of Information as Seen by a User." *The Use of Information* A. Van der Laan & A.A. Winters (Eds.). New York: North-Holland, 1984.

Cornwall, A. *Making Spaces, Changing Places: Situating Participation in Development.* Report No. 170. Brighton: Institute of Development Studies, University of Sussex, 2002.

Coursey, D. "E-Government: Trends, Benefits, and Challenges." *The Municipal Yearbook 2005*. Washington, DC: International City/County Management Association: 14–21, 2005.

Coursey, D., & D.F. Norris. " Models of E-Government: Are They Correct? An Empirical Assessment." *Public Administration Review*, May/June: 524–536, 2009.

Crampton, T. "How Facebook Ended My Marriage." 2007. Retrieved from http://www.thomascrampton.com/uncategorized/how-facebook-ended-my-marriage/

Cronin, B. "The Information Society." *Aslib Proceedings*, 38(4), April 1986.

Crossley, N. *Intersubjectivity: The Fabric of Social Becoming*. London: Sage, 1996.

Curran, J. *Media and Power*. London: Routledge, 2002.

Cutter, C.A. *Rules for a Dictionary Catalogue*. Washington: U.S. Government Printing Office, 1904.

Dance, F.E.X. "The Concept of Communication." *Journal of Communication*, 20, 1970.

Davidson, D. "Actions, Reasons and Causes." *The Philosophy of Action*. A. Van der Laan & E. White (Ed.). Oxford: Oxford University Press, 1968.

Davis, L.H. *Theory of Action*. Englewood Cliffs, NJ: Prentice-Hall, 1979.

Dean, J. "Cyber Salons and Civil Society: Rethinking the Public Sphere in Transnational Technoculture." *Public Culture*, 13(2): 243–265, 2001.

Dean, J. "Why the Net Is not a Public Sphere." *Constellations*, 10(1): 95–112, 2003.

Department of Veterans Affairs. Retrieved from http://www.vba.va.gov/.

Derr, R.L. "The Concept of Information in Ordinary Discourse." *Information Processing and Management*, 21(6), 1985.

Dewey, J. *The Quest for Certainty*. New York: Minton Batch, 1929.

Dibble, J. "A Rape in Cyberspace: How an Evil Clown, a Haitian Trickster Spirit, Two Wizards, and a Cast of Dozens Turned a Database Into a Society." *The Village Voice*. December 23, 1993.

Dictionary of Computing. Oxford: Oxford University Press, 1986.

Eco, U. *The Name of the Rose*. London: Pan, 1984.

Elias, N. *The Civilizing Process: The History of Manners*. Vol. 1. E. Jephcott (Trans.). Oxford: Blackwell, 1978.

Ellul, J. *The Technological Society*. New York: Vintage, 1964.

Fiske, J. *Introduction to Communication Studies*. London: Methuen, 1982.

Flanagin, A.J., C. Flanagin, & J. Flanagin. "Technical Code and the Social Construction of the Internet." *New Media & Society*, 12(2): 179–196, 2010.

Foskett, A.C. "E.J. Coates, The British Technology Index and the Theory of Subject Headings: The Man Who Loved Cat Springing." *Readings in Library Cataloguing*. R.K. Olding (Ed.). Melbourne: F.W. Cheshire, 1966.

Foskett, A.C. *The Subject Approach to Information*. London: Clive Bingley, 1969.

Foucault, M. *Discipline and Punish*. New York: Pantheon, 1977.

Fox, C.J. *Information and Misinformation: An Investigation of the Notions of Information, Misinformation, Informing and Misinforming*. Westport, CT: Greenwood, 1983.

Fraser, N. "Rethinking the Public Sphere: A Contribution to the Critique of Actually Existing Democracy." *Habermas and the Public Sphere*. C. Calhoun (Ed.). Cambridge: MIT Press,

1993.

Froomkin, M. "Critical Theory of Cyberspace." *Harvard Law Review*, 116: 749–873, 2003.

Fung, A. "Survey Article: Recipes for Public Spheres: Eight Institutional Design Choices and their Consequences." *The Journal of Political Philosophy*, 11(3): 338–367, 2003.

Interview with A.R. Galloway, (Oct 27, 2009) conducted via email by Henrique Costa of the Brazilian Digital Culture Forum. Retrieved from http://cultureandcommunication.org/galloway/InterviewBrazilOct09.pdf

Galloway, A. R. *Protocol: How Control Exists After Decentralization*. Cambridge: MIT Press, 2004.

Galloway, A.R. "Protocol." *Theory, Culture & Society*, 23(2–3): 317–320, 2006.

Galloway, A. R. "The Unworkable Interface." *New Literary History*, 39: 931–955, 2009.

Galloway, A. R., & E. Thacker. *The Exploit: A Theory of Networks*. Minneapolis: University of Minnesota Press, 2007.

Galvin, T.J. "The Significance of Information Science for the Theory and Practice of Librarianship." *Libri*, 34(2), 1984.

Garrido, M.I., & A. Halavais. "Activist in 140 Words: Twitter and International Organizations." *Internet Research 10.0–Internet Critical*, Milwaukee, 7–10, October, 2009.

Geiger, R.S. "Does Habermas Understand the Internet? The Algorithmic Construction of the Blogo/Public Sphere." *Gnovis*, 10(1), Fall 2009. Retrieved from http://gnovisjournal.org/journal/does-habermas-understand-internet-algorithmic-construction-blogopublic-sphere

Gergen, K.J. *Toward Transformation in Social Knowledge*. New York: Springer-Verlag, 1982.

Gibson, R.K, S. Ward, & A. Rommele. *Electronic Democracy: Mobilisation, Participation and Organisation via New ICTs*. London: Taylor & Francis, 2004.

Giddens, A. *The Constitution of Society*. Cambridge: Polity, 1984.

Gillan, K., J. Pickerall, & F. Webster. *Anti-war Activism: New Media and Protest in the Information Age*. New York: Palgrave Macmillan, 2008.

Give Your Voice. Retrieved from http://www.give-your-voice.eu/.

Gode, A. "What Is Communication?" *Journal of Communication*, 9, 1959.

Grönlund, Å. *Electronic Government: Design, Applications, and Management*. Hershey, PA: Idea Group, 2002.

Habermas, J. *Knowledge and Human Interests*. London: Heinemann, 1981.

Habermas, J. *The Theory of Communicative Action: Reason and the Rationalization of Society, Vol. 1*. Boston: Beacon, 1984.

Habermas, J. *The Structural Transformation of the Public Sphere: An Inquiry into a Category of Bourgeois Society*. Trans. T. Burger with assistance from F. Lawrence. Cambridge: MIT Press, 1989.

Habermas, J. "Concluding Remarks." *Habermas and the Public Sphere*. C. Calhoun, L. Florence, & R. Mirchandani (Condensed and Edited). Cambridge: MIT Press, 1992a.

Habermas, J. "Further Reflections on the Public Sphere." *Habermas and the Public Sphere*. C. Calhoun (Ed.). Cambridge: MIT Press, 1992b.

Habermas, J. "Political Communication in Media Society: Does Democracy Still Enjoy an Epistemic Dimension? The Impact of Normative Theory on Empirical Research." *Journal of*

Communication Theory, 16(4): 411–426, 2006.

Habermas, J. "How to Save the Quality Press?" SightandSound.com - Let's Talk European. Trans. Jab (John Lambert) (The article originally appeared in German in the *Süddeutsche Zeitung* on May 16, 2007.). 2007. Retrieved from http://www.signandsight.com/features/1349.html.

Habermas, J., & M. Cooke. *On the Pragmatics of Communication*. Cambridge: MIT Press, 2000.

Harre, R. *Social Being*. Oxford: Basil Blackwell, 1979.

Hawes, L.C. "Elements of a Model for Communication Processes." *Quarterly Journal of Speech*, 59, 1973.

Hegel, G.W.F. *Hegel's Philosophy of Right*. T.M. Knox (Trans.). London: Oxford University Press, 1981.

Hekman, S.J. *Weber, the Ideal Type, and Contemporary Social Theory*. Notre Dame: University of Notre Dame Press, 1983.

Hempel, C.G. *Aspects of Scientific Explanation*. New York: Free Press, 1965.

Hempel, C.G. *Philosophy of Natural Science*. Englewood Cliffs, NJ: Prentice-Hall, 1966.

Hillman, D.J. "Customized User Services via Interactions with LEADERMART." *Information Storage and Retrieval*, 9, 1973.

Hindess, B. "Interests in Political Analysis." *Power, Action and Belief*. J. Law (Ed.). London: Routledge & Kegan Paul, 1986a.

Hindess, B. "Action and Social Relations." *Sociological Theory in Transition*. M.L. Wardell & S. Turner (Eds.). Boston: Allen Unwin, 1986b.

Hindess, B. *Choice, Rationality and Social Theory*. London: Unwin Hyman, 1988.

Hintikka, J. "The Varieties of Information and Scientific Explanation." B. Von Rootselaar, & J.F. Staal (Eds.). *Logic, Methodology and Philosophy of Science*, 3, 1968.

Hirst, P. *Law, Socialism and Democracy*. London: Harper Collins, 1986.

Hjorland, B. "Information: Objectives or Subjective/Situational." *Journal of the American Society for Information Science and Technology*, 58(10): 1448–1456, 2007.

Hobbes, T. *The English Works of Thomas Hobbes*, Vol. 4. W. Molesworth (Ed.). London: John Bohn, 1839–1845.

Hoben, J.B. "English Communication at Colgate Re-examined." *Journal of Communication*, 4, 1954.

Hulme, E.W. "Principles of Book Classification." *Readings in Library Cataloguing*. R.K. Olding (Ed.). Melbourne: F.W. Cheshire, 1966.

Humphreys, S. "The Challenges of Intellectual Property for Users of Social Networking Sites: A Case Study of Ravelry." *Proceedings of the 12th International Conference on Entertainment and Media in the Ubiquitous Era*, in Tampere: 125–130, Finland, 2008.

Humphreys, S. "The Economies within an Online Social Network Market: A Case Study of Ravelry." *Paper presented at the Australia and New Zealand Communication at Colgate Re-examined*, 2009.

Innis, H. *The Bias of Communication*. Toronto: Toronto University Press, 1951.

Irani, Z., P.E.D. Love, & S. Jones. "Learning Lessons from Evaluating eGovernment: Reflective Case Experiences That Support Transformational Government." Strategic Information

Systems, 17: 155–164, 2009.

Jameson, F. *Postmodernism, or, the Cultural Logic of Late Capitalism*. Durham, NC: Duke University Press, 1991.

Jenkins, H. *Textual Poachers: Television Fans and Participatory Culture*. New York: Routledge, Chapman & Hall, 1992.

Johnson, J. (pseudonym for Latour, B). "Mixing Humans and Nonhumans Together: The Sociology of a Door-Closer." *Social Problems*, 35(3): 298–310, June 1988.

Jonas, H. "A Critique of Cybernetics." *Social Research*, 20, 1953.

Kant, I. *Critique of Judgement*. New York: Herder & Herder, 1959.

Kittler, F.A. "From Discourse Networks to Cultural Mathematics: An Interview with Friedrich A. Kittler." *Theory, Culture & Society*, 23(17), 2006.

Kochen, M. "Stability in the Growth of Knowledge." *Introduction to Information Science*. T. Saracevic (Ed.). New York: Bowker, 1970.

Kochen, M. "Information and Society." *Annual Review of Information Science and Technology*, 18: 278, 1983.

Kochen, M. "Information Science Research: The Search for the Nature of Information." *Journal of the American Society for Information Science*, 35(3), 1984.

Krippendorf, K. "Paradox and Information." *Progress in Communication Sciences*. B. Dervin & M.J. Voigt (Eds.). Norwood, NJ: Ablex, 1984.

Lamberton, D.M. "The Economics of Information and Organization." *Annual Review of Information Science and Technology*, 1984.

Lancaster, F.W. *Information Retrieval Systems*. New York: John Wiley, 1968.

Lancaster, F.W. *Vocabulary Control for Information Retrieval*. Washington, DC: Information Resources, 1972.

Landry, B.C. *A Theory of Indexing*, 2 Volumes. Colombus, OH: Computer and Information Science Research Centre, Ohio State University, 1971.

Lathi, B.P. *Modern Digital and Analog Communication Systems*. New York: Holt, Rinehart & Winston, 1983.

Latta, R. *Leibniz: The Monadology and Other Philosophical Writings*. London: Oxford University Press, 1898.

Leighninger, M. *The Promise and Challenge of Neighborhood Democracy: Lessons from the Intersection of Government and Community*. Orlando, FL: Grassroots Grantmakers, 2008.

Lessig, L. *Code and Other Laws of Cyberspace*. New York: Basic, 1999.

Lessig, L. "The Architecture of Innovation." *Duke Law Journal*, 51: 1783–1788, 2002.

Levesque, H.J. "Knowledge Representation and Reasoning." *Annual Review of Computing Science*, 1, 1986.

Levine, P., A. Fung, & J. Gastil. "Future Directions for Public Deliberation." *Journal of Public Deliberation*, 1(1): 1–13, 2005.

Levitan, K.B. "Applying a Holistic Framework to Synthesize Information Science Research." *Progress in Communication Sciences*, Vol. 2. Norwood, NJ: Ablex, 1980.

Levy, S.R. *Knowledge and Communication Sciences*. PhD Thesis. Los Angeles: University of California, 1974.

Lewis, C.T., & C. Short. *Latin Dictionary.* Oxford: Oxford University Press, 1900.

Licklider, J.C.R., & R.W. Taylor. "The Computer as a Communication Device." *Science and Technology,* April 1968.

Li Ming. "On Information." *Social Sciences in China,* 6(2), June 1985.

Littlejohn, S.W. *Theories of Human Communication.* Belmont, CA: Wadsworth, 1983.

Lords of the Blog. Retrieved from http://lordsoftheblog.net/

Lovink, G. "Publish Now: The Cultural Politics of Blogs and Web 2." Paper presented at the Centre for Research in Entertainment, Arts, Technology, Education and Communications (CREATEC) Colloquium, December 17–18, in Edith Cowan University, Perth, Western Australia, 2008a.

Lovink, G. "Toward Open and Dense Networks: An Interview with Geert Lovink." *Digital Media and Democracy: Tactics in Hard Times.* M. Boler (Ed.). Cambridge, London: MIT Press, 2008b.

Lyon, D. *The Information Society: Issues and Illusions.* Cambridge: Polity, 1988.

Lytle, R.H. "Information Resource Management: 1981–1986." *Annual Review of Information Science and Technology,* 21: 310, 1986.

Machlup, F. *Knowledge and Knowledge Production,* Vol 1. Princeton, NJ: Princeton University Press, 1980.

Machlup, F. *Knowledge and Knowledge Production,* Vol 2. Princeton, NJ: Princeton University Press, 1982.

Machlup, F. *Knowledge and Knowledge Production,* Vol 3. Princeton, NJ: Princeton University Press, 1984.

Machlup, F., & U. Mansfield. "Cultural Diversity in Studies of Information." *The Study of Information.* F. Machlup & U. Mansfield (Ed.). New York: John Wiley, 1983.

MacIntyre, A. "The Idea of a Social Science." *Rationality.* B.R. Wilson (Ed.). Oxford: Basil Blackwell, 1977.

MacKenzie, D. *Material Markets: How Economic Agents Are Constructed.* Oxford: Oxford University Press, 2009.

Make the Future. Retrieved from http://www.jimgilliam.com.

Malmberg, B. *Structural Linguistics and Human Communication.* Berlin: Springer-Verlag, 1963.

Martin, R "Protesting in the 21st century - Success Stories." *Catapult*–ABC Online: 6 December, http://www.abc.net.au/catapult/stories/s1259653.htm, 2004.

Martindale, D. "Sociological Theory and the Ideal Type." *Symposium on Sociological Theory.* L. Gross (Ed.). New York: Harper & Row, 1959.

Marx, K. *The Eighteenth Brumaire of Louis Bonaparte,* 1852.

Marx, K. *Capital.* New York: Random House, 1906.

Mason, R. "Acxiom: The Company That Knows If You Own a Cat or if You're Right - Handed." *Telegraph.co.uk* http://www.telegraph.co.uk/finance/newsbysector/retailand consumer/company-that-knows-if-you-own-a-cat-or-if-youre-right-handed.html, 2009.

Masuda, Y. *The Information Society as Post Industrial Society.* Washington, DC: World Future Society, 1981.

McQuail, D. *Mass Communication Theory: An Introduction.* (3rd ed.) London, Thousand Oaks,

CA: Sage, 1994.

Mead, G.H. *Philosophy of the Act*. Chicago: University of Chicago Press, 1938.

Mead, G.H. "Mind, Self and Society." *Sociology*. L. Broom & P. Selznik (Eds.). New York, Harper & Row, 1963.

Meikle, G. *Future Active: Media Activism and the Internet*. New York; London: Routledge; Pluto, 2002.

Melody, W.H. "Information: An Emerging Dimension of Institutional Analysis." *Journal of Economic Issues*, 21(3), 1313–1339, 1987.

Metcalfe, J. *Subject Classifying and Indexing of Libraries and Literature*. London: Angus & Robertson, 1959.

Miller, G.A. "On Defining Communications: Another Stab." *Journal of Abnormal and Social Psychology*, 6, 1951.

Minsky, M.L. "Matter, Mind and Models." *Semantic Information Processing*. M. Minsky. (Ed.). Cambridge: MIT Press, 1968.

Minsky, M.L. "Computer Science and the Representation of Knowledge." *The Computer Age*. M.L. Dertouzos & J. Muses (Eds.). Cambridge: MIT Press, 1979.

Minsky, M.L. *The Society of Mind*. London: Heinemann, 1987.

More, E. "Communication Policy–Research and Education Agendas in the Australian Context." *Australian Communication Review*, 8(5), December 1987.

Moynihan, C. "Arrest Puts Focus on Protestors' Texting." *The New York Times*, October 5, 2009. Retrieved from http://www.nytimes.com/2009/10/05/nyregion/05txt.htm.

Mumford, L. *The Condition of Man*. New York: Harcourt, Brace & World, 1944.

Murdock, G. "The Return of the Gift: Participation and Exploitation on the Internet." Smythe Lecture Series. Simon Fraser University, March 25, 2010 Retrieved from http://www.cmns.sfu.ca/2010/02/16/smythe-lecture-series-present-graham-murdock/

Murdock, J.W., & D.M. Liston. "A General Model of Information Transfer." *American Documentation*, 18, 1967.

Nagel, T. *The Possibility of Altruism*. Princeton, NJ: Princeton University Press, 1970.

National Commission on Libraries and Information Science (NCLIS). *Public Sector/Private Sector Interaction in Providing Information Services*. Washington: NCLIS, 1982.

Newcomb, T. (1953) "An approach to the study of communicative acts." *Psychological Review*, 60: 393–404.

Newell, A. "The Knowledge Level." *Artificial Intelligence*, 18, 1982.

Nextgov. Retrieved from http://techinsider.nextgov.com/2009/05/open_the_government _proce.php

Nye, D.E. *Electrifying America: Social Meanings of a New Technology*. Boston, MA: MIT, 1992.

Oostveen, A.M. "Citizens and Activists." *Information, Communication and Society*, 13(6): 793–819, 2010.

Papacharissi, Z.A. *A Private Sphere: Democracy in a Digital Age*. Digital Media and Society Series. Cambridge: Polity, 2010.

Parkin, F. *Marxism and Class Theory: A Bourgeois Critique*. London: Tavistock, 1979.

Parliament 2. Retrieved from http://parliament2.ca/.

Parsons, T. *The Structure of Social Action*. New York: Free Press, 1967a.

Parsons, T. *Sociological Theory and Modern Society*. New York: Free Press, 1967b.

Paulsen, B.A. "Fundamental Relationships of Information, Communication, and Power With Respect to Organizations and Automated Information Processing." PhD Thesis. University of Colorado, 1980.

Pearce, W.B., & V.E. Cronen. *Communication, Action and Meaning*. New York: Praeger, 1980.

Pearson, K. *The Grammar of Science*. London: J.M. Dent, 1892.

Penman, R. *Communication Processes and Relationships*. London: Academic, 1980.

Peters, B.G. *The Future of Governing: Four Emerging Models*, University Press of Kansas, Lawrence, 1996.

Peters, B.G., & Pierre, J. "Governance without Government? Rethinking Public Administration," *Journal of Public Administration Research and Theory*, 8(20): 223–243, 1998.

PEW Internet and American Life Project. "The Internet's Role in Campaign 2008." 2009. Retrieved from http://www.pewinternet.org/Reports/2009/6-The-Internets-Role-in-Campaign-2008.aspx

Pickerill, J.. "Rethinking Political Participation: Experiments in Internet Activism in Australia and Britain." In *Electronic Democracy: Mobilisation, Organisation and Participation via new ICTs*. R. Gibson, A. Roemmele, & S. Ward (Eds.). London: Routledge, 2004.

Pickerill, J. "Radical Politics on the Net." *Parliamentary Affairs*, 59(2): 266–282, 2006.

Pierce, J.R. *Symbols, Signals and Noise*. New York: Harper, 1961.

Ploman, E.W., & L.C. Hamilton. *Copyright: Intellectual Property in the Information Age*. London: Routledge & Kegal Paul, 1980.

Popper, K. *The Open Society and Its Enemies*, Vol. 2. London: Routledge, 1962.

Porat, M. "Communication Policy in an Information Society." *Communications for Tomorrow*. G.O. Robinson (Ed.). New York: Praeger, 1978.

Poster, M. *The Second Media Age*. Cambridge: Polity, 1995.

Postigo, H. "Of Mods and Modders; Chasing Down the Value of Fan-Based Digital Game Modifications." *Games and Culture*, 2(4): 300–313, 2007.

Pratt, A.D. "The Information of the Image." *Libri*, 27(3), 1977.

Putnam, R. *Bowling Alone: The Collapse and Revival of American Community*. New York: Simon & Schuster, 2000.

Pylyshyn, Z. "Information Science: Its Roots and Relations as Viewed From the Perspective of Cognitive Science." *The Study of Information*. F. Machlup & U. Manfield (Eds.). New York: John Wiley, 1983.

Pylyshyn, Z. "What's in a Mind?" *Synthese*, 70(1), 1987.

Raber, D. *The Problem of Information: An Introduction to Information Science*. Lanham, MD: Scarecrow, 2003.

Ranganathan, S.R. "Self-Perpetuating Schemes of Classification." *Readings in Library Cataloguing*. R.K. Olding (Ed.). Melbourne: F.W. Cheshire, 1966.

Ravelry Retrieved from http://www.ravelry.com/discuss/for-the-love-of-ravelry/221585/51-75

Ravelry Retrieved from http://www.ravelry.com/about/privacy

Reddy, M.J. "The Conduit Metaphor: A Case of Frame Conflict in our Language about Language." *Metaphor and Thought.* A. Ortony (Ed.). Cambridge: Cambridge University Press, 1979.

Rettberg, J.W. *Blogging.* Cambridge: Polity, 2008.

Rheingold, H. *The Virtual Community: Homesteading on the Electronic Frontier.* Reading, MA: Addison-Wesley, 1993.

Rheingold, H. "Habermas Blows Off Question About the Internet and the Public Sphere." Smart Mobs. http://www.smartmobs.com/2007/11/05/habermas-blows-off-question-about-the-internet-and-the-public-sphere/

Ritchie, D. "Shannon and Weaver: Unravelling the Paradox." *Communication Research,* 13(2), April 1986.

Roberts, N. "A Search for Information Man." *Social Science Information Studies.* 2: 93–104, 1982.

Robertson, S.E. "A Theoretical Model of the Retrieval Characteristics of Information Retrieval Systems." PhD Thesis. London: University of London, 1975.

Rogers, E.M. *Diffusion of Innovation.* New York: Free Press, 1962.

Rosenberg, S. *Say Everything: How Blogging Began, What it's Becoming, and Why it Matters.* New York: Crown, 2009.

Rosenblueth, A., N. Wiener, & J. Bigelow. "Behavior, Purpose and Teleology." *Philosophy of Science,* 10(1), 1943.

Ruesch, J. "Technology and Social Communication." *Communication Theory and Research.* L. Thayer (Ed.). Springfield, IL: Charles C. Thomas, 1957.

Runciman, W.G. *A Critique of Max Weber's Philosophy of Social Science.* Cambridge: Cambridge University Press, 1972.

Sampson, J.R. *Adaptive Information Processing.* New York: Springer-Verlag, 1976.

Saunders, B.J. "From Indymedia to Indyjournalism- How Indymedia Is Evolving." *Proceedings Our Media- The 6th International OurMedia Conference,* OM6. Sydney, 2007.

Schacter, S. "Definition, Rejection and Communication." *Journal of Abnormal Social Psychology,* 46, 1951.

Schauer, F. *Free Speech: A Philosophical Inquiry.* London: Cambridge University Press, 1982.

Schere, M. "Obama and Twitter: White House Social-Networking," *Time,* May 6, 2009.

Schick, F. *Having Reasons: An Essay on Rationality and Sociality.* Princeton, NJ: Princeton University Press, 1984.

Schramm, W. "Communication Research in the United States." *The Science of Human Communication.* W. Schramm (Ed.). New York: Basic, 1963.

Schramm, W. *Men, Messages and Media.* New York: Harper & Row, 1973.

Schudson, M. "Changing Concepts of Democracy." *MIT Communications Forum,* 1998. Retrieved from http://web.mit.edu/comm-forum/papers/schudson.html.

Schutz, A. "The Well-Informed Citizen." *Social Research,* 13, 1946.

Schutz A. *Collected Papers,* Vol 2. A. Brodersen (Ed). The Hague: Martinus Nijhoff, 1964.

Schutz, A. *Collected Papers,* M. Natanson (Ed.). The Hague: Martinus Nijhoff, 1962/70.

Schutz, A. *The Phenomenology of the Social World.* Evanston, IL: Northwestern University Press, 1967.

Seidensticker, W.D. "Language as Communication." *The Southwestern Journal of Philosophy*, 2(3), 1974.

Shannon, C., & W. Weaver. *The Mathematical Theory of Communication*. Urbana, IL: University of Illinois Press, 1964.

Sharp, J.R. *Some Fundamentals of Information Retrieval*. London: Andre-Deutsch, 1965.

Shils, E. *Tradition*. Chicago: University of Chicago Press, 1981.

Shirky, C. *Here Comes Everybody: How Change Happens When People Come Together*. London: Penguin, 2008.

Skinner, Q. "'Social Meaning' and the Explanation of Social Action." *Philosophy, Politics and Society*. P. Laslett, W.G. Runciman, & Q. Skinner (Eds.). Oxford: Basil Blackwell, 1972.

Small Business Administration News and Media. Retrieved from http://www.sba.gov/news/

Smith, A. *The Geopolitics of Information*. New York: Oxford University Press, 1980.

Sondel, B. "Toward a Field Theory of Communication." *Journal of Communication*, 6, 1956.

Song, F.W. *Virtual Communities: Bowling Alone, Online Together*. Digital Formations Series, Vol. 54. New York: Peter Lang, 2009.

Sperber, D. *On Anthropological Knowledge*. London: Cambridge University Press, 1985.

Sperber, D., & D. Wilson. *Relevance: Communication and Cognition*. Oxford: Basil Blackwell, 1986.

Steiner, P. "On the Internet, Nobody Knows You Are a Dog." Cartoon. *The New Yorker*, 69(20), July 5, 1993. Print.

Stevens, S.S. "A Definition of Communication." *Journal of the Acoustical Society of America*, 22, 1950.

Stigler, C.J. "The Economics of Information." *Economics of Information and Knowledge*. D.M. Lamberton (Ed.). Harmondsworth: Penguin, 1971.

Stonier, T. *The Wealth of Information: A Profile of the Post-industrial Economy*. London: Thames Methuen, 1983.

Stonier, T. "Towards a New Theory of Information." *Telecommunications Policy*, 10(4), 1986.

Stonier, T. "Towards a General Theory of Information." *Aslib Proceedings*, 41(2), February 1989.

Strawson, P.F. "On Referring." *Mind*, 1950.

Tady, M. Million Dollar Ad Bliz to Kill Net Neutrality, 2010. Retrieved from http://www.savetheinternet.com/blog/10/05/13/million-dollar-ad-blitz-kill-net-neutrality

The Future Melbourne Wiki. Retrieved from http://www.futuremelbourne.com.au/wiki/view/FMPlan

The Planning Mosman's Future: A Community Conversation. Retrieved from http://www.mosmanroundtable.net/mosplan/

Thompson, J. *A History of the Principles of Librarianship*. London: Clive Bingley, 1977

Timmers, P. "Agenda for eDemocracy—An EU Perspective. European Commission." 2008. Retrieved from http://ec.europa.eu/information_society/activities/egovernment/docs/pdf/agenda_for_edemocracy.pdf

Toffler, A. *The Third Wave*. New York: William Morrow, 1980.

Torres, L., Pina, V. & Royo, S. "E-government and the Transformation of Public Administration in EU Countries." *Online Information Review*, 29(5): 531-553, 2005.

Tracey, M. *The Decline and Fall of Public Service Broadcasting*. Oxford: Oxford University Press, 1998.

Tran, A. "Social media and return on investment: Greenpeace to PETA; Multiple case study from a not for profit perspective." Masters of Professional Communication, Edith Cowan University, 2009.

Tribus, M. "Thirty Years of Information Theory." *The Study of Information*. F. Machlup & U. Mansfield (Eds.). New York: John Wiley, 1983.

Turkle, S. *Life on the Screen: Identity in the Age of the Internet*. New York: Simon & Schuster, 1995.

Turner, S. *The Suppression of Reasons in Sociological Description*. St. Petersburg, FL: University of South Florida, Department of Sociology, Center for Interdisciplinary Studies in Culture and Society, 1984.

Ursom, J.O. "Motives and Causes." *The Philosophy of Action*. E. White (Ed.). Oxford: Oxford University Press, 1968.

Ursul, A.D. "Intensifikatsiya i Informatsiya" [Intensification and Information]. Nauchno-Texhnicheskaya Informatsiya [*Information Processes and Systems*], 9, (Series 2, 1–7). [Translated by Professor N. Standish, University of Wollongong, for the author], 1983.

US Department of Education. Retrieved from http://edpubs.ed.gov/webstore/Content/search.asp

Van Rijsbergen, C.J. *Information Retrieval*. London: Butterworths, 1975.

Wallas, G. "Property Under Socialism." G.B. Shaw, S. Oliver, & S. Webb, (Eds.). *Fabian Essays in Socialism*. London: Fabian Society, 1920.

Warren, M. & H. Pearse. *Designing Deliberative Democracy*. Cambridge: Cambridge University Press, 2008.

Weber, M. *The Methodology of the Social Sciences*. E. Shils & H. Finch (Eds.). New York: Free Press, 1949.

Weber, M. "Class, Status, Party." *A Reader in Social Stratification*. R. Bendix & S.M. Lipset (Eds.). New York: Free Press, 1953.

Wersig, G. & G. Windel. "Information Science Needs a Theory of Information Actions." *Social Science Information Studies*, 5: 11–23, 1985.

What Makes It Tick? Automotive Principles Simply Explained, Ontario: General Motors, 1947.

White House. Retrieved from http://www.whitehouse.gov/the_press_office/TransparencyandOpenGovernment/

Whitehouse 2. Retrieved from http://www.whitehouse2.org/

Wicken, J.S. "Entropy and Information: Suggestions for Common Language." *Philosophy of Science*, 54: 176–193, 1987.

Wiener, N. *The Human Use of Human Beings*. New York: Avon, 1950.

Wiener, N. *Cybernetics*. New York: John Wiley, 1951.

Williams, B. "Leviathan's Program." *The New York Review of Books*. June 11, 1987.

Willson, M. *Technically Together: Rethinking Community within Techno-Society*. Digital Formations Series, Vol.28. New York: Peter Lang, 2006.

Winch, P. *The Idea of a Social Science: And its Relations to Philosophy*. London: Routledge, 1973.

Wittgenstein, L. *Philosophical Investigations*. Oxford: Basil Blackwell, 1953.

Yovits, M.C., & J.G. Abilock. "A Semiotic Framework for Information Science Leading to the Development of a Quantitative Measure of Information." *Information Utilities: Proceedings of the 37th ASIS annual meeting*, Vol. 2. P. Zunde (Ed.). Washington: American Society for Information Science, 1974.

Zimmer, M. "Renvois of the Past, Present and Future: Hyperlinks and the Structuring of Knowledge from the Encyclopèdie to Web 2.0." *New Media & Society*, 11(1 & 2): 95–114, 2009.

Zimmer, M. "Google on Wi-Fi Privacy Invasions: "No Harm, No Foul." Michael Zimmer.Org. http://michaelzimmer.org/2010/05/19/google-on-wi-fi-privacy-invasions-no-harm-no-foul/, 2010.

Zittrain, J. *The Future of the Internet–And How to Stop It*. London: Yale University Press, 2008.

Index

• D •

• O •

• N •

• P •

•Y•

•Z•